BUDDHISM TODAY
Issues & Global Dimensions

Buddhism Today

Issues & Global Dimensions

By

Madhusudan Sakya

CYBER TECH PUBLICATIONS
4264/3, Ansari Road, Daryaganj, New Delhi-110002 (India)
Ph.: 011-23244078, 011-43559448 Fax: 011-23280028
E-Mail: cyberpublicationsdelhi@yahoo.com
Website: www.cybertechpublications.com

Buddhism Today
Issues & Global Dimensions

Madhusudan Sakya

First Edition 2011

Asian Offset Printers

Published by
G.S. Rawat for Cyber Tech Publications
4264/3, Ansari Road, Daryaganj, New Delhi-110002 (India)
Ph.: 011-23244078, 011-43559448 Fax: 011-23280028
E-Mail: cyberpublicationsdelhi@yahoo.com
cyberpublications@gmail.com
Website: www.cybertechpublications.com

Contents

Preface

> "Moderation in temper is a virtue, but moderation in principle is always a vice."

Buddhism is an ancient religion, propounded by Lord Gautama Buddha and has a large number of followers in Asia and far east as well as in western countries.

It is significant to note that Buddhism, its doctrines, philosophy, tenets, practices, schools, and scriptures are researched and debated by academics and philosophers all across the world. A plethora of literature is available in various forms.

Buddhism, though concentrated mianly in Asia with large number of followers have by now reached global dimensions. As the name of the title suggests, we have compiled here vital information on some key issues and Buddhism in different countries. The following chapters make core of the study—Introduction; Place of Tantra; Hinayana School of Buddhism; Miscellaneous Issues; Buddhism in China and Taiwan; Buddhism in Korea; South Asia; Buddhism in Myanmar and Thailand; Some Southeast Asian Countries; Tibetan Buddhism; Buddhism in Japan; Buddhism in the West and Bibliography etc.

Hopefully, this venture will prove successful in furnishing vital authentic information on Buddhism, and scholars and laymen will be benefitted by it equally.

In course of gathering authoritative information we have consulted piles of literature on Buddhism, in form of encyclopaedias, books, articles, research papers, reports, discourses etc. available in printed and digital forms. In fact the real credit for this exercise ought go to the original contributors on whose works this project is devised and developed. I am deeply beholden to them all and the web sources also.

In fact, I was also immensely benefitted by the guidance, assistance and inspiration of my former teachers, colleagues and friends. I am grateful to them also. I am equally grateful to my publishers for evincing interest in this project and materialising this elegantly in the present form, that too within shortest possible time.

—Author

PART I

1

Introduction

> "The best preacher in the heart; the best teacher is time; the best book is the world; the best friend is God."
>
> —*The Talmud*

Every religion aims at showing right path of living to all its followers having spirituality at the centre-stage. It is apt here to quote Elbert Hubbard who says "preachers for death. The wise teacher tell men that they should forsake sin to prepare for life."

As the title of the present book suggests, here first we will discuss some essential elements of Buddhism and later we will come to its acceptance by masses and how it spread in different countries of the world.

First, it is pertinent to note that the idea of an eternal Buddha is a notion popularly associated with the Mahayana scripture, the Lotus Sutra, and is also found in other Mahayana sutras.

Remarkably, *Lotus Sutra* portrays the Buddha as indicating that he became awakened countless, immeasurable, inconceivable myriads of trillions of aeons ("kalpas") ago and that his lifetime is "forever existing and immortal". From the human perspective, it seems as though the Buddha has always existed. The sutra itself, however, does not directly employ the phrase "eternal Buddha"; yet similar notions are found in other Mahayana scriptures, notably the Mahaparinirvana Sutra, which presents the Buddha as the ultimately real, eternal ("nitya"/ "sâúvata"), unchanging, blissful, pure Self (Atman) who, as the Dharmakaya, knows of no beginning or end.

Notably, commenting on this sutra, Dr. Guang Xing writes:

> 'One of the main themes of the *Mahayana Mahaparinirvana Sutra* is that the Buddha is eternal, a theme very much in contrast with the Hinayana idea that the Buddha departed for ever after his final nirvana. The Mahayanists assert the eternity of the Buddha in two ways in the *Mahaparinirvana Sutra*. They state that the Buddha is the *dharmakaya*, and hence eternal. Next, they re-interpret the liberation of the Buddha as *mahaparinirvana* possessing four attributes: eternity, happiness, self and purity. In other words, according to the Mahayanists, the fact that the Buddha abides in the *mahaparinirvana* means not that he has departed for ever, but that he perpetually abides in intrinsic quiescence. The Buddha abiding in intrinsic quiescence is none other than the *dharmakaya* ... This *dharmakaya* is the *real* Buddha. It is on this doctrinal foundation that the *Mahaparinirvana Sutra* declares:"the dharmakaya has [the attributes of] eternity (*nitya*), happiness (*sukha*), self (*atman*) and purity (*subha*) and is perpetually free from birth, old age, sickness, death and all other sufferings ... It exists eternally without change ..."'

The *All-Creating King Tantra* additionally contains a panentheistic vision of Samantabhadra Buddha as the eternal, primordial Buddha, the Awakened Mind of bodhi, who declares: "From the primordial, I am the Buddhas of the three times [i.e. past, present and future]."

Shin Buddhism

In Shin Buddhism, Amida Buddha is viewed as the eternal Buddha who manifested as Shakyamuni in India and who is the personification of Nirvana itself.

The Shin Buddhist priest, John Paraskevopoulos, in his monograph on Shin Buddhism, writes:

> 'In Shin Buddhism, Nirvana or Ultimate Reality (also known as the "Dharma-Body" or *Dharmakaya* in the original Sanskrit) has assumed a more concrete form as (a) the Buddha of Infinite Light (*Amitabha*) and Infinite Life (*Amitayus*)and (b) the "Pure Land" or "Land of Utmost Bliss" (*Sukhavati*), the realm over which this Buddha is said to preside ... Amida is the Eternal Buddha who is said to have taken form as Shakyamuni and his teachings in order to become known to us in ways we can readily comprehend.'

In the similar vein John Paraskevopoulos elucidates the notion of Nirvana, of which Amida is an embodiment, in the following terms:

> '... [Nirvana's] more positive connotation is that of a higher state of being, the dispelling of illusion and the corresponding joy of liberation. An early Buddhist scripture describes Nirvana as: ... the far shore, the subtle, the very difficult to see, the undisintegrating, the unmanifest, the peaceful, the deathless, the sublime, the auspicious, the secure, the destruction of craving, the wonderful, the amazing, the unailing, the unafflicted, dispassion, purity, freedom, the island, the shelter, the asylum, the refuge ... (*Samyutta Nikaya*)'

This Nirvana is seen as eternal and of one nature, indeed as the essence of all things. Paraskevopoulos tells of how the *Mahaparinirvana Sutra* speaks of Nirvana as eternal, pure, blissful and true self:

> 'In Mahayana Buddhism it is taught that there is fundamentally one reality which, in its highest and purest dimension, is experienced as Nirvana. It is also known, as we have seen, as the Dharma-Body (considered as the ultimate form of Being) or "Suchness" (*Tathata* in Sanskrit) when viewed as the essence of all things ... "The Dharma-Body is eternity, bliss, true self and purity. It is forever free of all birth, ageing, sickness and death" (*Nirvana Sutra*)'.

To attain this Self, however, it is needful to transcend the 'small self' and its pettiness with the help of an 'external' agency, Amida Buddha. This is the view promulgated by the Jodo Shinshu founding Buddhist master, Shinran Shonin. John Paraskevopoulos comments on this:

'Shinran's great insight was that we cannot conquer the self by the self. Some kind of external agency is required: (a) to help us to shed light on our ego as it really is in all its petty and baneful guises; and (b) to enable us to subdue the small 'self' with a view to realising the Great Self by awakening to Amida's light.'

When that Great Self of Amida's light is realised, Shin Buddhism is able to see the Infinite which transcends the care-worn mundane. John Paraskevopoulos concludes his monograph on Shin Buddhism thus:

> 'It is time we discarded the tired view of Buddhism as a dry and forensic rationalism , lacking in warmth and devotion ... By hearing the call of Amida Buddha we become awakened to true reality and its unfathomable working ... to live a life that dances jubilantly in the resplendent light of the Infinite.'

DHARMA (BUDDHISM)

Dhamma in Buddhism has two primary meanings:

- the teachings of the Buddha which lead to enlightenment (The Universal law of nature)

- the constituent factors of the experienced world (The characteristic of elements)

What is called Buddhism in the west has been referred to in India (the teachings' place of origin) and the East generally for many centuries as Buddha-Dharma. This term has no sectarian connotations but simply means "Path of Awakening" and thus conforms to a universal understanding of dharma. The teachings are means of getting the hearer to question their own cherished beliefs and view of life; when through investigation and insight is opened the door to truth, the teaching can be put aside.

"Dharma" is sometimes taken to denote the sayings of the Buddha and his early disciples (e.g. the Vinaya and Sutta Pitaka of the Pali Canon), or more broadly to include the later traditions of interpretation and addition that the various schools of Buddhism have developed to help explain and expand upon the Buddha's teachings. In later tradition, this was seen as the 84,000 different teachings (the Kangyur/ bka.'gyur) that the Buddha gave to various types of people based on their needs. Alternately, "Dharma" may be seen as an ultimate and transcendent truth which is utterly beyond worldly things, somewhat like the Greek logos, seeing the dharma as referring to the "truth" or ultimate reality or "the way things are". The Dharma is one of the Three Jewels of Buddhism in which practitioners of Buddhism seek refuge (what one relies on for his/her lasting happiness).

The three jewels of Buddhism are the Buddha (mind's perfection of enlightenment), the Dharma (teachings and methods), and the Sangha (awakened beings who provide guidance and support).

The Buddha's Dharma Body

It is pertinent to note that the qualities of the Dharma

(Law, truth) is the same as the qualities of the Buddha and forms his "truth body" or "Dhamma Kaya": In the Samyutta Nikaya, Vakkali Sutta, Buddha said to his disciple Vakkali that,

> "Yo kho Vakkali dhamma passati so ma passati"
>
> *O Vakkali, whoever sees the Dhamma, sees me [the Buddha]*
>
> Another reference from the Agganna Sutta of the *Digha Nikaya,* says to his disciple Vasettha:
>
> "Tathâgatassa h'etam Vasettha adivacanam Dhammakayo iti pi ...":
>
> *O Vasettha! The Word of Dhammakaya is indeed the name of the Tathagata*

The Teaching of the Buddha also has six supreme qualities:

1. Svâkkhâto ("well proclaimed"). The Dhamma is not a speculative philosophy, but is the Universal Law found through enlightenment and is preached precisely. Therefore it is excellent in the beginning (sîla – Sanskrit úîla – moral principles), excellent in the middle (samâdhi – concentration) and excellent in the end (paññâ - Sanskrit prajñâ . . . Wisdom).
2. Sandimmhiko ("able to be examined"). The Dhamma can be tested by practice and therefore he who follows it will see the result by himself through his own experience.
3. Akâliko ("immediate"). The Dhamma is able to bestow timeless and immediate results here and now, for which there is no need to wait until the future or next existence.
4. Ehipassiko ("which you can come and see" — from the phrase ehi, paœya "come, see!"). The Dhamma

welcomes all beings to put it to the test and come see for themselves.

5. Opanayiko ("leading one close to"). The Dhamma is capable of being entered upon and therefore it is worthy to be followed as a part of one's life. In the "Vishuddhimagga" this is also referred to as "Upanayanam."
6. Paccatta veditabbo viññshi ("To be personally known by the wise"). The Dhamma can be perfectly realized only by the noble disciples (Ariyas) who have matured and enlightened enough in supreme wisdom.

Knowing these attributes, Buddhists believe that they will attain the greatest peace and happiness through the practice of the Dhamma. Each person is therefore fully responsible for himself to put it in the real practice. Here the Buddha is compared to an experienced and skilful doctor, and the Dhamma to proper medicine. However efficient the doctor or wonderful the medicine may be, the patients cannot be cured unless they take the medicine properly. So the practice of the Dhamma is the only way to attain the final deliverance of Nibbâna. These teachings ranged from understanding karma (Pâli: kamma) (cause and effect) and developing good impressions in one's mind, to reach full enlightenment by recognizing the nature of mind.

Other uses include dharma, normally spelled in transliteration with a small "d" (this differentiation is impossible in the South Asian scripts used to write Sanskrit), which refers to a *phenomenon* or *constituent factor* of human experience. This was gradually expanded into a classification of constituents of the entire material and mental world. Rejecting the substantial existence of permanent entities which are qualified by possibly changing qualities, Buddhist Abhidharma philosophy, which enumerated seventy-five dharmas, came to propound that these "constituent factors" are the only type of entity that truly exists.

This notion is of particular importance for the analysis of human experience: Rather than assuming that mental states inhere in a cognizing subject, or a soul-substance, Buddhist philosophers largely propose that mental states alone exist as "momentary elements of consciousness", and that a subjective perceiver is assumed. One of the central tenets of Buddhism, is the denial of a separate permanent "I", and is outlined in the three marks of existence. The three signs: 1. Dukkha - Suffering, 2. Anitya (Anicca) - Change/Impermanence, 3. Anâtman (Anatta) - Non-self. At the heart of Buddhism, is the realization of no "self" or "I" (and hence the delusion) as a separate self-existing entity.

Dharma in the Buddhist scriptures has a variety of meanings, including "phenomenon", and "nature" or "characteristic".

Dharma also means 'mental contents', and is paired with *citta*, which means heart/mind. In major sutras (for example, the Mahasatipatthana sutra), the *dharma/citta* pairing is paralleled with the pairing of *kaya* (body) and *vedana* (feelings or sensations, that which arise within the body but experienced through the mind).

Dharma means the source of things and Truth.

Dharma is also used to refer to the teachings of the Buddha, not in the context of the words of one man, even an enlightened man, but as a reflection of natural law which was re-discovered by this man and shared with the world. A person who lives their life with an understanding of this natural law, is a "dhammic" person, which is often translated as "righteous".

The Buddha would teach the Four Noble Truths, the Noble Eightfold Path, the Three Marks of Existence, and other guidelines in order to achieve the freedom and liberation from suffering.

SANGHA

Sangha is a word in Pali or Sanskrit that can be translated roughly as "association" or "assembly," "company" or "community" with common goal, vision or purpose.

The term is commonly used in several senses to refer to Buddhist or Jain groups.

Traditionally, in Buddhism Sangha almost always has one of two meanings: most commonly, Sangha means the *monastic Sangha* of ordained Buddhist monks or nuns. In a stricter sense, Sangha can mean the assembly of all beings possessing some high degree of realization, referred to as the *arya-sangha* or "noble Sangha". This article deals primarily with the subject of the *monastic Sangha*.

Buddhists traditionally consider monastic life to provide the environment most conducive to advancing toward enlightenment, and the Sangha is responsible for maintaining, translating, advancing, and spreading the teachings of the Buddha.

According to the same tradition for a country or nation to be considered as truly Buddhist, the majority of the nation must be Buddhist and include at least a fourfold sangha of bhikkhus, bhikkhunis, upasakas and, upasikas.

That is why there is also a tradition of yogic tantric practitioners who are laypeople but still Buddhist practitioners.

In Buddhism, the Buddha, the Dharma and the Sangha each are described as having certain characteristics. These characteristics are chanted either on a daily basis and/or on Uposatha days, depending on the school of Buddhism. In Theravada tradition they are a part of daily chanting:

The Sangha: "The Sangha of the Blessed One's disciples (Savakas) is:

1. practising the good way
2. practising the upright way
3. practising the knowledgeable or logical way
4. practising the proper way;

that is, the four pairs of persons, the eight types of individuals - This Sangha of the Blessed One's disciples is:

1. worthy of gifts
2. worthy of hospitality
3. worthy of offerings
4. worthy of reverential salutation
5. the unsurpassed field of merit for the world."

The Sangha of monks and the Sangha of nuns were originally established by Gautama Buddha in the 5th century BCE in order to provide a means for those who wish to practise the Dhamma full time, in a direct and highly disciplined way, free from the restrictions and responsibilities of the household life.

The Sangha also fulfils the function of preserving the Buddha's original teachings and of providing spiritual support for the Buddhist lay-community. The key feature of Buddhist monasticism is the adherence to the vinaya which contains an elaborate set of rules of conduct including complete chastity and eating only before noon. Between midday and the next day, a strict life of scripture study, chanting, meditation, and occasional cleaning forms most of the Sangha's duties. Transgression of rules carries penalties ranging from confession to permanent expulsion from the Sangha. The founder of Japanese Tendai sects took the decision to reduce the number of rules down to about 60 (Enkai).

In Kamakura Era, many sects (Zen, Pureland and Nichiren) which originated from Tendai sect abolished vinaya entirely. Therefore Japanese Zen, Pureland and Nichiren, are led by priests (or minister) rather than by monks. Monks and nuns may own only the barest minimum of possessions due to their samaya as renunciates (ideally, three robes, an alms bowl, a cloth belt, a needle and thread, a razor for shaving the head, and a water filter). In practice, they often have a few additional personal possessions.

Traditionally, Buddhist monastics eschew ordinary clothes and wear robes. Originally the robes were sewn together from rags and stained with earth. The idea that robes were dyed with saffron seems unlikely to be true since it was and still is a very expensive commodity, and monks were poor. The color of modern robes varies from community to community (saffron is characteristic for southeast Asian Theravada and Mahayana groups, maroon in Tibet, gray in Korea, black in Japan etc.)

Notably, the word which is usually translated as monk is *bhikkhu* in Pali or *bhikshu* in Sanskrit. The feminine form is *bhikkhuni* or *bhikshuni*. These words literally mean "beggar", and it is traditional for bhikkhus to beg their food. In most places this has become an elaborate ritual, where lay people feed monastics in order to obtain merit which will ensure them a fortunate rebirth.

Although monastics in India traditionally did not work for income, this changed when Buddhism moved to east Asia, so that in China and the surrounding countries monks often engage in agriculture. The idea that all Buddhists, especially monks and nuns practice vegetarianism is a Western misperception. In some Sanskrit sutras meat eating is strongly discouraged whilst in Pali Sutras the Buddha specifically rejected a suggestion by a senior monk to impose vegetarianism on the Sangha.

The Buddha himself is recorded as having consumed meat. The Buddha allowed Sangha members to eat whatever food is donated to them by laypeople, except that they may not eat meat if they know or suspect the animal was killed specifically for them. Consequently, the Theravadan tradition (Sri Lanka, Thailand, Laos, Cambodia and Burma) which follows the Pali scriptures does not practice vegetarianism though an individual may do so at his or her personal choice.

On the other hand, the Mahayana and Vajrayana traditions accept both Theravada and Mahayana scriptures, and consequently the practice will vary depending on their interpretation of the sutras. In particualr, East Asian monastics take on the bodhisattva vows from the Brahma Net Sutra which has a vow of vegetarianism as part of the Triple Platform Ordination where they receive the sramanera/sramanerika, bhikshu/bhikshuni and bodhisattva vows, whereas the Tibetan lineages transmit the bodhisattva vows from Asanga's Yogacarabhumi, which does not include a vow of vegetarianism. In some areas such as China, Korea and Vietnam one expects the Sangha to practice strict vegetarianism while in other areas such as Japan or Tibet one does not.

Remarkably, the lay community is responsible for the production of goods and services in society, and for the production and raising of children. According to Mahayana sutras, the Buddha always maintained that lay persons were capable of great wisdom in the Buddhadharma and of reaching enlightenment. In the west, there is a misconception that Theravada regards enlightenment to be an impossible goal outside the Sangha. This is incorrect.

In Theravada suttas, it is clearly recorded that the Buddha's uncle—who was a lay follower—reached enlightenment by hearing the Buddha's discourse. The distinction between Sangha and lay persons has always been important and forms the *Parisa*, Buddhist community. Here, monastics teach and counsel the laity at request while laymen and laywomen offer donations for their future support. This inter-connectedness serves as a marriage and has sustained Buddhism to this day.

Women in the Sangha

Although always maintaining that women were just as capable of attaining enlightenment as men, the canonical texts depict the Buddha as being reluctant to permit women to join the Sangha. After several entreaties from his aunt and foster-mother, Maha Pajapati Gotami, who wished to become ordained, and from his cousin and aide Ananda, who supported her cause, the Buddha relented and ordained Maha Pajapati and several others as nuns.

It is interesting to note that this was one of the few issues about which the Buddha is recorded to have changed his mind. The Buddha later established the condition that each new ordination would be sanctioned by at least five bhikkhunis. There have been several theories regarding the Buddha's reluctance to ordain women, including the possibility that it was due to fears that a community of women would not be safe in the society of his day. According to the scriptures the reason the Buddha himself gave was that the admission of women would weaken the Sangha and shorten its lifetime, and he laid down strict rules subordinating nuns to monks.

Before the modern era, the Bhikkhuni Sangha spread to most Buddhist countries including Burma (also known as Myanmar), with the notable exceptions being Tibet and Thailand. However, in Sri Lanka, it died out in the 11th century during a civil war and was not revived. Consequently, as Theravada Buddhism spread to Thailand, the Theravada Sangha consisted only of monks.

Notably, in recent decades, there has been a serious attempt to revive the Theravada Bhikkhuni Sangha with the assistance of Mahayana bhikkhunis from the Chinese lineage. These were introduced from Sri Lanka in 433 C. E., following the Dharmaguptaka Vinaya, and subsequently spread to Korea, Taiwan, Vietnam, and Japan. This has resulted in a small but thriving community of nuns in Sri Lanka, who in turn ordained the first Theravada Buddhist nun in the history of Thailand, Ven. Dhammananda.

However, the validity of these ordinations is strongly disputed by some of the conservative Theravada establishment. Meanwhile, a similar process has produced the first fully ordained bhikkhunis in Tibetan Buddhism, where only the novice ordination for bhikkhunis existed. In the west, where feminism has been a strong influence, there have been many remarkable Buddhist nuns: three notable examples are Pema Chodron , Ayya Khema and Tenzin Palmo.

The first bhikkhuni ordination in Australia in the Theravadin tradition was held in Perth on October 22nd at Bodhinyana Monastery. Venerable Ajahn Vayama together with Venerables Nirodha, Seri and Hasapanna were ordained as bhikkhunis by a dual sangha act of bhikkhus and bhikkhunis in full accordance with the pali vinaya.

It is remarkable that some commentators noted that Sangha is occasionally (and mistakenly) used in the West to refer to any sort of Buddhist community. This is problematic in a theological sense because a collection of Buddhists does not amount to a triple gem where other Buddhists could take refuge. It is suggested by these commentators that the terms parisa or gana would be a more appropriate reference to a community of Buddhists.

REFERENCES

1. Dr. Guang Xing, *The Concept of the Buddha*, RoutledgeCurzon, London, 2005, p. 89.
2. John Paraskevopoulos, *Call of the Infinite: The Way of Shin Buddhism*, Sophia Perennis Publications, California, 2009, pp. 16-17.
3. John Paraskevopoulos, *Call of the Infinite: The Way of Shin Buddhism,* California, 2009.

2

Place of Tantra

Tantra is a philosophy according to which Shakti is usually the main deity worshipped, and the universe is regarded as the divine play of *Shakti* and *Shiva*. The word Tantra also applies to any of the scriptures (called "Tantras") commonly identified with the worship of Shakti. Tantra deals primarily with spiritual practices and ritual forms of worship, which aim at liberation from ignorance and rebirth.

Tantrism has influenced the Hindu, Sikh, Bön, Buddhist, and Jain religious traditions. Tantra in its various forms has existed in India, Nepal, China, Japan, Tibet, Korea, Cambodia, Burma, Indonesia and Mongolia. Despite reluctance to support a rigorous definition of tantra, David Gordon White offers the following definition:

Basically, Tantra is that Asian body of beliefs and practices which, working from the principle that the universe we experience is nothing other than the concrete manifestation of the divine energy of the Godhead that creates and maintains that universe, seeks to ritually appropriate and channel that energy, within the human microcosm, in creative and emancipatory ways.

There are a number of different definitions of tantra from various viewpoints, not all of them necessarily consistent.

Robert Brown notes that the term *tantrism* is a construction of Western scholarship and that:

> In fact, it is not a concept that comes from within the religious system itself, although it is generally recognized internally as different from the Vedic tradition. This immediately makes it suspect as an independent category. Rather than a single coherent system, Tantra is an accumulation of practices and ideas which is characterized by the use of ritual, by the use of the mundane to access the supra-mundane, and by the identification of the microcosm with the macrocosm.

The Tantric practitioner seeks to use the *prana* (divine power) that flows through the universe (including one's own body) to attain purposeful goals. These goals may be spiritual, material or both. Most practitioners of tantra consider mystical experience imperative. Some versions of Tantra require the guidance of a guru. In the process of working with energy, the *Tantrika*, or tantric practitioner, has various tools at hand. These include *yoga*, to actuate processes that will "yoke" the practitioner to the divine.

Also important are visualizations of deity, and verbalisation or evocation through *mantras*, which may be construed as seeing, listening internally, and singing power into a stronger state within the individual, resulting in an ever-increasing awareness of cosmic vibration through daily practice. Identification with and internalisation of the divine is enacted, through a total identification with deity, such that the aspirant "becomes" the *Ishta-deva* or meditational deity.

Obviously, Tantrism is a quest for spiritual perfection and magical power. Its purpose is to achieve complete control of oneself, and of all the forces of nature, in order to attain union with the cosmos and with the divine. Long training is generally required to master Tantric methods, into which pupils are typically initiated by a guru. *Yoga*, including breathing techniques and postures (*asana*), is employed to subject the body to the control of the will.

Mudras, or gestures; *mantras* or syllables, words and phrases; *mandalas* and *yantras*, which are symbolic diagrams of the forces at work in the universe, are all used as aids for meditation and for the achievement of spiritual and magical power. During meditation, the initiate identifies herself or himself with any of the numerous Hindu gods and goddesses representing cosmic forces. The initiate visualizes them and takes them into her or his mind so that she or he unites with them, a process likened to sexual courtship and consummation. In fact, some Tantric monks use females partners to represent goddesses.

Also, in left-handed Tantra (*Vamachara*), ritual sexual intercourse is employed—not for pleasure—but as a way of entering into the underlying processes and structure of the universe.

Relation with Vedic Tradition

The Tantric tradition may be considered as either parallel to, or intertwined with, the Vedic tradition. The primary sources of written Tantric lore are the *agama*, which generally consist of four parts, delineating metaphysical knowledge (*jnana*), contemplative procedures (*yoga*), ritual regulations (*kriya*), and ethical and religious injunctions (*charya*). Schools and lineages affiliate themselves with specific *agamic* traditions.

It is apt here to quote André Padoux who notes that in India, tantrism is marked by a rejection of orthodox Vedic tenets. Maurice Winernitz, in his review of the literature of tantra, points out that while Indian tantric texts are not positively hostile to the Vedas, they propound that the precepts of the Vedas are too difficult for our age, and so, for that reason, an easier cult and an easier doctrine have been revealed in them. Some orthodox Brahmans who accept the authority of the Vedas reject the authority of the Tantras.

N.N. Bhattacharyya explains:

> It is to be noticed that although later Tantric writers wanted to base their doctrines on the Vedas, the orthodox followers of the Vedic tradition invariably referred to Tantra in a spirit of denunciation, stressing its anti-Vedic character.

Tantra exists in *Shaiva*, *Vaisnava*, *Ganapatya*, Saurya and *Shakta* forms, amongst others. Strictly speaking, within individual traditions, tantric texts are classified as *Shaiva gamas*I, *Vaishnava Pñcartra Sanhitâs*, and *Shakta Tantras*, but there is no clear dividing line between these works, and on a practical basis the expression *Tantra* generally includes all such works of sort.

Yoga

It is remarkable that the paths of Tantra & Yoga are contradictory, they do intersect at some common philosophies and goals. During his discourse on Vijnana Bhairava Tantra, Osho tries to differentiate between these two paths: As Robert Svoboda attempts to summarize the three major paths of the Vedic knowledge, he writes:

> *"Because every embodied individual is composed of a body, a mind and a spirit, the ancient Rishis of India who developed the Science of Life organized their wisdom into three bodies of knowledge: Ayurveda, which deals mainly with the physical body; Yoga, which deals mainly with spirit; and Tantra, which is mainly concerned with the mind. The philosophy of all three is identical; their manifestations differ because*

> *of their differing emphases. Ayurveda is most concerned with the physical basis of life, concentrating on its harmony of mind and spirit. Yoga controls body and mind to enable them to harmonize with spirit, and Tantra seeks to use the mind to balance the demands of body and spirit."*

Buddhist Tantra

According to Tibetan Buddhist Tantric master Lama Thubten Yeshe:

> ...each one of us is a union of all universal energy. Everything that we need in order to be complete is within us right at this very moment. It is simply a matter of being able to recognize it. This is the tantric approach.

It is remarkable that Linguistically as well as phonologically the three words *mantram*, *tantram* and *yantram* are related in the ancient traditions of India. *Mantram* denotes the chant, or "knowledge." *Tantram* denotes philosophy, or ritual actions. *Yantram* denotes the means (or the machine) by which a human is expected to lead his life.

According to Tantra, "being-consciousness-bliss" or *Satchidananda* has the power of both self-evolution and self-involution. *Prakriti* or "reality" evolves into a multiplicity of creatures and things, yet at the same time always remains pure consciousness, pure being, and pure bliss. In this process of evolution, *Maya* (illusion) veils Reality and separates it into opposites, such as conscious and unconscious, pleasant and unpleasant, and so forth. If not recognized as illusion, these opposing determining conditions bind, limit and fetter *(pashu)* the individual *(jiva)*. Generally speaking, the Hindu god and goddess Shiva and Shakti are perceived as separate and distinct.

However, in Tantra, even in the process of evolution, Reality remains pure consciousness, pure being and pure bliss, and Tantra denies neither the act nor the fact of this process. In fact, Tantra affirms that both the world-process itself, and the individual *jiva*, are themselves Real. In this respect, Tantra distinguishes itself both from pure dualism and from the qualified non-dualism of Vedanta. Evolution, or the "outgoing current," is only half of the functioning of *Maya*.

Involution, or the "return current," takes the *jiva* back towards the source, or the root of Reality, revealing the infinite. Tantra is understood to teach the method of changing the "outgoing current" into the "return current," transforming the fetters created by *Maya* into that which "releases" or "liberates."

This view underscores two maxims of Tantra: "One must rise by that by which one falls," and "the very poison that kills becomes the elixir of life when used by the wise."

In fact, the Tantric aim is to sublimate rather than to negate relative reality. This process of sublimation consists of three phases: purification, elevation, and the "reaffirmation of identity on the plane of pure consciousness." The methods employed by *Dakshinachara* (right-hand path) interpretations of Tantra are very different from the methods used in the pursuit of the *Vamachara* (left-hand path).

Ritual Practices

Because of the wide range of communities covered by the term *tantra*, it is challenging and problematic to describe tantric practices definitively. Avalon (1918) does provide a useful dichotomy of the "Ordinary Ritual" and the "Secret Ritual".

The ordinary ritual or *puja* may include any of the following elements:

Mantra and Yantra: As in other Hindu and Buddhist yoga traditions, *mantra* and *yantra* play an important role in Tantra. The *mantra* and *yantra* are instruments to invoke specific Hindu deities such as Shiva, Shakti, or Kali. Similarly, *puja* may involve focusing on a *yantra* or *mandala* associated with a deity.

Identification with Deities: Tantra, as a development of early Hindu-Vedic thought, embraced the Hindu gods and goddesses, especially Shiva and Shakti, along with the *Advaita* philosophy that each represents an *aspect* of the ultimate Para Shiva, or Brahman. These deities may be worshipped externally with flowers, incense, and other offerings, such as singing and dancing. But, more importantly, these deities are engaged as *attributes* of *Ishta Devata* meditations, the practitioners either visualizing themselves *as* the deity, or experiencing the *darshan* (the vision) of the deity. These Tantric practices form the foundation of the ritual temple dance of the *devadasis*, and are preserved in the *Melattur* style of *Bharatanatyam* by Guru Mangudi Dorairaja Iyer.

Secret Ritual

It is pertinent to note that Secret ritual may include any or all of the elements of ordinary ritual, either directly or substituted, along with other sensate rites and themes such as a feast (representing food, or sustenance), coitus (representing sexuality and procreation), the charnel grounds (representing death and transition) and defecation, urination and vomiting (representing waste, renewal, and fecundity). It is this sensate inclusion that prompted Zimmer's praise of Tantra's world-affirming attitude:

Notably, in the Tantra, the manner of approach is not that of Nay but of Yea ... the world attitude is affirmative

... Man must approach through and by means of nature, not by rejection of nature.

In Avalon's *Chapter 27: The Pañcatattva (The Secret Ritual)* of *Sakti and Sakta* (1918), he states that the Secret Ritual (which he calls *Panchatattva*, *Chakrapuja* and *Panchamakara*) involves:

> Worship with the Pañcatattva generally takes place in a Cakra or circle composed of men and women... sitting in a circle, the Shakti (or female practitioner) being on the Sadhaka's (male practitioner's) left. Hence it is called Cakrapuja. ...There are various kinds of Cakra – productive, it is said, of differing fruits for the participator therein.

Avalon also provides a series of variations and substitutions of the *Panchatattva* (*Panchamakara*) "elements" or *tattva* encoded in the Tantras and various tantric traditions, and affirms that there is a direct correlation to the Tantric Five Nectars and the *Mahâbhûta*.

Use of Sex

Notably, sexual rites of Vamamarga may have emerged from early Hindu Tantra as a practical means of catalyzing biochemical transformations in the body to facilitate heightened states of awareness. These constitute a vital offering to Tantric deities. Sexual rites may have also evolved from clan initiation ceremonies involving transactions of sexual fluids.

Here the male initiate is inseminated or ensanguinated with the sexual emissions of the female consort, sometimes admixed with the semen of the guru. The *Tantrika* is thus transformed into a son of the clan (*kulaputra*) through the grace of his consort. The clan fluid (*kuladravya*) or clan nectar (*kulamrita*) is conceived as flowing naturally from her womb. Later developments in the rite emphasize the primacy of bliss and divine union, which replace the more bodily connotations of earlier forms. Although popularly equated with Tantra in its entirety in the West, such sexual rites were historically practiced by a minority of sects.

For many practicing lineages, these *maithuna* practices progressed into psychological symbolism. When enacted as enjoined by the Tantras, the ritual culminates in a sublime experience of infinite awareness for both participants. Tantric texts specify that sex has three distinct and separate purposes—procreation, pleasure, and liberation. Those seeking liberation eschew frictional orgasm for a higher form of ecstasy, as the couple participating in the ritual lock in a static embrace. Several sexual rituals are recommended and practiced.

These involve elaborate and meticulous preparatory and purificatory rites. The sexual act itself balances energies coursing within the *pranic ida* and *pingala* channels in the subtle bodies of both participants. The *sushumna nadi* is awakened and *kundalini* rises upwards within it.

This eventually culminates in *samadhi*, wherein the respective individual personalities and identities of each of the participants are completely dissolved in a unity of cosmic consciousness. Tantrics understand these acts on multiple levels. The male and female participants are conjoined physically, and represent *Shiva* and *Shakti*, the male and female principles. Beyond the physical, a subtle fusion of *Shiva* and *Shakti* energies takes place, resulting in a united energy field.

On an individual level, each participant experiences a fusion of one's own *Shiva* and *Shakti* energies.

Western Views

The first Western scholar to take the study of Tantra seriously was Sir John Woodroffe (1865–1936), who wrote about Tantra under the pen name Arthur Avalon. He is generally held as the "founding father of Tantric studies." Unlike previous Western scholars, Woodroffe was an ardent advocate for Tantra, defending Tantra against its many critics and presenting Tantra as an ethical philosophical system greatly in accord with the Vedas and Vedanta. Woodroffe himself practised Tantra as he saw and understood it and, while trying to maintain his scholastic objectivity, was considered a student of Hindu Tantra (in particular *Shiva-Shakta*) tradition.

Following Sir John Woodroffe, a number of scholars began to actively investigate Tantric teachings. These included a number of scholars of comparative religion and Indology, such as: Agehananda Bharati, Mircea Eliade, Julius Evola, Carl Jung, Giuseppe Tucci and Heinrich Zimmer.

According to Hugh Urban, Zimmer, Evola and Eliade viewed Tantra as "the culmination of all Indian thought: the most radical form of spirituality and the archaic heart of aboriginal India", and regarded it as the ideal religion of the modern era. All three saw Tantra as "the most *transgressive* and *violent* path to the sacred."

Following these first presentations of Tantra, other more popular authors such as Joseph Campbell helped to bring Tantra into the imagination of the peoples of the West. Tantra came to be viewed by some as a "cult of ecstasy", combining sexuality and spirituality in such a way as to act as a corrective force to Western repressive attitudes about sex.

As Tantra has become more popular in the West it has undergone a major transformation. For many modern readers, "Tantra" has become a synonym for "spiritual sex" or "sacred sexuality", a belief that sex in itself ought to be recognized as a sacred act which is capable of elevating its participants to a more sublime spiritual plane. Though pop-tantra may adopt many of the concepts and terminology of Indian Tantra, it often omits one or more of the following: the traditional reliance on *guruparampara* (the guidance of a guru), extensive meditative practice, and traditional rules of conduct—both moral and ritualistic.

In this connection, Hugh Urban writes:

> Since at least the time of Agehananda Bharati, most Western scholars have been severely critical of these new forms of pop Tantra. This "California Tantra" as Georg Feuerstein calls it, is "based on a profound misunderstanding of the Tantric path. Their main error is to confuse Tantric bliss ... with ordinary orgasmic pleasure.

Urban goes on to say that he himself doesn't consider this "wrong" or "false" but rather "simply a different interpretation for a specific historical situation."

REFERENCES

1. Avalon, Arthur (1918). *Sakti and Sakta*. Ganesh and Co. http://www.sacred-texts.com/tantra/sas/index.htm.
2. Avalon, Arthur (1972). *Tantra of the great liberation – Mahanirvana Tantra*. New York: Dover Publications.
3. Bhattacharyya, N. N. (1999). *History of the Tantric Religion*. New Delhi: Manohar.
4. Bühnemann, Gudrun (1988). *The Worship of MahgaGapati According to the Nityotsava*. Institut für Indologie.
5. Harper, Katherine Anne and Robert L. Brown (ed.) (2002). *The Roots of Tantra*. State University of New York Press

6. Norbu, Chögyal Namkhai (1999). *The Crystal and The Way of Light: Sutra, Tantra and Dzogchen*. Snow Lion Publications.
7. Saraswati, Swami Satyananda (2000). *Sure Ways to Self Realization*. Yoga Publications Trust.
8. Urban, Hugh (2003). *Tantra: Sex, Secrecy, Politics, and Power in the Study of Religions*. University of California Press.
9. Wangyal Rinpoche, Tenzin; Dahlby, Mark (1998). *The Tibetan Yogas of Dream and Sleep*. N.Y.: Snow Lion Publications.
10. White, David Gordon (ed.) (2000). *Tantra in Practice*. Princeton University Press.
11. Winternitz, Maurice (1972). *History of Indian Literature*. New Delhi: Oriental Books Reprint Corporation.
12. Yeshe, Lama Thubten (1987). *Introduction to Tantra:The Transformation of Desire* (2001, revised ed.). Boston: Wisdom Publications.

3

Hinayana School of Buddhism

Etymologically, the word Hînayâna is formed of *hîna*: "low", "inferior", "deficient", "defective;" and *yâna*: "vehicle", where "vehicle" means "a way of going to enlightenment". The Pali Text Society's Pali-English Dictionary (1921-25) defines *hîna* in even stronger terms, with a semantic field that includes "poor, miserable; vile, base, abject, contemptible," and "despicable." In the Chinese, Korean, Vietnamese and Japanese languages, the term means small vehicle (*hina* meaning "small", *yana* meaning "vehicle"), and in the Tibetan (*theg chung*) and Mongolian (*Baga Holgon*) terms for Hinayana also mean "small" or "lesser" vehicle.

Hînayâna is sometimes said to be referring solely to the Early Buddhist Schools, and not to the current Theravada school, while sometimes it is held to be also cognate with the modern Theravada tradition. The legitimacy of using the term Hinayana to refer to the early Buddhist schools is disputed while use of "Hinayana" to refer to the contemporary Theravada is seen as pejorative.

The term appeared around the 1st or 2nd century CE. Its use in scholarly publications is controversial .

It is pertinent to note that hold that the term was

coined to be purposely pejorative. For example, the MacMillan Library Reference Encyclopedia of Buddhism mentions that it is a polemical term coined by Mahâyâna Buddhists to denigrate their opponents.

Scholar Isabelle Onians asserts that although "the Mahâyâna ... very occasionally referred contemptuously to earlier Buddhism as the Hinayâna, the Inferior Way," "the preponderance of this name in the secondary literature is far out of proportion to occurrences in the Indian texts." She notes that the term Srâvakayâna was "the more politically correct and much more usual" term used by Mahâyânists. Jonathan Silk has argued that the term "Hïnayana" was used to refer to whomever one wanted to criticize on any given occasion, and did not refer to any definite grouping of Buddhists. There remains an open and active debate regarding the issue of whether Hînayâna was coined to be pejorative or merely classificatory.

The arguments for the term as being pejorative largely depends upon the etymological roots of the prefix 'Hîna': Hîna- is defined as such: "inferior, less, low, base, mean, incomplete, deficient, wanting and so on." Since the meaning of 'hina' covers both a pejorative and non-pejorative meaning, it is difficult to come to a definite conclusion.

The term could have been chosen because it provided both meanings. There are Mahayana Sutras and traditions which repeatedly admonish the trainee Bodhisattva not to criticise any of the Buddhist schools. The mere fact that there is such a strong admonishment against criticising the Hinayana indicates that it was either a common attitude, or that there was a degree of defensiveness within Mahayana regarding this issue. By the 3rd Century CE, in the ethics chapter of Asanga's Bodhisattvabhumi, we find an explicit injunction not to criticise or reject the Hînayâna texts or traditions, where Trainee Bodhisattvas are instructed not to "disparage the Hînayâna, or over-encourage others to learn Mahayana".

Candragomin wrote a very influential twenty verse summary of Asanga's Ethics, written or summarised as a set of vows to be taken by a trainee Bodhisattve. The 15th Verse (derived from Asanga's chapter on ethics) cites "rejecting the Sravakayana" as a root downfall. Candragomin's vows were adopted by the Indo-Tibetan Mahayana tradition via Atisha, and are still used today by the Gelugpa and Kagyupa schools.

It is obvious, as Hinayana represents a specifically Mahayana point of view and is often seen as a polemical term, other terms have been suggested to describe the Buddhist schools that did not adopt the Mahayana sutras. Among the terms that have been used as substitutes for "Hînayâna" are the following:

- *Srâvakayâna Buddhism*—The term most often historically used Mahâyâna texts to refer to early Buddhist schools. This term refers to the "srâvakas," meaning disciples, followers, or hearers. They who followed the Buddha and sought solely to eliminate suffering, thus culminating in Arahantship. This term originates (like the term Hinayana) from within Mahâyâna Buddhism, and thus faces some of the same objections as "Hînayâna", though it is less obviously derogatory. Srâvakayâna can also refer to a tendency or intention found in an individual; this is, one might be a member of a Mahâyâna school, but be personally following a Srâvakayâna path. Srâvakayâna is also contrasted with the term "Bodhisattvayâna".

- *Early Buddhism*—refers to the variations within Buddhism (both Pre-sectarian Buddhism as the Early Buddhist schools) that were current before the Mahayana movement emerged.
- *Early Buddhist schools*—This term properly covers all the schools that existed before the emergence of the Mahâyâna. The arising of the Mahayana school of Buddhism (1st / 2nd century CE) went together with the adoption of new (previously not-existing) sutras, and introduced new (or emphasized old but not very central) philosophies such as the Bodhisattva and having the intention of liberating all sentient beings. Since this constituted a serious break with the previous traditions and customs that the earlier schools had in common, the Mahayana is seen as a 'reformist' or revolutionary movement, and not included in any lists of the early schools. Thus, there is a large correlation between the earlier schools and the label 'Hinayana'.

  Also the Mahayana itself never groups itself with the previously existing schools. Some of the later 'early schools' might have arisen (meaning: split off) from another, older, early school, and might have come into existence at about the same time as the Mahayana. However, these schools kept to the larger framework and attitude of the earlier schools.
- *Eighteen Schools (or Twenty Schools)*—This term is historically oriented, based on the lists of the various Early Buddhist schools. However, the list itself is numerically inexact since the exact number and the names of the schools differ between the various lists. These were the schools that the emerging Mahayana-movement was familiar with because

they were existing at that time. Subsequently, these eighteen schools split up further into a larger number, and the Hinayana label could have also been applied to those later split-offs. Also, the Mahayana writer Bhavya (Bhavaviveka) says in the Tarkajvala that Mahayana is oncluded in the eighteen schools.

- *Southern Buddhism*—This frequently used geographical designation is appropriately applied to the Theravâda, whose centers in Sri Lanka and Southeast Asia are located south of the centers of Mahayana (China, Tibet, Japan).

  In its early period, however, there was significant overlap between the geographical regions of Mahayana and the early schools.

- *Pâli Buddhism*—This term only applies to the Theravâda, whose scriptures (the Pâli canon) are in the Pâli language. The other "Hînayâna" schools wrote either in Sanskrit, in other Prakrits (notably Gândhârî) or in Buddhist Hybrid Sanskrit, a mixed language with both Sanskrit and Prakrit elements.

- *Nikâya Buddhism*—This recently invented term was intended to cover the same ground as Hînayâna, referring to the nikâyas or "schools" into which Buddhism was split by the beginning of the Common Era. It could also be interpreted as "Buddhism as taught in the Nikâyas", the five primary divisions of the Tipimaka, although this second usage of the term is only used among the Theravâda—other schools used the term Âgamas— so if used in the latter sense "Nikaya Buddhism" would be a misnomer when applied to non-Theravâda early schools such as the Sarvastivada and Sammitiya.

- *Theravâda*—This term properly refers to only one school among many non-Mahâyâna schools that once existed, many of which espoused philosophical notions contrary to those of the Theravâdins. It would be altogether inaccurate to refer to such Buddhists as the Sarvâstivâdins as Theravâdins. Some scholars, such as Dr. Walpola Rahula, have pointed out that there was small contact between early Mahâyânists and Theravâdins, and have suggested that the term "Hînayâna" was never intended to include the Theravâda. Judging by the content of Mahâyâna polemic, it seems certain that other sects of northern India were the primary targets of the "Hînayâna" critique.
- *Mainstream Buddhism*—this term might be considered derogatory by Mahayanists, as it seems to suggest they are fringe (when in fact they are the majority)
- Sectarian Buddhism

Hinayana as Doctrine, Practitioner or Thought

It has been used by both past and present Mahayanists as a name to refer variously to one or more *doctrines*, *traditions*, *practitioners* or *thoughts* that are generally concerned with the achievement of Nirvana as a Sâvakabuddha ('Arahant') or a Pratyeka-Buddha, as opposed to the achievement of liberation as a Samyaksambuddha, wherein the Samyaksambuddha (according to Mahayana lore) is deemed to operate from a basis of vowing to effect the spiritual liberation of all beings and creatures from the suffering of samsara (not just himself or a small number of others).

1. Hînayâna as *doctrine* would (from a Mahâyâna

perspective) include the Sutras taught by Buddha that admonish the practitioner to follow the úrâvaka path—i.e., all non-Mahâyâna sutras. In such teachings there is no emphasis on pledging to emancipate the totality of sentient beings from the pain and bondage of samsara - the focus is more on practice for individual liberation. In the early Sutra Pitika as preserved in the Pali Canon and the Âgamas, "Srâvaka" just translates as "follower" or "disciple": *any* disciple of Buddha would be a úrâvaka. There is thus no mention of a "úrâvakayâna" as "úrâvaka" refers to *all* disciples, not to a limited class of disciples. Although Paccekabuddhas are mentioned in the Jataka tales, the Buddha never admonishes his disciples to strive to become Paccekabuddhas—they are, in fact, beings who realize Buddhahood without reference to the teachings of other Buddhas.

2. Hînayâna as a *tradition* in general would include those schools who solely follow the sutras of the Pali Canon or the Âgamas (being, Pre-sectarian Buddhism and the Early Buddhist Schools). Recent scholars have also used the name Nikaya Buddhism to refer to these schools. Some of these schools actively rejected the Mahayana sutras during the time of the rise of the Mahayana, around 2,000 years ago.

3. Hînayâna as *practitioner* would be an individual of any school (including Mahayana) who practices to eliminate suffering according to basic Buddhist teachings; if successful, he is called an Arahant. (Similarly, a follower of a bodhisattva path in any school would be Mahayana in this sense.)

As a follower of what Mahayana terms "Hinayana",

> he or she will not strive to become a Buddha, nor will he or she take the Mahayana Bodhisattva-vow of pledging to come back into samsara countless times in the future in order to liberate all other sentient beings from suffering. Also, the 'Pratyeka-Buddha' is regarded by Mahayana as being Hinayanist. Mahayana only considers the ideal of a Samyaksambuddha 'Great'; the other enlightened ideals are considered by Mahayana orthodoxy to be (depending on the translation) either 'inferior' or 'low'.

Remarkably, within Buddhism the differing interpretations of Hînayâna have consequences that are sometimes quite far-reaching. It is primarily the interpretation of Hînayâna as a tradition that has led to the most concern, especially as many people have seen the term as a slur against Pre-sectarian Buddhism, Theravada.

Emergence

Apparently, the distinction between vehicles and paths arises in early Mahayana sutras, such as the *Lotus Sutra*, where it is stated that there is one *path* - the path to Nirvana -, but there are different *vehicles*. The vehicles are described (by Mahayana) as representing the fruit of the two types of Buddha found in the Pali Canon, plus the path of the Arahants.

For instance, in Chapter three of the *Lotus Sutra*, there is a parable of a father promising three carts to lure sons out of a burning building, where the goat-cart represents the Sravaka-vehicle; the deer-cart, Pratyeka-Buddhahood; and the bullock-cart, Samyaksambuddha-hood.

According to early Mahayana (as found in the Lotus

sutra), it is the *vehicles* that are taught as a method for journeying on the path to enlightenment. It is here that we can see the basis for term being used to indicate differences of doctrine.

The Lotus Sutra declares that the bullock-cart is "supremely restful", implying that the goat-cart and the deer-cart are inferior to the bullock-cart. This is where we begin to see the terminological origins for the term *Hînayâna*: The Sravakayana and the Pratyekabuddhayana as vehicles inferior to the superior bullock-cart of the *Mahayana*. The Dharmakshema Mahaparinirvana Sutra also speaks of the inferior nature of the Hinayana when compared to the higher level of the Mahayana.

In that sutra the Buddha states:

> "Noble son, there are also two groups of people within this great congregation: those who seek the Inferior Way (*hînayâna*) and those who seek the Great Way (*mahâyâna*). In past days I turned the lesser Wheel of the Dharma for the Úrâvakas, but now here in Kuúinagara I turn the great Wheel of the Dharma for Bodhisattvas."

The term first appeared in the Mahayana Prajñâpâramitâ literature. Possibly the earliest instance appears in the *Perfection of Wisdom in 8,000 Lines* (*Acmasâhasrikâ Prajñâpâramitâ Sûtra*), believed by scholars to have been composed some time between the 1st century BCE and the 1st century CE. Chapter 11 ("Mara's Deeds") depicts a conversation between Buddha and the arhat Subhuti, wherein Buddha admonishes those Bodhisattvas who disavow this sutra in favor of certain unnamed Buddhist sutras. In the following passage, the term *hinayana* is translated as "inferior vehicle" (emphasis added). "Subhuti, do these Bodhisattvas appear to be very intelligent who, having obtained and met with the irreversible, the great vehicle, and then again abandon this, turn away from this, and prefer an inferior vehicle [...] this is seen as being done to these Bodhisattvas by Mara."

In the early centuries CE, the Mahayana tradition was making efforts not to criticize or condemn the Hînayâna vehicles:

Lotus Sutra (Ch.14):

> "A bodhisattva [...] does not hold other Buddhists in contempt, not even those who follow the Hinayana path, nor does he cause them to have doubts or regrets by criticizing their way of practice or making discouraging remarks."

However, the Buddha also emphasises that the Bodhisattva should only preach the Mahâyâna in response to queries, not the Hinayana:

> "If there are objections or queries, one is not to answer them by resort to the Dharma of the Lesser Vehicle [*Hinayana*], but one is to explain only in terms of the Greater Vehicle [*Mahayana*], causing persons to gain knowledge of all modes" (*Scripture of the Lotus Blossom of the Fine Dharma*, tr. by Leon Hurvitz, Columbia UP, 1976, pp. 213-214).

The SaCdhinirmocana Sûtra, the foundational Mahâyâna Yogâcâra text, contains praise for both úrâvakas and bodhisattvas its introductory chapter. The relevant section on srâvakas is reproduced below.

> "[The Buddha] was accompanied by an immeasurable multitude of great word-hearers (úrâvakas), all of whom were docile sons of the Buddha. Their thinking was well liberated. Their understanding was well liberated. Their discipline was well purified, and they had set their aim upon joy in doctrine (Dharma). They had heard much, and retained and accumulated what they had heard. They

> thought good thoughts, spoke good words, and did good deeds. Their wisdom was swift, quick, incisive, salvific, penetrating, great, expansive, unequaled. Having perfected that wisdom gem, they were endowed with the three knowledges of remembering former lives, of the divine eye, and of the destruction of contaminants.
>
> They had attained the happiness of the highest state in the present world. They dwelled in the field of pure merit. Their deportment was tranquil and in no way imperfect. The perfection of their great patience and gentleness was without decrease. Already good, they revered and practiced the holy teachings of the Tathâgata."

However, should be noted that the SaCdhinirmocana Sûtra does draw distinctions between the various accomplishments of úrâvakas, pratyekabuddhas, bodhisattvas, and fully enlightened buddhas. This distinction is again drawn in the Yogâcârabhûmi Úâstra, an encyclopedic and definitive Yogâcâra text, which has divisions for the respective stages of úrâvakas, pratyekabuddhas, and bodhisattvas.

Philosophical Differences

Mahayanists were primarily in philosophical dialectic with the Vaibhâúika-Sarvâstivâda, which had by far the most "comprehensive edifice of doctrinal systematics" of the nikaya schools. With this in mind it is sometimes argued that the Theravada would not have been considered a "Hinayana" school by Mahayanists because unlike the now-extinct Sarvastivada school, the primary object of Mahayana criticism, the Theravada school does not claim the existence of independent dharmas; in this it maintains the attitude of early Buddhism.

Some contemporary Theravadin figures have thus indicated a sympathetic stance toward the Mahayana philosophy found in the Heart Sutra and the Fundamental Stanzas on the Middle Way. The Mahayanists were bothered by the substantialist thought of the Sarvastivadins and Sautrantikas, and in emphasizing the doctrine of emptiness, Kalupahana holds that they endeavored to preserve the early teaching.

The Theravadins too refuted the Sarvastivadins and Sautrantikas (and other schools) on the grounds that their theories were in conflict with the non-substantialism of the canon. The Theravada arguments are preserved in the Kathavatthu.

Most western scholars regard the Theravada school to be one of the Hinayana schools referred to in Mahayana literature, or regard Hinayana as a synonym for Theravada.

These scholars understand the term to refer to schools of Buddhism that did not accept the teachings of the Mahayana Sutras as authentic teachings of the Buddha. At the same time, scholars have objected to the prejorative connotation of the term Hinayana and some scholars do not use it for any school.

Some Theravada Buddhists have opposed the identification of Theravada with Hinayana.

As Walpola Rahula noted in his *Gems of Buddhist Wisdom*:

We must not confuse Hînayâna with Theravâda because the terms are not synonymous. Theravâda Buddhism went to Sri Lanka during the 3rd Century B.C. when there was no Mahâyâna at all. Hînayâna sects developed in India and had an existence independent from the form of Buddhism existing in Sri Lanka. Today there is no Hînayâna sect in existence anywhere in the world.

Therefore, in 1950 the World Fellowship of Buddhists inaugurated in Colombo unanimously decided that the term Hînayana should be dropped when referring to Buddhism existing today in Sri Lanka, Thailand, Burma, Cambodia, Laos, etc. This is the brief history of Theravâda, Mahayâna and Hînayâna. The Theravada school remained a presence on the Indian mainland long after its establishment in Sri Lanka, however. In addition, since the time of Rahula's writing considerable evidence has emerged indicating that Theravadins and Mahayanists interacted extensively in Sri Lanka throughout the first millennium CE, so any suggestion that there was no contact between the two would be incorrect.

4

Miscellaneous Issues

"If a man can have only one kind of sense, let him have common sense. If he has that and uncommon sense too, he is not far from genius."

—*Henry Word Beecher*

Here in the chapter we will discuss some salient features of Buddhism from modern day perspective. These include animals in Buddhisms, Vegetarianism, cuisines, eschatology, humanism, socialism, anarchism, economics, atomism, sexuality, fourteen unanswerable questions etc.

The position and treatment of animals in Buddhism is important for the light it sheds on Buddhists' perception of their own relation to the natural world, on Buddhist humanitarian concerns in general, and on the relationship between Buddhist theory and Buddhist practice.

Animals in Buddhist Doctrine

First, it is remarkable that Animals have always been regarded in Buddhist thought as sentient beings, different in their intellectual ability than humans but no less capable of feeling suffering. Furthermore, animals possess Buddha nature (according to the Mahâyâna school) and therefore an equal potential to become enlightened.

Moreover, the doctrine of rebirth held that any human could be reborn as an animal, and any animal could be reborn as a human. An animal might be a reborn dead relative, and if you looked far enough back in one's infinite series of lives, you would eventually perceive every animal to be related to you in some way. The Buddha expounded that sentient beings currently living in the animal realm have been our mothers, brothers, sisters, fathers, children, friends in past rebirths.

One could not, therefore, make a hard distinction between moral rules applicable to animals and those applicable to humans; ultimately humans and animals were part of a single family. They are all interconnected. In cosmological terms, the animals were believed to inhabit a distinct "world", separated from humans not by space but by state of mind. This world was called *Tiryagyoni* in Sanskrit, *Tiracchânayoni* in Pâli.

Rebirth as an animal was considered to be one of the unhappy rebirths, usually involving more than human suffering. Buddhist commentarial texts depict many sufferings associated with the animal world: even where no human beings are present, they are attacked and eaten by other animals or live in fear of it, they endure extreme changes of environment throughout the year, and they have no security of habitation.

Those that live among humans are often slaughtered for their bodies, or taken and forced to work with many beatings until they are slaughtered at the end of their lives. On top of this, they suffer from ignorance, not knowing or understanding what is happening to them with any clarity, and unable to do very much about it, acting primarily on instinct.

Animals in the Jatakas

The Jâtaka stories which tell of past lives of the Buddha in folktale fashion, frequently involve animals as peripheral or main characters, and it is not uncommon for the Bodhisattva (the past-life Buddha) to appear as an animal as well. The stories sometimes involve animals alone, and sometimes involve conflicts between humans and animals; in the latter cases, the animals often exhibit characteristics of kindness and generosity that are absent in the humans.

It is pertinent to note that the first of the five precepts bans the taking of life. As most narrowly interpreted, it applies primarily to the killing of human beings; however, the broader interpretation is that it applies to all sentient beings, which includes those in the animal realm in its broadest sense, i.e., not just mammals, but all animal taxa including insects, and invertebrates. From the beginnings of Buddhism, there were regulations intended to prevent the harming of sentient beings in the animals realm for various reasons. The Buddha taught that all sentient beings, including those in the animal realm, possess Buddha nature and therefore can attain enlightenment and that from infinite rebirths, all animals have been our past relatives, sisters, mothers, brothers, fathers and children.

Therefore it is against the first precept to harm, kill or eat sentient beings as it is the same as harming, killing or eating the flesh of our own child or mother. Monks were forbidden from intentionally killing an animal, or drinking water with living creatures (such as larvae) in it. Concern for animals is attested back to the beginnings of Buddhist history. The first Buddhist monarch of India, Ashoka, includes in his Edicts an expression of concern for the number of animals that had been killed for his meals, and expresses an intention to put an end to this killing. He also includes animals with humans as the beneficiaries of his programs for obtaining medicinal plants, planting trees and digging wells. In his fifth Pillar Edict, Ashoka decrees the protection of a large number of animals that were not in common use as livestock; protects from slaughter young animals and mother animals still milking their young; protects forests from being burned, expressly to protect the animals living in them; and bans a number of other practices hurtful to animals. In this Ashoka was carrying out the advice to the Cakravartin king given in the *Cakkavattisîhanâda-sutta* (DN.26) that a good king should extend his protection not merely to different classes of people equally, but also to beasts and birds.

Vegetarianism

A basic precept in Buddhism is that of non-harm. Actions which result in the taking of life, directly or indirectly, contradict this basic Buddhist precept.

Many Buddhists in many countries, including monks, are not vegetarians. However in recent years attitudes are changing. In January 2007, the 17th Karmapa, Ogyen Trinley Dorje, instructed all his monasteries & centres to become vegetarian. There has been some contention about interpretations of the sûtras. One interpretation is that eating of meat is not explicitly prohibited in the suttas and Vinaya of the Pâli canon which encourage monks to accept whatever food they are given. However, monks are forbidden from accepting animal flesh if they know, believe or suspect that the animal in question was killed especially for them, i.e., if the visits of begging monks have become an occasion for the slaughter of animals.

In the Lankâvatâra & Angulimâla sutra the Buddha explicitly prohibits the eating of meat, fish and any animal products which are the result of harming and killing of any sentient being. The Buddha states the only time it is acceptable for a monastic to accept and eat the flesh of sentient beings is for medicinal purposes only if the animal died in accordance with the Dharma, meaning the animal died of natural causes.

In Mahâyâna Chinese Buddhism and in those countries to which Chinese Buddhism has spread (Korea, Japan, Vietnam), Buddhist monks are more strictly vegetarian. One of the scriptural sources for this prohibition is the Mahâyâna Lankâvatâra Sûtra. This sûtra condemns meat-eating in the strongest terms; among several other reasons, it is stated that it should be avoided because the presence of a meat-eater causes terror in animals, who believe them to be likely to kill them.

Although vegetarianism is not expressly commanded in the Pâli canon, it is evidently viewed as an ideal state from which human beings have fallen; the Aggañña Sutta (DN.27) explains how human beings, originally sustained on various kinds of vegetable matter, as the result of increasing wickedness began to live by hunting, which was originally thought of as a demeaning occupation.

In Buddhism, the views on vegetarianism vary from school to school. According to Theravada, the Buddha allowed his monks to eat pork, chicken and beef if the animal was not killed for the purpose of providing food for monks. Theravada also believes that the Buddha allowed the monks to choose a vegetarian diet, but only prohibited against eating human, elephant, horse, dog, snake, lion, tiger, leopard, bear, and hyena flesh. Buddha did not prohibit any kind of meat-eating for his lay followers. In Vajrayana, the act of eating meat is not always prohibited.

The Mahayana schools generally recommend a vegetarian diet, for they believe that the Buddha insisted that his followers should not eat meat or fish. The accepted legend of the Buddha's death also says that he died after accepting tainted meat from his hosts while traveling. The relevant word to describe this food, however, is contested as to meaning: it is not the usual term for meat (*mamsa*), but *sukara-maddava*, which translates as "pig's delight".

There is a divergence of views within Buddhism as to whether vegetarianism is required, with some schools of Buddhism rejecting such a requirement. The first precept in Buddhism is usually translated as "I undertake the precept to refrain from taking life." Some Buddhists see this as implying that Buddhists should not eat meat, other Buddhists argue that this is not the case. Some Buddhists do strongly oppose meat-eating on the basis of scriptural injunctions against flesh-eating in Mahayana sutras.

Buddha in the *Anguttara Nikaya* 3.38 Sukhamala Sutta, describes his family being wealthy enough to provide non-vegetarian meals even to his servants. After becoming Buddha, he accepted any food offered with respect as alms, including meat, but there is no reference of him eating meat during his seven years as an ascetic.

On one occasion, according to the scriptures, a general sent a servant to purchase meat specifically to feed the Buddha. The Buddha declared that

> ... meat should not be eaten under three circumstances: when it is seen or heard or suspected (that a living being has been purposely slaughtered for the eater); these, Jivaka, are the three circumstances in which meat should not be eaten, Jivaka! I declare there are three circumstances in which meat can be eaten: when it is not seen or heard or suspected (that a living being has been purposely

> slaughtered for the eater); Jivaka, I say these are the three circumstances in which meat can be eaten.
>
> —Jivaka Sutta, MN 55

Remarkably, in this particular sutta, Buddha instructs to a monk or nun to accept, without any discrimination, whatever food is offered in receiving alms offered with good will, including meat, whereas the Buddha declares the meat trade to be wrong livelihood in the Vanijja Sutta, AN 5:177.

Monks, a lay follower should not engage in five types of business. Which five? Business in weapons, business in human beings, business in meat, business in intoxicants, and business in poison. These are the five types of business that a lay follower should not engage in. But this is not, strictly speaking, a dietary rule. The Buddha, on one particular occasion, specifically refused suggestions by Devadatta to institute vegetarianism in the Sangha.

According to Kassapa Buddha (a previous Buddha before Shakyamuni Buddha)

> "[t]aking life, beating, wounding, binding, stealing, lying, deceiving, worthless knowledge, adultery; this is stench. Not the eating of meat." (Amagandha Sutta).

There were monastic guidelines prohibiting consumption of 10 types of meat. Those are humans, elephants, horses, dogs, snakes, lions, tigers, leopards, bears and hyenas because these animals can be provoked by the smell of the flesh of their own kind or the eating of such flesh would generate a bad reputation for the Sangha. According to the story of the Nirvana Sutra, a Mahayana Buddhist scripture purporting to give the Buddha's final teachings, the Buddha insisted that his followers should not eat any kind of meat or fish, even those not included in the 10 types, and that even vegetarian food that has been touched by meat should be washed before being eaten.

Also, it is not permissible for the monk or nun just to pick out the non-meat portions of a diet and leave the rest: the whole meal must be rejected. However, this scripture is of late origin and is thus not accepted in Theravada Buddhism. Also many Buddhist teachers refrain from eating meat (and fish and egg), while many other Buddhist teachers do eat meat.

Eating Meat Versus Killing

In Buddhism, what is most important is to recognise that being alive, by its very nature, is the cause of direct or indirect suffering and death to other beings (samsara). One should avoid gluttony and greedy consumption, while maintaining a healthy diet and lifestyle which is conducive to attaining enlightenment. In the Pali Canon, the Buddha refused suggestion by Devadatta to institute vegetarianism in the monastic code. Mahayana Buddhism argues that if one pursues the path of the Bodhisattva for enlightenment, one should avoid meat eating to cultivate compassion for all living beings. Similarly, in Theravada Buddhism, avoiding meat eating for the purpose of cultivation of metta (loving kindness) is also seen to be in accord with Buddhist Dharma. In most Buddhist branches, one may adopt vegetarianism if one so wishes but it is not considered skillful practice to verbally attack another person for eating meat.

Remarkably, in Chinese Mahayana, vegetarianism is seen as a prerequisite for pursuing the path of the Bodhisattva. The argument for vegetarianism is made more forcefully, often to the extent of accusing those who eat meat of lacking compassion. Chinese Mahayanists do not accept the Pali suttas as definitive when they conflict with the Mahayana sutras, and consequently some do not accept that Gautama Buddha ever ate meat or permitted eating it, in accordance with the Lankavatara Sutra.

Theravada

In the Pali Canon, Buddha explicitly declared meat-eating to be karma neutral and once explicitly refused suggestion by Devadatta to institute vegetarianism in the monks' Vinaya.

Buddha's advice on meat eating was directed specifically to monks. In his comment, he stated that monks and nuns are not allowed to eat meat if they have seen, heard or suspect that the meat was killed specifically for them. Theravada commentaries explain the Buddha was making a distinction between direct destruction of life and eating of already dead meat.

Moreover, they point out that the cultivation of vegetables also involves proxy killing. In fact, any act of consumption would cause some degree of proxy killing. Hence, the Buddha advised his followers to avoid gluttony or any other act of craving which lead to overconsumption. However, Theravadins argue that it is acceptable to practice vegetarianism based on brahmavihara. Theravada canon does not contain Buddha making a reference for lay followers' meat eating. The distinction is rather crucial as monks and nuns beg for alms, eating left over foods of lay household.

In this case, therefore, economic chain of proxy killing is largely absent. On the other hand, monks and nuns must stop collecting alms once they judge that enough amount for daily sustenance has been collected and they are not allowed to cherry pick food. Instead they must eat whatever given to them, which include meat.

Mahayana

Notably, certain Mahayana sutras do present the Buddha as very vigorously and unreservedly denouncing the eating of meat, mainly on the grounds that such an act is linked to the spreading of fear amongst sentient beings (who can allegedly sense the odour of death that lingers about the meat-eater and who consequently fear for their own lives) and violates the bodhisattva's fundamental cultivation of compassion. Moreover, according to the Buddha in the Angulimaliya Sutra, since all beings share the same "Dhatu" (spiritual Principle or Essence) and are intimately related to one another, killing and eating other sentient creatures is tantamount to a form of self-killing and cannibalism.

The sutras which inveigh against meat-eating include the *Nirvana Sutra,* the *Shurangama Sutra,* the *Brahmajala Sutra,* the *Angulimaliya Sutra,* the *Mahamegha Sutra,* and the *Lankavatara Sutra,* as well as the Buddha's comments on the negative karmic effects of meat consumption in the *Karma Sutra*. In the Mahayana Mahaparinirvana Sutra, which presents itself as the final elucidatory and definitive Mahayana teachings of the Buddha on the very eve of his death, the Buddha states that "the eating of meat extinguishes the seed of Great Kindness", adding that all and every kind of meat and fish consumption (even of animals found already dead) is prohibited by him. He specifically rejects the idea that monks who go out begging and receive meat from a donor should eat it: ". . . it should be rejected . . . I say that even meat, fish, game, dried hooves and scraps of meat left over by others constitutes an infraction . . . I teach the harm arising from meat-eating." The Buddha also predicts in this sutra that later monks will "hold spurious writings to be the authentic Dharma" and will concoct their own sutras and falsely claim that the Buddha allows the eating of meat, whereas he says he does not.

A long passage in the Lankavatara Sutra shows the Buddha speaking out very forcefully against meat consumption and unequivocally in favor of vegetarianism, since the eating of the flesh of fellow sentient beings is said by him to be incompatible with the compassion that a Bodhisattva should strive to cultivate. In several other Mahayana scriptures, too (e.g., the Mahayana jatakas), the Buddha is seen clearly to indicate that meat-eating is undesirable and karmically unwholesome. Some suggest that the rise of monasteries in Mahayana tradition to be a contributing factor in the emphasis on vegetarianism. In the monastery, food was prepared specifically for monks.

In this context, large quantities of meat would have been specifically prepared (killed) for monks. Henceforth, when monks from the Indian geographical sphere of influence migrated to China from the year 65 CE on, they met followers who provided them with money instead of food. From those days onwards Chinese monastics, and others who came to inhabit northern countries, cultivated their own vegetable plots and bought food in the market.

This remains the dominant practice in China, Vietnam and part of Korean Mahayanan temples. Mahayana lay buddhists often eat vegetarian diets on the vegetarian dates. There are different arrangement of the dates, from several days to three months in each year.

Vajrayana

In Tibetan Buddhism, a strong emphasis was placed on number of esoteric tantras which were transmitted from Northern India. In these tantras, it is clearly stated that the practice of Vajrayana would make vegetarianism unnecessary.

A number of tantric texts frequently recommend alcohol and meat—though not all take such passages literally. Many traditions of the Ganachakra which is a type of Panchamakara puja prescribe the offering and ingestion of meat and alcohol. The Tibetan position is that it is not necessary to be vegetarian if one practices Vajrayana, but that it is necessary to be vegetarian if one practices the Mahayana path. The 14th Dalai Lama and other esteemed lamas invite their audiences to adopt vegetarianism when they can.

When asked in recent years what he thinks of vegetarianism, the 14th Dalai Lama has said: "It is wonderful. We must absolutely promote vegetarianism." The Dalai Lama became a vegetarian and promoted vegetarianism. In 1999, it has been published that the Dalai Lama would only be vegetarian every other day and partakes of meat regularly. When he is in Dharamsala, he is vegetarian, but not necessarily when he is outside Dharamsala. Paul McCartney has taken him to task for this and wrote to him to urge him to return to strict vegetarianism but " [The Dalai Lama] replied saying that his doctors had told him he needed [meat], so I wrote back saying they were wrong."

Arjia Rinpoche became vegetarian in 1999.

On 3 January 2007, 17th Karmapa, Urgyen Trinley Dorje, strongly urged vegetarianism upon his students, saying that generally, in his view, it was very important in the Mahayana not to eat meat and that even in Vajrayana students should not eat meat: There are many great masters and very great realized beings in India and there have been many great realized beings in Tibet also, but they are not saying, "I'm realized, therefore I can do anything; I can eat meat and drink alcohol." It's nothing like that. It should not be like that. According to the Kagyupa school, we have to see what the great masters of the past, the past lamas of Kagyupas, did and said about eating meat. The Drikung Shakpa [sp?] Rinpoche, master of Drikungpa, said like this, "My students, whomever are eating or using meat and calling it tsokhor or tsok, then these people are completely deserting me and going against the dharma." I can't explain each of these things, but he said that anybody that is using meat and saying it is something good, this is completely against the dharma and against me and they completely have nothing to do with dharma. He said it very, very strongly.

Japan initially received Chinese Buddhism through Korea in 6th century. And in 9th century, Emperor Saga made a decree prohibiting meat consumption except fish and birds.

This remained the dietary habit of Japanese until the introduction of European dietary customs in 19th century. Again around the 9th century, two Japanese monks (Kûkai and Saichô) introduced Vajrayana Buddhism into Japan and this soon became the dominant Buddhism among the nobility. In particular, Saichô, who founded the Tendai sect of Japanese Buddhism, reduced the number of vinaya code to 66.

During the 12th century, a number of monks from Tendai sects founded new sects (Zen, Pure Land and Nichiren) of Buddhism, and de-emphasised vegetarianism - although Ch'an and Zen do tend generally to look favourably upon vegetarianism.

Buddhist Views Today

In the modern world, attitudes toward vegetarianism vary by location. In the Theravada countries of South East Asia and Sri Lanka, monks are obliged by the vinaya to accept almost any food that is offered to them, including meat unless they suspect the meat was slaughtered specifically for them; while in China, Korea and Vietnam, monks are expected to eat no meat. In Taiwan, Buddhist monks, nuns, and most lay followers eat no animal products or the fetid vegetables - traditionally garlic, *Allium chinense*, asafoetida, shallot, and *Allium victorialis* (victory onion or mountain leek), although in modern times this rule is often interpreted to include other vegetables of the onion genus, as well as coriander - this is called Su vegetarianism. Some Zhaijiao lay adherents do not eat any meat. In Japan, some clergy practice vegetarianism, and most will do so at least when training at a monastery, but otherwise they typically do eat meat. In Tibet, where vegetables have been historically very scarce, and the adopted vinaya was the Nikaya Sarvâstivâda, vegetarianism is very rare, although the Dalai Lama and other esteemed lamas invite their audiences to adopt vegetarianism whenever they can. Chatral Rinpoche in particular, has stated that anyone who wishes to be his student must be vegetarian. Many followers of Mahayana Buddhism (including monks) also eat meat despite the emphatic denunciation of the practice found in some major Mahayana sutras. Part of the reason is that there are many hundreds of Mahayana sutras and the position on vegetarianism depends on one's position on the authority of any particular sutra.

The Japanese Pure Land puts a heavy emphasis on the Pure Land sutras and aims to achieve enlightenment by reincarnating into the Pure Land where one's enlightenment is assured. Therefore, vegetarianism holds very little relevance for them, either. The Vajrayana of Tibet and the Japanese Shingon sect consider that tantric practice makes vegetarianism unnecessary. In the West, of course, a wide variety of practices are followed. Lay Buddhists generally follow dietary rules less rigorously than monastics. Overall, it can be said that the debate over whether Buddhists should ideally be vegetarian or not continues.

Release of Animals

In East Asian Buddhism and particularly in China, the release of animals, particularly birds or fish, into their natural environment became an important way of demonstrating Buddhist piety. In China it was known as *fang sheng*. This practice is based on a passage in the Mahâyâna Sûtra of Brahma's Net (Ch: Fanwang Jing), which states that "...all the beings in the six paths of existence are my parents. If I should kill and eat them, it is the same as killing my own parents. ... Since to be reborn into one existence after another is the permanent and unalterable law, we should teach people to release sentient beings." In the later Ming dynasty, societies "for releasing life" were created, which built ponds in which to release fish that were redeemed from fishermen for this purpose. They also bought other animals which were sold in the markets and released them.

CUISINE

Buddhist cuisine is an East Asian cuisine which is followed by some believers of Buddhism. It is primarily vegetarian, in order to keep with the general Buddhist precept of ahimsa (non-violence). Parts of Ancient India were also Buddhist, and many Indians remain vegetarian.

Buddhism, along with Jainism, recognizes that even eating vegetables could contribute to the indirect killing of living beings because animal life is destroyed by tilling the soil or the use of pesticides. Jainism consequently considers death by starvation (only after undergoing 12 years of strict asceticism) as the ultimate practice of non-violence, while Buddhism considers extreme self-mortification to be undesirable for attaining enlightenment. Both Mahayana and Theravada thinking is that eating meat in and of itself does not constitute a violation of the Five Precepts which prohibit one from directly harming life.

When monks and nuns who follow the Theravadan way feed themselves by alms, they must eat whatever leftover foods which are given to them, including meat. (The Pali/Sanskrit term for monks and nuns means "one who seeks alms".) The exception to this alms rule is when monks and nuns have seen, heard or known that animal(s) have been specifically killed to feed the alms-seeker, in which case consumption of such meat would be karmically negative. The same restriction is also followed by lay Buddhists and is known as the consumption of the "triply-clean meat". On the other hand, when lay communities specifically purchase meat for the consumption of monks and nuns, the permissibility of meat eating differ among Buddhist sects. The Theravada Pali Canon records instances of Buddha eating meat that was specifically purchased for him.

This act was deliberately performed by the Buddha to demonstrate that, if need be, a Buddhist can bend the rules in times of emergency or inconvenience. Obstinately observing vegetarianism or Buddhist rules in times when you cannot conflicts with Mahayana philosophy because obstinacy or attachment for anything, is considered to be "stubbornness", which will become an obstacle to nirvana or enlightenment.

However, if one undertakes a vow to be a Buddhist vegetarian, one is expected to follow this vow until it is humanly impossible to continue one's vegetarian diet. Acceptance of authenticity of the Pali Sutras differ within Mahayana sects, and the Mahayana sutras do not record Buddha eating meat. While no Mahayana sects consider the Pali sutras to be inauthentic, Chinese Buddhist sects tend to consider this particular part of writing in Pali sutras to be false. Japanese Buddhist sects generally accept that Buddha ate meat.

Still, both Mahayana and Theravada Buddhists consider that one may practice vegetarianism as part of cultivating Bodhisattvas's paramita. Since Mahayana Buddhists recognise the consumption of meat to be cruel and devoid of compassion, some Mahayana Buddhists are vegetarians. Numbers of Mahayana sutra record Buddha praising the virtue of avoiding meat. However, Tibetan Buddhism believes that tantric practice makes vegetarianism unnecessary.

All Japanese Kamakura sects of Buddhism (Zen, Nichiren, Jodo) have relaxed Mahayana vinaya, and as a consequence, do not practice vegetarianism but rather pescetarianism. Chinese Buddhism and part of Korean Buddhism strictly adhere to vegetarianism.

Buddhism and other Food Considerations

East Asian "Buddhist" cuisine differ from Western vegetarian cuisine in one aspect, that is avoidance of killing plant life. Buddhist vinaya for monks and nuns prohibit harming of plants. Therefore, strictly speaking, no root vegetables (such as potatoes, carrots or onion) are to be used as this will result in death of vegetables. Instead, vegetables such as beans or fruits are used. However, this stricter version of diet is often practiced only on special occasion. Some Mahayana Buddhists in China, Japan and Vietnam specifically avoid eating strong-smelling plants, traditionally garlic, *Allium chinense*, asafoetida, shallot, and *Allium victorialis* (victory onion or mountain leek), and refer to these as "Nd*f* 'Five Acrid And Strong Smelling Vegetables' or " 'Five Spices' as they tend to excite senses. This is based on teachings found in the Brahma Net Sutra, the Surangama Sutra and the Lankavatara Sutra (chapter 8). In modern times this rule is often interpreted to include other vegetables of the onion genus, as well as coriander.

The food that a strict Buddhist takes, even if he/she is not a vegetarian, is also specific. For many Chinese Buddhists, beef and the consumption of large animals and exotic species is avoided. Then there would be the aforementioned sanjingrou rule. One restriction on food that is not known to many is the abstinence from eating animal innards and organs. This is known as N41 (*xia shui*), and is not to be confused with the term for sewage. Alcohol and/or other drugs are also avoided by many Buddhists because of their effects on the mind and "mindfulness". It is part of the Five Precepts which dictate that one is not to consume "addictive materials". The definition of "addictive" depends on each individual but most Buddhists consider alcohol, tobacco and contraband drugs to be addictive.

Sources for Buddhist Foods

Buddhist vegetarian chefs have become extremely creative in imitating meat using prepared wheat gluten, also known as "seitan" or "wheat meat", soy (such as tofu or tempeh), agar, and other plant products. Some of their recipes are the oldest and most-refined meat analogues in the world. Soy and wheat gluten are very versatile materials, because they can be manufactured into various shapes and textures, and they absorb flavourings (including, but not limited to, meat-like flavourings), whilst having very little flavour of their own. With the proper seasonings, they can mimic various kinds of meat quite closely. Some of these Buddhist vegetarian chefs are in the many monasteries which serve *wu hun* and mock-meat (also known as 'meat analogues') dishes to the monks and visitors (including non-Buddhists who often stay for a few hours or days, to Buddhists who are not monks, but staying overnight for anywhere up to weeks or months). Many Buddhist restaurants also serve vegetarian, vegan, non-alcoholic, and/or *wu hun* dishes. Some Buddhists eat vegetarian only once per week or month, or on special occasions such as annual visits to an ancestor's grave. To cater to this type of customer, as well as full-time vegetarians, the menu of a Buddhist vegetarian restaurant usually shows no difference from a typical Chinese or far-Eastern restaurant, except that in recipes originally made to contain meat, a chicken flavoured soy or wheat gluten might be served instead.

BUDDHIST ESCHATOLOGY

Buddhist eschatology, as subscribed by some Buddhist schools, derives from purported Gautama Buddha's prediction that his teachings would disappear after 5000 years. According to the Sutta Pitaka, the "ten moral courses of conduct" will disappear and people will follow the ten amoral concepts of theft, violence, murder, lying, evil speaking, adultery, abusive and idle talk, covetousness and ill will, wanton greed, and perverted lust resulting in skyrocketing poverty and the end of the worldly laws of true dharma. During the Middle Ages, the span of time was expanded to 5,000 years. Commentators like Buddhaghosa predicted a step-by-step disappearance of the Buddha's teachings. During the first stage, arahants would no longer appear in the world.

Later, the content of the Buddha's true teachings would vanish, and only their form would be preserved. Finally, even the form of the Dharma would be forgotten. During the final stage, the memory of the Buddha himself would be forgotten, and the last of his relics would be gathered together in Bodh Gaya and cremated. Some time following this development a new Buddha named Maitreya will arise to renew the teachings of Buddhism and rediscover the path to Nirvana.

Maitreya is believed to currently reside in the Tucita heaven, where he is awaiting his final rebirth in the world. The decline of Buddhism in the world, and its eventual re-establishment by Maitreya, are in keeping with the general shape of Buddhist cosmology.

Like Hindus, Buddhists generally believe in a cycle of creation and destruction, of which the current epoch represents only the latest step.

The historical Buddha Shakyamuni is only the latest in a series of Buddhas that stretches back into the past. The belief in the decline and disappearance of Buddhism in the world has exerted significant influence in the development of Buddhism since the time of the Buddha. In Vajrayana Buddhism and various other forms of esoteric Buddhism, the use of tantra is justified by the degenerate state of the present world.

The East Asian belief in the decline of the Dharma (called mappo in Japanese) was instrumental in the emergence of Pure Land Buddhism. Within the Theravada tradition, debate over whether Nirvana was still attainable in the present age helped prompt the creation of the Dhammayutt Order in Thailand.

HUMANISTIC BUDDHISM

Humanistic Buddhism is a modern Buddhist philosophy practiced mostly by Mahayana Buddhists. It is the integration of people's spiritual practice into all aspects of their daily lives. Buddhist monastics such as Taixu, Yinshun and Hsing Yun pioneered the start of the propagation of Humanistic Buddhism. Humanistic Buddhism claims to encompass all of the Buddhist teachings from the time of Gautama Buddha to the present. Its goal is to live the bodhisattva way, which means to be an energetic, enlightened, and endearing person who strives to help all sentient beings liberate themselves.

It focuses on issues of the world rather than on how to leave the world behind; on caring for the living, rather than the dead; on benefiting others, rather than benefiting oneself and on universal salvation, rather than cultivation for only oneself.

Taixu, a reformist pioneer in early 20th century Chinese Buddhism, was one of the first to popularize the term "Buddhism for Human Life" though may not have been the inventor of this term. The first two characters, "human" and "life", indicating his criticism of several aspects of late Ming dynasty and early Republican Chinese Buddhism that he wished to correct, namely, an emphasis on spirits and ghosts (viz "human"), and funeral services and rites (viz "life"). His disciples continued this emphasis.

Taixu also used the term "Buddhism for the Human World", or popularly "Humanistic Buddhism". It appears that at first the two terms were largely interchangeable. One of Taixu's disciples, Yin Shun, used the term "Humanistic Buddhism" to indicate a criticism against the "deification" of Buddhism, which was another common feature of much of Chinese Buddhism, in his articles and books. It was Yinshun, and other disciples of Taixu, who brought both of these two terms to Taiwan in the wake of the Republican's defeat during the civil war against the Chinese Communist Party.

It was in Taiwan that the term "Humanistic Buddhism" became the most commonly used term, particularly amongst the religious leaders who originally hailed from the Mainland. The term has also been translated as "Engaged Buddhism" or "Socially Engaged Buddhism," attributed mainly to Thich Nhat Hanh and his rendering of the Chinese into Vietnamese as *Nhân gian ph-t giáo*. Both share historical and structural features in emphasizing the relief of suffering in the here and now.

An international conference on "Humanistic and Engaged Buddhism - Patterns and Prospects" was held May 18–24, 2009 at Foguang University in Ilan, Taiwan to reflect on the history, teachings, practices, and future of these movements.

Pure Land in the Human World

The proponents of this reformation was not seen as a rejection of other forms of Buddhism, but a reinterpretation. One classic example, is the idea of "creating a Pure Land in the human world" which can be seen as a new interpretation to the Pure Land form of Chinese Buddhism. This latter school, of course, being one of the most popular forms of Chinese Buddhism for over 1000 years, particularly amongst the laity. Many of the forms and practices are maintained, however, the aim is redirected - rather than practicing in the hope (or vow) of rebirth in Amitabha Buddha's Pure Land, the practitioner seeks to better themselves and society, to create a Pure Land here on earth. This interpretation is also quite well justified in many Mahayana scriptures, which indicate that the bodhisattva (Mahayana practitioner) "travels from Pure Land to Pure Land, learning from the Buddhas and bodhisattvas", before creating their own one, as an expedient means to liberate sentient beings.

According to Venerable Master Hsing Yun, Humanistic Buddhism has the following six characteristics:

1. Humanism: The Buddha was neither a spirit—coming and going without leaving a trace— nor a figment of one's imagination. The Buddha was a living human being. Just like the rest of us, he had parents, a family, and he lived a life. It was through his human existence that he showed his supreme wisdom of compassion, ethical responsibility, and prajna-wisdom. Thus, he is a Buddha who was also (in the past) a human being.

2. Emphasis on Daily Life: In his teachings, the Buddha placed great importance on daily life as spiritual practice. He provided guidance on everything, from how to eat, dress, work, and live, to how to walk, stand, sit, and sleep. He gave clear directions on every aspect of life, from relations among family members and between friends to how we should conduct ourselves in the social and political arenas.

3. Altruism: The Buddha was born into this world to teach, to provide an example, and to bring joy to all beings. He nurtured all beings, for he always had the best interests of others in his mind and heart. In short, his every thought, word, and action arose from a heart filled with deep care and concern for others.

4. Joyfulness: The Buddhist teachings give people joy.

Through the limitless compassion of his heart, the Buddha aimed to relieve the suffering of all beings and to give them joy.

5. Timeliness: The Buddha was born for a great reason: to build a special relationship with all of us who live in this world. Although the Buddha lived some 2,500 years ago and has already entered nirvana, he left the seed of liberation for all subsequent generations. Even today, the Buddha's ideals and teachings serve as timely, relevant guides for us all.

6. Universality: The entire life of the Buddha can be characterized by the Buddha's spirit of wanting to liberate all beings, without exclusion. [The Buddha loved beings of all forms, whether they were animals or humans, male or female, young or old, Buddhist or not Buddhist, etc.]

Yinshun was the key figure in the doctrinal exposition of Buddhism, and thus Humanistic Buddhism, in Taiwan. However, he was not particularly active in the social or policital spheres of life. This was to be carried out by a younger generation: Hsing Yun, Sheng-yen, Wei Chueh and Cheng Yen. These four figures, collectively known as the "Four Heavenly Kings of Taiwanese Buddhism", head the "Four Great Mountains", or monasteries, of modern Taiwanese Buddhism: Fo Guang Shan, Dharma Drum Mountain, Chung Tai Shan, and Tsu Chi.

BUDDHIST SOCIALISM

Buddhist socialism is a political ideology which advocates socialism based on the principles of Buddhism. Buddhist socialists have called for state provision of the Buddhist requisites of food, shelter, clothing and medicine, for the abolition or amelioration of class distinctions, for campaigns for morality based on Buddhist traditions, and for workers and peasants to overcome the love of property.

People who have been described as Buddhist socialists include Buddhadasa Bhikkhu, S.W.R.D. Bandaranaike, U Nu and Norodom Sihanouk.

Tenzin Gyatso, the Fourteenth Dalai Lama of Tibet has said that:

> "Of all the modern economic theories, the economic system of Marxism is founded on moral principles, while capitalism is concerned only with gain and profitability. (...) The failure of the regime in the former Soviet Union was, for me, not the failure of Marxism but the failure of totalitarianism. For this reason I still think of myself as half-Marxist, half-Buddhist."

ANARCHISM

It is pertinent to note that observers believe certain Buddhist teachings form a philosophical ground for anarchism.

Buddhism is rooted in three fundamental truths of the universe, the dharma seals, viz.:

1. Everything is in a constant state of change, nothing is permanent. (anicca)
2. That "suffering" exists everywhere in Samsara. (dukkha)
3. That everything is devoid of a "self." (anatta)

Thus, there can be no "perfect State"; from this Buddhist anarchists infer that it is only possible to try to approach an ideal community for all. Any man-made institution is impermanent as well as imperfect, as people and the world change constantly. Further, no material wealth or political power will grant people permanent happiness—

unenlightened satisfaction is an illusion that only perpetuates samsara.

Individual liberty, while a worthy goal for anarchists, is nevertheless incomplete, to the extent that it precludes our common humanity, since there is, ultimately, no "self" that is inherently distinct from the rest of the universe. That being said, the aim of a *bodhisattva* is to try to minimize the amount of suffering that goes on during the lives of conscious beings. The socialist anarchist argues that both the state and capitalism generate oppression and, therefore, suffering. The former, the state, is an institution that frames the desire for power, and the latter, capitalism, the desire for material wealth. Trying to control other human beings, in the view of Buddhist anarchists, will only cause them to suffer, and ultimately causes suffering for those who try to control.

Trying to hold on to and accumulate material wealth, likewise, increases suffering for the capitalist and those they do business with. Compassion, for a Buddhist, springs from a fundamental selflessness. Compassion for humanity as a whole is what inspires the Buddhist towards activism; however, most, if not all, political groups tend to go against the Eightfold Path that steers Buddhist thought and action.

Thus, anarchism, lacking a rigid ideological structure and dogmas, is seen as easily applicable for Buddhists. Those who have seen the conjunction of anarchism and Buddhism (in various ways) arguably include Uchiyama Gudo, Edward Carpenter, Ananda Coomaraswamy, Lala Hardayal, Liu Shipei, John Cage, Kenneth Rexroth, Allen Ginsberg, Diane di Prima, Gary Snyder, Jackson MacLow, Peter Lamborn Wilson, John Moore, Kerry Wendell Thornley, Max Cafard, William Batchelder Greene, as well as the pro-Situationist Ken Knabb and others.

The anarchist thinker Peter Kropotkin saw primitive Buddhist communities as embodying the principle of mutual aid, and Matthew Turner noted that some Buddhist priests were involved in the anarchist movement in Japan in the early part of the 20th century.

Eisai the founder of Rinzai school in Japan held quite a different view as regards the state (which is otherwise universally abhorred by all forms of anarchists) as shown in *Ko-zen-go-koku-ron* (*The Protection of the State by the Propagation of Zen*). This, however, has not prevented the promotion of Zen Anarchism as "whatever you make it" or of Zen Anarchists as "scholar warriors" with little reference to Zen Buddhism itself, but rather promoting a literary and psychological view rooted in Japanese militaristic tradition. Parts of Japanese anarchism embraced this militarism and became ultra-nationalists

Anarchism and Hindu Fundamentalism

The Indian anarchist Har Dayal understood the realisation of ancient *Aryan* culture as anarchism, which he also saw as the goal of Buddhism. A prominent Sanskrit scholar influenced by Swami Dayananda Saraswati (founder of Arya Samaj), he wished to create a movement which he saw as replicating a return to ancient vedic culture. He was active in the Industrial Workers of the World in San Francisco and was a central figure in the Ghadar movement which attempted to overthrow the British in India by reconciling Western concepts of social revolution - particularly those stemming from Mikhail Bakunin - with Buddhism. It should be noted that the relationship between Buddhism and Hinduism remains a controversial issue.

The controversy includes the usage of the term "Aryan", which does not necessarily carry racial connotations in

Buddhism (where it more often means "noble" - see also aristocracy which comes from the same Aryan root).

"Dharma Bums"

In the 1950s, California saw the rise of a strand of Buddhist anarchism emerging from the Beat movement. Gary Snyder and Diane di Prima were a product of this. Snyder was the inspiration for the character Japhy Rider in Jack Kerouac's novel the *The Dharma Bums* (1958). Snyder spent considerable time in Japan studying Zen Buddhism, and in 1961 published *Buddhist Anarchism* where he described the connection he saw between these two concepts originating in different parts of the world: "The mercy of the West has been social revolution; the mercy of the East has been individual insight into the basic self/void."

He advocated "using such means as civil disobedience, outspoken criticism, protest, pacifism, voluntary poverty and even gentle violence" and defended "the right of individuals to smoke hemp, eat peyote, be polygymous, polyandrous or homosexual" which he saw as being banned by "the Judaeo-Capitalist-Christian-Marxist West".

ECONOMICS

Buddhist economics is a set of economic principles partly inspired by Buddhist beliefs that individuals ought to do good work in order to ensure proper human development.

The term was coined by Ernst Schumacher in 1955, when he traveled to Burma as an economic consultant for Prime Minister U Nu, and is used almost exclusively by followers of Schumacher and by Theravada Buddhist writers such as Prayudh Payutto and Phrabhavanaviriyakhun.

Schumacher's essay "Buddhist Economics" was first

published in 1966 in *Asia: A Handbook,* and republished in Schumacher's influential collection *Small Is Beautiful: Economics as if People Mattered* (1973).

The efforts by the government of Bhutan are often considered an expression of Buddhist economics: for example, alongside traditional economic indicators, Bhutan uses 'Gross national happiness' to measure quality of life and non-economic well-being.

ATOMISM

Buddhist atomism is a school of atomistic Buddhist philosophy that flourished on the Indian subcontinent during two major periods. During the first phase, which began to develop prior to the 4th century BCE, Buddhist atomism had a very qualitative, Aristotelian-style atomic theory. This form of atomism identifies four kinds of atoms, corresponding to the standard elements. Each of these elements has a specific property, such as solidity or motion, and performs a specific function in mixtures, such as providing support or causing growth.

Like the Hindus and Jains, the Buddhists were able to integrate a theory of atomism with their theological presuppositions. The second phase of Buddhist atomism, which flourished in the 7th century CE, was very different from the first. Indian Buddhist philosophers, including Dharmakirti and Dignâga, considered atoms to be point-sized, durationless, and made of energy. In discussing Buddhist atomism, Stcherbatsky writes:

> ... The Buddhists denied the existence of substantial matter altogether. Movement consists for them of moments, it is a staccato movement, momentary flashes of a stream of energy... "Everything is evanescent," ... says the Buddhist, because there is no stuff ... Both systems [Sânkhya and

> later Indian Buddhism] share in common a tendency to push the analysis of Existence up to its minutest, last elements which are imagined as absolute qualities, or things possessing only one unique quality. They are called "qualities" (guna-dharma) in both systems in the sense of absolute qualities, a kind of atomic, or intra-atomic, energies of which the empirical things are composed. Both systems, therefore, agree in denying the objective reality of the categories of Substance and Quality, ... and of the relation of Inference uniting them. There is in Sânkhya philosophy no separate existence of qualities. What we call quality is but a particular manifestation of a subtle entity. To every new unit of quality corresponds a subtle quantum of matter which is called guna "quality", but represents a subtle substantive entity. The same applies to early Buddhism where all qualities are substantive ... or, more precisely, dynamic entities, although they are also called dharmas ("qualities").

ON SEXUALITY

Most variations of Buddhism do not go much into details of right and wrong regarding sexuality and other activities of life. The historical Buddha advised his students to avoid *sexual misconduct*, but at the same time largely avoided to define how to have sex. The interpretation of sexual misconduct will thus vary between the different schools and traditions, the cultures and even between individual teachers within the respective traditions. Another variation in the view of sexuality is dependent if the Buddhist practitioner is an ordained monk or nun, since monastic Buddhism has very strict regulation regarding celibacy. Lay Buddhists do not have these regulations, since sex is a very natural part of having a life in society with family and children. In Vajrayana, sexual intercourse can even be a part of the way to enlightenment, the goal of Buddhism.

Celibacy and Monasticism

Those who choose to practice Buddhism as ordained monks and nuns, also chose to live in celibacy. Sex is the downfall that could end a monk or nun's career, and seen as the most serious monastic transgression. There are four principal transgressions: sex, theft, murder, and boasting of superhuman perfections, where sex is listed first. *Sexual misconduct* for monks and nuns even include masturbation. In the case of monasticism, chastity is seen as a necessity in order to reach the enlightenment.

Lay Buddhism

The most common formulation of Buddhist ethics are the Five Precepts and the Eightfold Path, which say that one should neither be attached to nor crave sensual pleasure. These precepts take the form of voluntary, personal undertakings, not divine mandate or instruction. The third of the Five Precepts is "To refrain from committing sexual misconduct. However, the "sexual misconduct" is such a broad term, and is subjected to interpretation relative to the social norms of the followers. In fact, Buddhism in its fundamental form, does not define what is right and what is wrong in absolute terms for lay followers. Therefore the interpretation of what kinds of sexual activity is acceptable for a layperson, is not a religious matter as far as Buddhism is concerned.

Sexual Yoga

According to some Tibetan authorities, the physical practice of sexual yoga is necessary at the highest level for the attainment of Buddhahood. The use of sexual yoga is highly regulated. It is only permitted after years of training. The physical practice of sexual yoga is extremely rare, and has been historically. A great majority of Tibetans believe that the only proper practice of tantric texts is metaphorically, not physically, in rituals and during meditative visualizations.

The dominant Gelug sect of Tibetan Buddhism holds that sexual yoga as an actual physical practice is the only way to attain Buddhahood in one lifetime. The founder of the sect Tsongkhapa did not, according to tradition, engage in this practice, but instead attained complete enlightenment at the moment of death, that being according to this school the nearest possible without sexual yoga.

The school also taught that they are only appropriate for the most elite practitioners, who had directly realized emptiness and who had unusually strong compassion. The next largest school in Tibet, the Nyingma, holds that this is not necessary to achieve Buddhahood in one lifetime. The fourteenth Dalai Lama of the Gelug sect, holds that the practice should only be done as a visualization. Shingon, along with all non-tantric forms of Buddhism, does not recognize sexual yoga.

Homosexuality

Asian societies shaped by Buddhist traditions take a strong ethical stand in human affairs and sexual behavior in particular. However, unlike most other world religions, most variations of Buddhism do not go into details about what is right and what is wrong in what it considers mundane activities of life.

Details of accepted or unaccepted human sexual conduct are not specifically mentioned in any of the religious scriptures in the Pali language. The most common formulations of Buddhist ethics are found the Five Precepts and the Eightfold Path, which state that one should neither be attached to nor crave sensual pleasure. These precepts take the form of voluntary, personal undertakings, not divine mandate or instruction. The third of the Five Precepts is "To refrain from committing sexual misconduct. However, "sexual misconduct" is a broad term, and is subject to interpretation relative to the social norms of the followers. In fact, Buddhism in its fundamental form does not define what is right and what is wrong in absolute terms for lay followers. Therefore the determination of whether or not homosexuality is acceptable for a layperson is not a religious matter as far as fundamental Buddhism is concerned.

Among Buddhists there is a wide diversity of opinion about homosexuality. Buddhism teaches that sensual enjoyment and desire in general, and sexual pleasure in particular, are hindrances to enlightenment. Buddhist monks and nuns of most traditions are expected to refrain from all sexual activity and take vows of celibacy. Some Buddhist orders may specifically prohibit transgender, homosexually active, or homosexually oriented people from ordination but accept homosexuality among laypersons.

Thailand

In Thailand, traditional accounts propose that "homosexuality arises as a karmic consequence of violating Buddhist proscriptions against heterosexual misconduct. These karmic accounts describe homosexuality as a congenital condition which cannot be altered, at least in a homosexual person's current lifetime, and have been linked with calls for compassion and understanding from the non-homosexual populace."

There are two broad schools of thought on homosexuality are current among contemporary Thai Buddhist writers, one accepting, the other unaccepting. AIDS in the 1980s brought about a shift of perception in Thailand regarding homosexuals, with a shift in Buddhist attitudes from relative tolerance of homosexuality to condemnation. Since 1989 gays are prohibited from being ordained.

Dalai Lama

The current Dalai Lama interprets sexual misconduct to include lesbian and gay sex, and indeed any sex other than penis-vagina intercourse, including oral sex, anal sex, and masturbation. However, he also explained in an interview with OUT Magazine that "If someone comes to me and asks whether homosexuality is okay or not, I will ask 'What is your companion's opinion?'. If you both agree, then I think I would say 'if two males or two females voluntarily agree to have mutual satisfaction without further implication of harming others, then it is okay'".

Western Buddhism is often relatively gay-friendly, and the interpretation of what is sexual misconduct is an individual decision and not subject to judgement by any central authority, a view of accepting all peoples, but rejecting certain types of sexual acts is more predominant. When applying buddhist philosophy to the question of homosexuality, western Buddhists often emphasize the importance the Buddha placed on tolerance, compassion, and seeking answers within one's self.

The phrase 'fourteen unanswerable questions', in Buddhism, refers to fourteen common philosophical questions that Buddha refused to answer, according to Buddhist Sanskrit texts. Pali texts give only ten.

Fourteen Questions

Questions referring to the world: concerning the existence of the world in time

- Is the world eternal?

- or not?
- or both?
- or neither?

Pali texts omit "both" and "neither".

Questions referring to the world: concerning the existence of the world in space

- Is the world finite?
- or not?
- or both?
- or neither?

Pali texts omit "both" and "neither".

Questions referring to personal experience

- Is the self identical with the body?
- or is it different from the body?

Questions referring to life after death

- Does the Tathagata exist after death?
- or not?
- or both?
- or neither?

Buddha's Answer to the Questions, According to the Scriptures

The Buddha remained silent when asked these fourteen questions. He described them as a net and refused to be drawn into such a net of theories, speculations, and dogmas. He said that it was because he was free of bondage to all theories and dogmas that he had attained liberation. Such speculations, he said, are attended by fever, unease, bewilderment, and suffering, and it is by freeing oneself of them that one achieves liberation.

Implications

The fourteen questions imply two basic attitudes toward the world. The Buddha speaks of these two attitudes in his dialogue with Mahakashyapa, when he says that there are two basic views, the view of existence and the view of nonexistence. He said that people are accustomed to think in these terms, and that as long as they remain entangled in these two views they will not attain liberation.

The propositions that the world is eternal, that the world is infinite, that the Tathagatha exists after death, and that the self is independent of the body reflect the view of existence. The propositions that the world is not eternal, that the world is finite, that the Tathagata does not exist after death, and that the self is identical with the body reflect the view of nonexistence. These two views were professed by teachers of other schools during the time of the Buddha. The view of existence is generally the view of the Brahmins; that of nonexistence is generally the view of the materialists and hedonists.

When the Buddha refuses to be drawn into the net of these dogmatic views of existence and nonexistence, he has two things in mind: the ethical consequences of these two views, and the fact that the views of absolute existence and nonexistence do not correspond to the way things really are. The eternalists view this self as permanent and unchanging. When the body dies, this self will not die because the self is by nature unchanging. If that is the case, it does not matter what this body does: actions of the body will not affect the destiny of the self. This view is incompatible with moral responsibility because if the self is eternal and unchanging, it will not be affected by wholesome and unwholesome actions. Similarly, if the self were identical with the body and the self dies along with the body, then it does not matter what the body does. If you believe that existence ends at death, there will be no constraint upon action. But in a situation where things exist through interdependent origination, absolute existence and nonexistence are impossible.

Another example drawn from the fourteen unanswerable questions also shows that the propositions do not correspond to the way things really are. Take the example of the world. According to Buddhist teaching, the world does not exist absolutely or does not exist absolutely in time. The world exists dependent on causes and conditions—ignorance, craving, and clinging. When ignorance, craving, and clinging are present, the world exists; when they are not present, the world ceases to exist. Hence the question of the absolute existence or nonexistence of the world is unanswerable. Existence and nonexistence, taken as absolute ideas, do not apply to things as they really are. This is why the Buddha refuses to agree to absolute statements about the nature of things. He saw that the absolute categories of metaphysics do not apply to things as they really are.

Now we will discuss, Buddhism in different countries of the world.

REFERENCES

1. Dreyfus, Georges (1997). *Recognizing Reality: Dharmakirti's Philosophy and Its Tibetan Interpretations*. New York: State University of New York Press.
2. Higgins, Winton. "Buddhist Sexual Ethics". BuddhaNet

Magazine. http://www.buddhanet.net/winton_s.htm. Retrieved 2007-01-15.

3. Jackson, Peter (1995). *Thai Buddhist accounts of male homosexuality and AIDS in the 1980s.* The Australian Journal of Anthropology, Vol.6 No.3, pp.140–153. December 1995. Text online.
4. Khamhuno. 1989 (B.E. 2532). *Gay Praakot Nai Wongkaan Song* ("Gays Appear in Sangha Circles"). Sangkhom Saatsanaa (Religion and Society Column). Siam Rath Sutsapdaa (Siam Rath Weekly), November 18, 1989 (B.E. 2532). 36 (22):37–38.
5. Lopez, Donald S. Critical Terms for the Study of Buddhism. Chicago: The University of Chicago Press. 2005.
6. Olson, Carl. The Different Paths of Buddhism: A Narrative-Historical Introduction. New Jersey: Rutgers University Press. 2005.
7. Page, Tony (1998), *Buddhism and Animals* (Nirvana Publications, London).
8. Peter Harvey, *An Introduction to Buddhist Ethics.* Cambridge University Press, 2000.
9. Phelps, Norm. (2004). *The Great Compassion: Buddhism and Animal Rights.* Lantern Books.
10. Queen, Chris; King, Sallie (1996). *Engaged Buddhism: Buddhist Liberation Movements in Asia.* New York: Albany State University Press. p. 36.
11. Rangdrol, Shabkar Natshok. (Translated by Padmakara Translation Group.) *Food of Bodhisattvas: Buddhist Teachings on Abstaining from Meat.* Shambhala Publications, 2004.
12. Releasing life (chapter 4: 'The Debate'): published by The Corporate Body of the Buddha Educational Foundation,
13. Routledge *Encyclopedia of Buddhism*, p. 781.
14. Saddhatissa, Hammalawa (December 1987). *Buddhist Ethics: The Path to Nirvana.* Wisdom Pubns; New Ed edition. pp. 88.
15. Stcherbatsky, F. Th. 1962 (1930). *Buddhist Logic.* Volume 1. New York: Dover.
16. Thomas Laird, *The Story of Tibet.* Grove Press, 2006, p. 81.
17. Vegetarianism: Living a Buddhist life series (2004) by: Bodhipaksa.

PART II

5

Buddhism in China and Taiwan

CHINA

China has a large number of followers of Buddhism. Chinese Buddhism refers collectively to the various schools of Buddhism that have flourished in China proper since ancient times. Buddhism has played an enormous role in shaping the mindset of the Chinese people, affecting their aesthetics, politics, literature, philosophy and medicine. At the peak of the Tang Dynasty's vitality, Chinese Buddhism produced numerous spiritual masters.

It is pertinent to note that recent research indicates that Buddhism had already been established in China during the reign of the first emperor, Qin Shihuang. The emperor is said to have suppressed Buddhism and Buddhist temples in the same way other philosophical schools were suppressed. Han Wei, a noted researcher from the Shaanxi Provincial Institute of Archaeology, found evidence for this in *Records of the Grand Historian*, along with corresponding historical, linguistic, and archaeological evidence.

According to this study, Buddhism was already popular in the interior regions of China by the time its suppression began in 213 BCE. Silk Road Archaeologist Wang Jianxin has stated that Han's research sounds "reasonable". According to some European historians, Mauryan emperor Ashoka the Great sent the royal monk Massim Sthavira to Nepal, Bhutan, and China to spread Buddhism around 265 BCE. However, it has not been widely confirmed that these missionaries arrived in China or that they were responsible for establishing the teachings of Buddhism there.

Remarkably, a number of popular accounts in historical Chinese literature have lead to the popularity of certain legends regarding the introduction of Buddhism into China. According to the most popular account, Emperor Ming (58–75 CE) precipitated the first introduction of Buddhist teachings into China. After dreaming of a golden man with a shining halo, he questioned his advisors about the dream. One advisor told him about the existence of a man called the Buddha in regions to the west. The emperor then sent an envoy to Tianzhu (Southern India) to inquire about the teachings of the Buddha. Buddhist scriptures were said to have been returned to China on the backs of white horses, after which White Horse Temple was named.

Two Indian monks also returned with them, named Dharmarakca and Kaúyapa MâtaEga, together with sutras containing 600,000 Sanskrit words. An 8th century Chinese mural in Dunhuang portrays Emperor Han Wudi (156–87 BCE) worshiping statues of a golden man; "golden men brought in 120 BCE by a great Han general in his campaigns against the nomads". This depiction comes from traditional accounts in the *Shiji* and the *Book of Han*.

The first documented translation of Buddhist scriptures into Chinese occurs in 148 CE with the arrival of the Parthian prince-turned-monk An Shigao. He worked to establish Buddhist temples in Loyang and organized the translation of Buddhist scriptures into Chinese, testifying to the beginning of a wave of Central Asian Buddhist proselytism that was to last several centuries. An Shigao translated Buddhist texts on basic doctrines, meditation, and abhidharma. An Xuan, a Parthian layman who worked alongside An Shigao, also translated an early Mahâyâna Buddhist text on the bodhisattva path.

Mahâyâna Buddhism was first widely propagated in China by the Kushan monk Lokaksema (active ca. 164–186 CE), who came from the ancient Buddhist kingdom of Gandhâra. Lokaksema translated important Mahâyâna sûtras such as the *Asmasâhasrikâ Prajñâpâramitâ Sûtra*, as well as rare, early Mahâyâna sûtras on topics such as samâdhi, and meditation on the buddha Aksobhya. These translations from Lokaksema continue to give insight into the early period of Mahâyâna Buddhism.

Initially, Buddhism in China faced a number of difficulties in becoming established. The concept of monasticism and the aversion to social affairs seemed to contradict the long-established norms and standards established in Chinese society. However, Buddhism was often associated with Taoism in its ascetic meditative tradition. For this reason, a concept-matching system was used by some early Indian translators, to adapt native Buddhist ideas onto Taoist ideas and terminology. During this time, Indian monks continued to travel along the Silk Road to teach Buddhism, and translation work was primarily done by foreign monks rather than Chinese.

Role of Kumârajîva

When the famous monk Kumârajîva was captured as booty during the Chinese conquest of the Buddhist kingdom of Kucha, he was imprisoned for many years. When he was released, he immediately took a high place in Chinese Buddhism and was appraised as a great master from the

West. He was especially valued by Emperor Yao Xing of the state of Later Qin, who gave him an honorific title and treated him like a god. Kumârajîva revolutionized Chinese Buddhism with his high quality translations, which are still praised for their flowing smoothness, clarity of meaning, subtlety, and literary skill. Due to the efforts of Kumârajîva, Buddhism in China became not only recognized for its practice methods, but also as high philosophy and religion.

Remarkably, the arrival of Kumârajîva also set a standard for Chinese translations of Buddhist texts, effectively doing away with previous concept-matching systems. The translations of Kumârajîva have often remained more popular than those of other translators. Among the most well-known are his translations of the *Diamond Sutra*, the *Amitabha Sutra*, the *Lotus Sutra*, the *Vimalakîrti Nirdesa Sûtra*, the *Mûlamadhyamakakârikâ*, and the *Acmasâhasrikâ Prajñâpâramitâ Sûtra*.

Around the time of Kumârajîva, the four major Sanskrit âgamas were also translated into Chinese. Each of the âgamas was translated independently by a different Indian monk. These âgamas comprise the only other complete surviving Sûtra Pimaka, which is generally comparable to the Pali Sutta Pitaka of Theravada Buddhism. The teachings of the Sûtra Pimaka are usually considered to be the earliest teachings of Buddhism and the core texts of the Early Buddhist Schools.

Early Chinese Buddhist Traditions

Due to the wide proliferation of Buddhist texts available in Chinese and the large number of foreign monks who came to teach Buddhism in China, various new and independent traditions emerged. Among the most influential of these was the practice of Pure Land Buddhism established by Hui Yuan, which focused on Amitâbha Buddha and his western pure land.

Another major early tradition was the Tiantai school, founded by Zhiyi, which is based upon the primacy of the *Lotus Sutra*, along with supplementary sûtras and commentaries. Zhiyi wrote several works that become important and widely-read meditation manuals in China.

Local Interpretation of Indian Texts

To thrive in China, Buddhism had to transform itself into a system that could exist within the Chinese way of life. Thus highly regarded Indian sutras that advocated filial piety became core texts in China. Buddhism was made compatible with ancestor worship and participation in China's hierarchical system. Works were written arguing that the salvation of an individual was a benefit to that individual's society and family and monks thus contributed to the greater good. It is conjectured that the shocking collapse of the Han Dynasty in 220 and the resulting period of social upheaval and political unrest known as the Three Kingdoms period may have helped the spread of Buddhism. Buddhism was a minor force, however, compared with Taoism which was directly associated with efforts to defy the emperor (cf. Yellow Turban Rebellion).

The Taoist Zhang family self-governed the Hanzhong Commandry for nearly 20 years until invasion by the renowned Chinese warlord Cao Cao. A reason for the lack of interest mostly stemmed from the ruling entity and gentry. All the rulers were Han Chinese and had simply never heard of or knew too little of the religion. The Nine-grade controller system, by which prominent individuals in each local administrative area were given the authority to rank local families and individuals in nine grades according to their potential for government service, further consolidated the importance of Confucianism. Taoism also remained a strong force among the population and philosophers. Subsequent chaotic periods of Sixteen Kingdoms (304 to 439 AD) and Southern and Northern Dynasties changed the situation, resulting in state support of Buddhism. Most rulers of the Wu, Hu, and the Northern dynasties originated from more than ten distinct ethnic groups including either non-Han Chinese "barbarians", or Han Chinese after generations of "barbarian" influence.

They did not propagate nor trust the combined philosophical concept of Confucianism and Taoism as zealously as their rivals in the south. Official support of Buddhism would eventually mould a new Chinese populace with a common ideology out of the diversely ethnic population, which would in turn consolidate these dynasties. It is instructive that Buddhism propagated faster in northern China than in the south. Social upheaval in northern China worked to break down cultural barriers between the elite ruling families and the general populace, in contrast to the south where elite clans and royal families firmly monopolized politics.

Taoist and Confucian political ideology had long consolidated the political status of elite clans in the south. Support of another religion would have unknown and possibly adverse effects, for which these clans would not risk their privileges. Furthermore pro-Buddhist policy would not be backed by the bureaucracy, which had been staffed by members of the clans. Southern rulers were in weaker positions to strive for their legitimacy - some were even installed by the clans.

It was not until the reign of Emperor Wu of the Liang Dynasty that saw the official support of Buddhism. Rebellion of Hou Jing near the end of Emperor Wu's reign wreaked havoc on the political and social privileges of the elite clans, which indirectly assisted the spread of Buddhism. But Buddhism spread pretty well in the peasant populace, both in the north and the south. The Tang capital of Chang'an (today's Xi'an) became an important center for Buddhist thought. From there Buddhism spread to Korea, and Japanese embassies of Kentoshi helped gain footholds in Japan.

The popularization of Buddhism in this period is evident in the many scripture-filled caves and structures surviving from this period. The Mogao Caves near Dunhuang in Gansu province, the Longmen Grottoes near Luoyang in Henan and the Yungang Grottoes near Datong in Shanxi are the most renowned examples from the Northern, Sui and Tang Dynasties.

The Leshan Giant Buddha, carved out of a hillside in the 8th century during the Tang Dynasty and looking down on the confluence of three rivers, is still the largest stone Buddha statue in the world.

Buddhist Scriptures

During the early Tang dynasty the monk Xuanzang journeyed to Nalanda in India and other important sites to bring back scriptures. He sought to propagate Mahayana Buddhism, and was especially involved in the Yogâcâra school. He translated central Yogâcâra texts such as the *Sandhinirmocana Sûtra* and the *Yogâcârabhûmi Sâstra*, as well as sutras important to other schools such as Mâdhyamaka (*Mahâprajñâpâramitâ Sûtra*) and the Pure Land tradition (*Bhaicajyaguruvaidûryaprabharâja Sûtra*). The proliferation of these sutras expanded the Chinese Buddhist canon significantly with high quality translations of some of the most important Indian Mahayana sutras.

Making duplications of Buddhist texts was considered to bring meritorious karma. Printing from individually carved wooden blocks and from clay or metal movable type proved much more efficient and eventually eclipsed hand copying. The *Diamond Sutra* of 868 CE, a Buddhist scripture discovered in 1907 inside the Mogao Caves, is the first dated example of block printing. Temple.

Arrivals of several prestigious monks in the early 5th century also contributed to the propagation of the religion and were welcomed by rulers of the Sixteen Kingdoms and Northern Dynasties. Fo Tu Cheng was entrusted by the tyrant Shi Hu of Later Chao. Kumarajiva was invited by Lü Guang, the founder of Later Liang, and later by Yao Xing, second ruler of Later Qin. Biographies of these monks, among others, were the subject of the *Memoirs of Eminent Monks*.

The direct experiential impact of contact with practicing monks should not be underestimated. Confucianism had no equivalent to holy men – the archetypical best and brightest was a wise government minister, not a saint. In this way Buddhism grew to become a major religion in China. By the beginning of the 6th century, Buddhism had grown in popularity to rival Taoism.

We know they were successful because the monks were soon accused of falling into extravagance and their lands and their properties were confiscated by Emperor Wu of the Northern Zhou dynasty and Wuzong of the Tang Dynasty.

The Kaiyuan's Three Great Enlightened Masters, Subhakarasimha, Vajrabodhi, and Amoghavajra, established Esoteric Buddhism in China from AD 716 to 720 during the reign of emperor Tang Xuanzong (or Hsuan-Tsung).

In fact, they came to Daxing Shansi, Great Propagating Goodness Temple, which was the predecessor of Temple of the Great Enlightener Mahavairocana. Daxing Shansi was established in the ancient capital Chang'an, today's Xi'an, and became one of the four great centers of scripture translation supported by the imperial court. They had translated many Buddhist scriptures, sutra and tantra, from Sanskrit to Chinese.

They had also assimilated the prevailing teachings of China, Taoism and Confucianism, with Buddhism, and had further evolved the practice of The Esoteric School. They brought to the Chinese a mysterious, dynamic, and magical teaching, which included mantra formulae and rituals to protect a person or an empire, to affect a person's fate after death, and, particularly popular, to bring rain in times of drought.

It is not surprising, then, that all three masters were well received by the emperor Tang Xuanzong, and their teachings were quickly taken up at the Tang court and among the elite. Mantrayana altars were installed in temples in the capital, and by the time of emperor Tang Taizong (Tai-Tsung, r. 762-779) its influence among the upper classes outstripped that of Taoism. Relations between Amoghavajra and Taizong were especially good. In life the emperor favored Amoghavajra with titles and gifts, and when the master died in 774, he honored his memory with a stupa, or funeral monument.

Subhakarasimha

Subhakarasimha (637-735), an eminent Indian Tantric master, arrived in the capital Chang'an in 716 and translated the Mahâvairocana Abhisanbodhi Tantra, better known as the Mahâvairocana Sûtra. Four years later another master,

Vajrabodhi (670-741), and his pupil Amoghavajra (705-775), would arrive and proceeded to translate other scriptures, thus establishing a second Mantrayâna tradition.

Vajrabodhi

Vajrabodhi (671-732), an Indian Buddhist master, and a graduate of the Nâlandâ Monastery, received complete empowerment and transmission from Nagabodhi, who in turn received from Nagarjuna. He was born of a South Indian Brahmin family, and his father was a priest for the royal house. Vajrabodhi probably converted to Buddhism at the age of sixteen, although some accounts place him at Nâlandâ at the age of ten. He studied all varieties of Buddhism and was said to have studied for a time under the famous Buddhist logician Dharmakîrti. Under Santijnana, Vajrabodhi studied Vajrayâna teachings and was duly initiated into yoga. Leaving India, Vajrabodhi traveled to Sri Lanka and Srivijaya (present-day Sumatra), where he apparently was taught a Vajrayâna tradition distinct from that taught at Nâlandâ. From Srivijaya he sailed to China via the escort of thirty-five Persian merchant-vessels and by AD 720 was ensconced in the Jian'fu Temple at the Chinese capital, Chang'an (present-day Xi'an). Accompanying him was his soon-to-be-famous disciple, Amoghavajra.

When Vajrabodhi arrived in Chang'an, Subhakarasimha had already been there for four years. Subhakarasimha was eighty some years old. Vajrabodhi was about thirty something, and Amoghavajra a teenager. Subhakarasimha and Vajrabodhi met and debated. Afterward, they bowed to each other as each other's teacher.

Like Subhakarasimha, who preceded him by four years, Vajrabodhi spent most of his time in ritual activity, in translating texts from Sanskrit to Chinese, and in the production of Esoteric art. Particularly important was his partial translation of the Sarva-Tathâgata-Tattva-Samgraha between the years 723 and 724.

This Yoga Tantra, along with the Mahâvairocana Sutra translated by Subhakarasimha the same year, provides the foundation of the Chen-Yen school in China and the Shingon and Esoteric branch of the Tendai schools in Japan. Like Subhakarasinha, Vajrabodhi had ties to high court circles and enjoyed the patronage of imperial princesses. He also taught Korean monk Hyecho, who went on to travel India. Vajrabodhi died in 732 and was buried south of the Longmen Grottoes. He was posthumously awarded the title Guoshi, 'National Master'.

Amoghavajra

Noted scholar Amoghavajra (705-774) was the most famous Yogacharya of his time. He was a prolific translator who became one of the most politically powerful Buddhist monks in Chinese history, acknowledged as one of the eight patriarchs of the doctrine in Shingon lineage. Born in Samarkand of an Indian father and Sogdian mother, he went to China at age 10 after his father's death. In 719, he was ordained into the Sangha by Vajrabodhi and became his disciple.

He also became Subhakarasimha's disciple a few years later. Both Subhakarasimha, the holder of the Garbhadhatu Womb Realm teachings, and Vajrabodhi, the holder of the Vajradhatu Thunderbolt Realm teachings transmitted the Dharma Lineage to Amoghavajra, who began the Not-Two Dharma Teachings of Garbhadhatu and Vajradhatu.

The Tang emperor granted Dharma instruments to Amoghavajra to setup the first Abhiseka-Bodhi-Mandala at Daxing Shansi, thus began the Chinese Esoteric School.

After Vajrabodhi's death in 732, and at his wish, Amoghavajra went on a pilgrimage in search of esoteric or tantric writings, visiting Ceylon, Southeast Asia and India. During this voyage, he apparently met Nagabodhi, master of Vajrabodhi, and studied the Tattvasamgraha system at length. He returned to China in 746 with some five hundred volumes, and baptized the Emperor Tang Xuanzong.

He was especially noted for rainmaking and stilling storms. In 749 he received permission to return home, but was stopped by imperial orders when in the south of China. In 750, he left the court to join the military governorship of Geshu Han, for whom he conducted large-scale tantric initiations at field headquarters. In 754, he translated the first portion of the Tattvasamgraha, the central text of Esoteric Buddhism, which became one of his most significant accomplishments.

He regarded its teachings as the most effective method for attaining enlightenment yet devised, and incorporated its basic schema in a number of writings. In 756, under emperor Suzong, Amoghavajra was recalled to the capital. He was captured in general An Lushan's rebellion but in 757 was freed by loyalist forces, whereupon he performed rites to purify the capital and consolidate the security of the Tang state.

Two years later, he initiated the emperor Suzong as a cakravartin. In 765, Amoghavajra used his new rendition of the Scripture for Humane Kings in an elaborate ritual to counter the advance of a 200,000-strong army of Tibetans and Uyghurs, which was poised to invade Chang'an. Its leader, Pugu Huaien, dropped dead in camp and his forces dispersed.

The opulent Jin'ge Temple on Mt. Wutai was completed

in 767, a pet project of Amoghavajra's, and one of his many efforts to promote the Bodhisattva Mañjuúrî as the protector of China. Amoghavajra continued to perform rites to avert disaster at the request of the emperor Tang Taizong. His time until 771 was spent translating and editing tantric books in 120 volumes, and the Yogachara rose to its peak of prosperity. He died greatly honored at 70 years of age, in 774, the twelfth year of Taizong, the third emperor under whom he had served.

On his death, three days of mourning were officially declared, and he posthumously received various exalted titles. He was given the title of the Thesaurus of Wisdom, Amogha Tripikata and the posthumous rank and title of a Minister of State. The Chinese monks Huilang, Huiguo and Huilin were among his most prominent successors.

Seventy-seven texts were translated by Amoghavajra according to his own account, though many more, including original compositions, are ascribed to him in the Chinese canons. Huiguo was the most well-known disciple of Amoghavajra. Both Amoghavajra and Huiguo were emperors' guru, in other words, they were National Masters. Huiguo's main residence was the Qinglong. Tang Emperor Wuzong, distrusting its popularity and magical claims, prohibited these new practices.

Tang State Repression of Buddhism

It is pertinent to note that there were several components that lead to opposition of Buddhism. One factor is the foreign origins of Buddhism, unlike Taoism and Confucianism. Han Yu wrote, "Buddha was a man of the barbarians who did not speak the language of China and wore clothes of a different fashion. His sayings did not concern the ways of our ancient kings, nor did his manner of dress conform to their laws. He understood neither the duties that bind sovereign and subject, nor the affections of father and son."

Other components included the Buddhists' withdrawal from society, since the Chinese believed that Chinese people should be involved with family life. Wealth, tax-exemption status and power of the Buddhist temples and monasteries also annoyed many critics. As mentioned earlier, persecution came during the reign of Emperor Wuzong in the Tang Dynasty. Wuzong was said to hate the sight of Buddhist monks, whom he thought were tax-evaders. In 845, he ordered the destruction of 4,600 Buddhist monasteries and 40,000 temples. About 250,000 Buddhist monks and nuns had to give up their monastery lives.

Wuzong cited that Buddhism was an alien religion, which is the reason he also persecuted the Christians in China. Ancient Chinese Buddhism never fully recovered from the persecution.

During Song Dynasty

Buddhist ideology began to merge with Confucianism and Taoism, due in part to the use of existing Chinese philosophical terms in the translation of Buddhist scriptures. Various Confucian scholars of the Song dynasty, including Zhu Xi (wg: Chu Hsi), sought to redefine Confucianism as Neo-Confucianism.

During Ming Dynasty

"By the Ming period (1368–1644) the preeminence of Chan had been so firmly established that almost the entire Buddhist clergy were affiliated with either its Lin-chi or Ts'ao-tung lineages, both of which claimed descent from Bodhidharma."

During Qing Dynasty

The official religion of the Qing court was the Gelukpa School of Tibetan Buddhism. Early in the Taiping rebellion, the Taiping rebels targeted Buddhism. In the Battle of Nanjing (1853), the Taiping army butchered thousands of monks in Nanjing. But from the middle of the Taiping rebellion, Taiping leaders took a more moderate approach, demanding that monks should have licences.

Chinese Buddhism: Modern Era

The 108-metre-high statue is the world's tallest of Guanyin Statue of Hainan was enshrined on April 24, 2005 with the participation of 108 eminent monks from various Buddhist groups in Taiwan, Hong Kong, Macao and Mainland China, and tens of thousands of pilgrims. The delegation also included monks from the Theravada and Tibetan Buddhist traditions.

China belongs to those countries that own most of the world's highest Buddhist statues. In April 2006 China organized the World Buddhist Forum and in March 2007 the government banned mining on Buddhist sacred mountains. In May of the same year, in Changzhou, world's tallest pagoda was built and opened. In March 2008 the Taiwan-based Tzu Chi Foundation was approved to open a branch in mainland China.

Theravada Buddhism and Tibetan Buddhism exist mainly among ethnic minorities in the southwest and the north.

Main Festivals

These are the holy days that Chinese Buddhists celebrate by visiting temples to make offerings of prayers, incense, fruits, flowers and donations. On such days they observe the moral precepts very strictly as well as a full day's vegetarian diet, a practice originally from China. Thee dates given are based on the Chinese Lunar system so that 1.1 means the *First day of the First lunar moon* and so on.

- 8.12 — Enlightenment Day of Sâkyamuni Buddha
- 1.1 — Birthday of Maitreya Buddha
- 9.1 — Birthday of Sakra, Lord of the Devas
- 8.2 — Renunciation Day of Sâkyamuni Buddha
- 15.2 — Mahâparinirvâna Day of Sâkyamuni Buddha
- 19.2 — Birthday of Bodhisattva Avalokitesvara (Guan Yin)
- 21.2 — Birthday of Bodhisattva Samantabhadra
- 4.4 — Birthday of Bodhisattva Mañjusrî
- 8.4 — Birthday of Sâkyamuni Buddha
- 15.4 — Vesak Day
- 3.6 — Birthday of Skanda (Wei Tuo)
- 10.6 — Birthday of Padmasambhava (Guru Rinpoche)
- 19.6 — Enlightenment Day of Bodhisattva Avalokitesvara
- 13.7 — Birthday of Bodhisattva Mahâsthâmaprâpta
- 15.7 — Ghost Festival
- 30.7 — Birthday of Bodhisattva Ksitigarbha
- 22.8 — Birthday of Dîpankara Buddha (an ancient buddha)
- 19.9 — Renunciation Day of Bodhisattva Avalokitesvara
- 30.9 — Birthday of Bhaisajyaguru Buddha (Medicine Buddha)

- 5.10 — Anniversary of the death of Bodhidharma
- 17.11 — Birthday of Amitâbha Buddha

TAIWAN

Buddhism is a major religion in Taiwan. More than 90 percent of Taiwanese people practice the Chinese traditional religion which integrates Buddhist elements, Confucian principles, local practices and Taoist tradition. (Roles for religious specialists from both Buddhist and Taoist traditions exist on special occasions such as childbirth and funerals). Of these, a smaller number identify more specifically with Chinese Buddhist teachings and institutions, without necessarily eschewing practices from other Asian traditions. One study proposes that 7 to 15 percent of Taiwanese are Buddhist in the strict sense. A distinguishing feature of this form of Buddhism is the practice of vegetarianism. Taiwan government statistics distinguish Buddhism from Taoism, giving almost equal numbers for both (in 2005, 8 million and 7.6 million, respectively, out of a total population of 23 million).

Many of Taiwan's self-declared "Buddhists" actually observe the more syncretistic practices associated with Chinese traditional religion. Self-avowed Buddhists may also be adherents of more localized faiths such as I-kuan Tao, which also emphasize Buddhist figures like Guanyin or Maitreya and espouse vegetarianism.

Four local Buddhist teachers whose institutions are especially significant are popularly likened to the "Four Heavenly Kings of Taiwanese Buddhism." They are:

- North (Jinshan, Taipei): Master Sheng-yen (, d. 2009) of Dharma Drum Mountain)

- South (Dashu, Kaohsiung): Master Hsing Yun of Fo Guang Shan
- East (Hualien): Master Cheng Yen of the Tzu Chi Foundation)
- West (Nantou): Master Wei Chueh of Chung Tai Shan)

Remarkably, several of these figures have been influenced by the Humanistic Buddhism of Master Yin Shun, a theological approach which has come to distinguish Taiwanese Buddhism. (Sheng-yen's tradition is formally Zen Buddhist; Yin Shun was inspired by Taixu, who is less well known in Taiwan.) Their missions have branches all over the world. In a reversal of the older historical relationship, these Taiwanese Buddhists have played important roles in the revival of Buddhism in China.

Buddhism was brought to Taiwan in the time of the Ming dynasty by settlers from Fukien and Kwangtung Provinces. It was discouraged by the Dutch colonial rulers who controlled Taiwan from 1624 until 1663, until Cheng Cheng-kung (Koxinga) drove the Dutch from Taiwan in 1663. His son Cheng Ching established the first Buddhist temple in Taiwan.

When the Qing dynasty took control of Taiwan by defeating of Cheng Ching's son, Ching Ning, in 1683, large numbers of monks came from Fukien and Kwangtung provinces to establish temples, and a number of different Buddhist sects flourished. Monastic Buddhism, however, would not arrive until the 19th century.

During the Japanese period (1895-1945), most Taiwan Buddhist temples came to affiliate with one of three central temples:

- North (Keelung): Yueh-mei Mountain, founded by Master Shan-hui
- Center (Miaoli): Fa-yun Temple, founded by Master Chueh-li
- South (Tainan): Kai-yuan Temple, also founded by Chueh-li

As a Japanese colony, Taiwan fell under the influence of Japanese Buddhism. Many temples experienced pressure to affiliate with Japanese lineages, including many whose status with respect to Buddhism or Taoism was unclear. (Emphasis on the Chinese folk religion was widely considered a form of protest against Japanese rule.) Attempts were made to introduce a married priesthood (as in Japan). These failed to take root, as emphasis on vegetarianism and/or clerical celibacy became another means of anti-Japanese protest. With Japan's defeat in World War II, Taiwan fell under the control of Chiang Kai-shek's government, resulting in contrary political pressures. In 1949, a number of mainland monks fled to Taiwan alongside Chiang's military forces, and received preferential treatment by the new regime.

During this period, Buddhist institutions fell under the authority of the government-controlled Chinese Buddhist Association. Originally established in 1947 (in Nanjing), it was dominated by "mainland" monks. Its authority began to decline in the 1960s, when independent Buddhist organizations began to be permitted; and especially since the 1987 lifting of martial law in Taiwan. One of the first private networks of Buddhist centers was that of Hsing Yun, who first attained popularity through radio broadcasts in the 1950s.

Another key figure was Cheng Yen, a nun who was

ordained by the aforementioned Yin Shun and later founded Tzu Chi, Taiwan's most important charity organization. It is difficult to overestimate the impact of her personal example on the image of Taiwan's sangha. Tzu Chi runs several hospitals in Taiwan, and conducts worldwide relief work.

A 1999 earthquake centered in Puli brought praise for Tzu Chi for its effective response, in contrast with that of the Taiwanese government. During the 1980s, Buddhist leaders pressed Taiwan's Ministry of Education to relax various policies preventing the organization of a Buddhist university. The eventual result was that in the 1990s—flush with contributions made possible by Taiwan's " miracle economy"—not one but half a dozen such schools emerged, each associated with a different Buddhist leader. Among them were Tzu Chi University, Hsuan-Chuang University, Huafan University, Fo Guang University, Nanhua University, and Dharma Drum Buddhist College.

The regulations of Taiwan's Ministry of Education prohibit recognized colleges and universities from requiring religious belief or practice, and these institutions therefore appear little different from others of their rank. (Degrees granted by seminaries, of which Taiwan has several dozen, are not recognized by the government.) In 2001, Master Hsin Tao of Ling Jiou Shan opened the Museum of World Religions in Taipei. In addition to exhibits on ten different world religions, the museum also features "Avatamsaka World," a model illustrating the Avatamsaka Sutra.

In 2009 Taiwan lost one if its most influential Buddhist teachers when Sheng-yen of the Dharma Drum Mountain monastery died.

In recent decades Vajrayana Buddhism has increased in popularity in Taiwan as Tibetan lamas from the four major Tibetan schools (Kagyu, Nyingma, Sakya and Gelug) have visited the island, including the 14th Dalai Lama, who visited the island thrice in 1997, 2001 and 2009. The True Buddha School is the largest Vajrayana sect in Taiwan, although at least seven established Buddhist organisations have charged that the group functions as a personality cult.

Recent Growth

Statistics provided by the Interior Ministry show that Taiwan's Buddhist population grew from 800,000 in 1983 to 4.9 million in 1995, a 600 percent increase against an overall population rise of about twelve percent. Additionally, in the same period the number of registered Buddhist temples increased from 1,157 to 4,020, and the number of monks and nuns was up 9,300 monks and nuns, up from 3,470 in 1983.14. This trend can be attributed to the activity of various charismatic teachers, such as those mentioned above.

REFERENCES

1. Chen, Kenneth Kuan Sheng. *Buddhism in China: A historical survey*. Princeton, N.J. , Princeton University Press, 1964.
2. Han, Yu. "Sources of Chinese Tradition. *Circa 800.*
3. Hill, John E. (2009) *Through the Jade Gate to Rome: A Study of the Silk Routes during the Later Han Dynasty, 1st to 2nd Centuries CE*. John E. Hill. BookSurge, Charleston, South Carolina.
4. Mullin, Glenn H.*The Fourteen Dalai Lamas: A Sacred Legacy of Reincarnations* (2001) Clear Light Publishers.
5. Welch, Holmes. *The practice of Chinese Buddhism*. Cambridge, Mass.: Harvard University Press, 1967.
6. Welch, Holmes. *The Buddhist revival in China*. Cambridge, Mass.: Harvard University Press, 1968.
7. Welch, Holmes. *Buddhism under Mao*. Cambridge, Mass.:

6

Buddhism in Korea

First it is significant to note that Korean Buddhism is distinguished from other forms of Buddhism by its attempt to resolve what it sees as inconsistencies in *Mahayana* Buddhism. Early Korean monks believed that the traditions they received from foreign countries were internally inconsistent. To address this, they developed a new holistic approach to Buddhism.

This approach is characteristic of virtually all major Korean thinkers, and has resulted in a distinct variation of Buddhism, which is called *Tongbulgyo* ("interpenetrated Buddhism") by Korean scholars.

Korean Buddhist thinkers refined their predecessors' ideas into a distinct form.

As it now stands, Korean Buddhism consists mostly of the *Seon* lineage.

Seon has a strong relationship with other *Mahayana* traditions that bear the imprint of Chinese *Ch'an* teachings, as well as the closely related Japanese *Zen*. Other sects, such as the *Taego*, the modern revival of the *Cheontae* lineage, the "Jingak" order (a modern esoteric sect), and the newly formed *Won*, have also attracted sizable followings.

It is pertinent to note that when Buddhism was originally introduced to Korea from Former Qin in 372, or about 800 years after the death of the historical Buddha, Shamanism was the indigenous religion. As it was not seen to conflict with the rites of nature worship, it was allowed to blend in with Shamanism. Thus, the mountains that were believed to be the residence of spirits in pre-Buddhist times became the sites of Buddhist temples.

Infact, Korean Shamanism held three spirits in especially high regard: Sanshin (the Mountain Spirit), Toksong (the Recluse) and Chilsong (the Spirit of the Seven Stars, the Big Dipper). Korean Buddhism accepted and absorbed these three spirits and, even today, special shrines are set aside for them in many temples. The Mountain Spirit receives particular recognition in an attempt to appease the local mountain spirits, on whose land the temple stands.

This blend of Buddhism and Shamanism became known as Korean Buddhism, although the fundamental teachings of the Buddha remained. Though it initially enjoyed wide acceptance, even being supported as the state ideology during the Goryeo period, Buddhism in Korea suffered extreme repression during the Joseon Dynasty, which lasted for several hundred years. During this period, Neo-Confucian ideology overcame the prior dominance of Buddhism. Only after Buddhist monks helped repel a Japanese invasion at the end of the 16th century did the persecution of Buddhism and Buddhist practitioners stop.

Buddhism in Korea remained subdued until the end of the Joseon period, when its position was strengthened somewhat by the Japanese occupation, which lasted from 1910 to 1945. After World War II, the Seon school of Korean Buddhism once again gained acceptance. As Christianity has become increasingly influential in Korea it is estimated that the declining proportion of the religious population among self-professed Buddhist community in South Korea now accounts for about 23% of the country's population. In officially atheist North Korea, Buddhists make up 2% of the population.

When Buddhism was introduced to Korea in the 4th century CE, the Korean peninsula was politically subdivided into three kingdoms: Goguryeo in the north, Baekje in the southwest, and Silla in the southeast. There is concrete evidence of an earlier introduction of Buddhism than traditionally believed. A mid-4th century tomb, unearthed near P'yÒngyang, is found to incorporate Buddhist motifs in its ceiling decoration.

Goguryeo

In 372 the monk Sundo (or Shundao in Chinese) was sent by Fu Jiân of Former Qin to the court of the King Sosurim of Goguryeo. He brought texts and statues with him and the Goguryeo royalty and their subjects quickly accepted his teachings. The Buddhism in China was in a rudimentary form, consisting of the law of cause and effect and the search for happiness. This had much in common with the predominant Shamanism, which likely led to the quick assimilation of Buddhism by the people of Goguryeo.

Baekje

In 384, the Serindian monk Marananta arrived in Baekje and the royal family received the similar strain of Buddhism he brought. King Asin proclaimed, "people should believe in Buddhism and seek happiness."

Gaya

A small, separate federation called Gaya emerged for a short time on the southern coast between Baekje and the fast growing Shilla. It fell to an invasion in the mid sixth century before reaching maturity, however, and was annexed by the Silla.

Silla

Buddhism did not enter the kingdom of Silla until the 5th century. The common people were first attracted to Buddhism here, but there was resistance among the aristocrats. In 527, however, a prominent court official named Ichadon presented himself to King Pophung and announced he had become Buddhist. The king had him beheaded, but when the executioner cut off his head, it is said that milk poured out instead of blood.

Paintings of this are in the temple at Haein-sa and a stone monument honoring his martyrdom is in the National Museum of Kyongju. During the reign of the next king, King Chinhung, the growth of Buddhism was encouraged — eventually being recognized as the national religion of Silla. Additionally, selected young men were physically and spiritually trained at Hwarangdo according to Buddhist principles to be able to defend the kingdom. King Chinhung later became a monk himself. Many Korean Buddhist monks traveled to China in order to study Buddhism in the late Three Kingdoms Period, especially in the late 6th century.

The monk Banya (562–613?) is said to have studied under the Tiantai master Zhiyi, and Gyeomik of Baekje and travelled to India to learn Sanskrit and study Vinaya. Monks of the period brought back numerous scriptures from abroad and conducted missionary activity throughout Korea and Japan. The date of the first mission to Japan is unclear, but it is reported that a second detachment of scholars was sent to Japan upon invitation by the Japanese rulers in 577. The strong Korean influence on the development of Buddhism in Japan continued through the Unified Silla period; only in the 8th or 9th century did independent study by Japanese monks begin in significant numbers.

Buddhist Schools of Thought

- the Samnon (or *Sanlun* in Chinese) school focused on the Indian *Mâdhyamika* (Middle Path) doctrine,
- the Gyeyul (or *Vinaya* in Sanskrit) school was mainly concerned with the study and implementation of moral discipline (*úîla*), and
- the Yeolban (or *Nirvâna* in Sanskrit) school, which was based in the themes of the *Mahâparinirvâna-sûtra*

Toward the end of the Three Kingdoms Period, the Wonyung (or *Yuanrong* in Chinese) school was formed. It would lead the actualization of the metaphysics of interpenetration as found in the Huayan jing and soon was considered the premier school, especially among the educated aristocracy. This school was later known as Hwaeom (or *Huayan* in Chinese) and was the longest lasting of these "imported" schools. It had strong ties with the Beopseong the indigenous Korean school of thought.

The monk Jajang is credited with having been a major force in the adoption of Buddhism as a national religion. Jajang is also known for his participation in the founding of the Korean sangha, a type of monastic community.

Another great scholar to emerge from the Silla Period was Won-hyo. He renounced his religious life to better serve the people and even married a princess for a short time and had a son. He wrote many treatises and his philosophy centered on the unity and interrelatedness of all things. He set off to China to study Buddhism with a close friend, Ui-sang, but only made it part of the way there. The legend is that Won-hyo awoke one night very thirsty, found a container with cool water, drank, and returned to sleep. The next morning he saw the container from which he had drunk was a human skull and he realized all enlightenment depended on the mind. He saw no reason to continue to China, so he returned home. His companion, Ui-sang, continued to China and after studying ten years, offered a poem to his master in the shape of a seal that geometrically represents infinity. The poem contained the essence of the Avatamsaka Sutra. Buddhism was so successful during this period that many kings converted and cities/places were even renamed after famous places during the time of Buddha.

Unified Silla Period (668–918)

In 668, the kingdom of Silla succeeded in unifying the whole Korean peninsula, giving rise to a period of political stability that lasted for about one hundred years. This led to a high point in the scholarly studies of Buddhism in Korea. In general, the most popular areas of study were *Wonyung*, *Yusik* (*Weishi*; "consciousness-only"; the East Asian form of *Yogâcâra*), *Jeongto* (Pure Land), and the indigenous Korean *Beopseong* ("dharma-nature school"). The monk Wonhyo taught the "Pure Land"-practice of *yeombul*, which would become very popular amongst both scholars and laypeople, and has had a lasting influence on Buddhist thought in Korea.

His work, which attempts a synthesis of the seemingly divergent strands of Indian and Chinese Buddhist doctrine, makes use of the *essence-function* (or *che-yong*) framework, which was popular in native East Asian philosophical schools. His work was instrumental in the development of the dominant school of Korean Buddhist thought, known variously as *Beopseong*, *Haedong* ("Korean") and later as *Jungdo* ("Middle way")

Wonhyo's friend Uisang went to Changan, where he studied under Huayan patriarchs Zhiyan (600–668) and Fazang (643–712). When he returned after twenty years, his work contributed to *Hwaeom* and became the predominant doctrinal influence on Korean Buddhism, together with Wonhyo's *tong bulgyo* thought.

Hwaeom principles were deeply assimilated into the Korean meditational school, the Seon school, where they made a profound effect on its basic attitudes. Influences from Silla Buddhism in general, and from these two philosophers in particular, even crept "backwards" into Chinese Buddhism. Wonhyo's commentaries were very important in shaping the thought of the preeminent Chinese Buddhist philosopher Fazang, and Woncheuk's commentary on the *SaCdhinirmocana-sûtra* had a strong influence in Tibetan Buddhism. As was the case in Tang China, as well as the Nara and early Heian period in Japan, which are roughly contemporary to the Silla period, the intellectual developments of Silla Buddhism also brought with them significant cultural achievements in many areas, including painting, literature, sculpture, and architecture.

During this period, many large and beautiful temples were built. Two crowning achievements were the temple Bulguksa and the cave-retreat of Seokguram. Bulguksa was especially famous for its jeweled pagodas, while Seokguram was known for the beauty of its stone sculpture. A new epoch in Korean Buddhism began during the latter Silla period with the birth of schools of *Seon* in Korea. In China, the movement toward a meditation-based view of practice, which came to be known as *chan*, had begun during the sixth and seventh centuries, and it was not long before the influence of the new meditational school reached Korea, where it was known as *Seon*. Meaning "meditation," the term is more widely known in the West in its Japanese variant *zen*.

Tension developed between the new meditational schools and the previously existing academically oriented schools, which were described by the term *gyo*, meaning "learning" or "study." Kim Kiaokak(630–729), a prince who became a monastic came to the region of Anhui to Mount Jiuhua in China. Many Chinese buddhists believe he was indeed the transformation body of Kcitigarbha.

Two uncles sent by his mother and wife to call him back also became a monastic there. His well-preserved, dehydrated body were seen at the monastery he built on Mount Jiuhua today. The two uncles, unable to resist wine and meat as they were official before becoming monastics, practice in another place in the mount. People built the palace of the two saints in their practice place to memorize them. Many Buddhists visited there. Beomnang (632–646), said to be a student of the Chinese master Daoxin (580–651), is generally credited with the initial transmission of *Seon* into Korea. *Seon* was popularized by Sinhaeng (704–779) in the latter part of the eighth century and by Doui (died 825) at the beginning of the ninth century. From then on, many Koreans studied *Chan* in China, and upon their return established their own schools at various mountain monasteries with their leading disciples.

Initially, the number of these schools was fixed at nine, and Korean *Seon* was termed the "nine mountains" (or *gusan*) school at the time. Eight of these were of the lineage of Mazu Daoyi (709–788), as they were established through connection with either him or one of his eminent disciples. The one exception was the Sumi-san school founded by Ieom (869–936), which had developed from the *Caotong* lineage.

Goryeo Period (918–1392)

Initially, the new Seon schools were regarded by the established doctrinal schools as radical and dangerous upstarts. Thus, the early founders of the various "nine mountain" monasteries met with considerable resistance, repressed by the long influence in court of the Gyo schools. The struggles which ensued continued for most of the Goryeo period, but gradually the Seon argument for the possession of the true transmission of enlightenment would gain the upper hand. The position that was generally adopted in the later Seon schools, due in large part to the efforts of Jinul, did not claim clear superiority of Seon meditational methods, but rather declared the intrinsic unity and similarities of the Seon and Gyo viewpoints.

Although all these schools are mentioned in historical records, toward the end of the dynasty, Seon became dominant in its effect on the government and society, and the production of noteworthy scholars and adepts. During the Goryeo period, Seon thoroughly became a "religion of the state," receiving extensive support and privileges through connections with the ruling family and powerful members of the court. Although most of the scholastic schools waned in activity and influence during this period of the growth of Seon, the *Hwaeom* school continued to be a lively source of scholarship well into the Goryeo, much of it continuing the legacy of Uisang and Wonhyo. In particular the work of Gyunyeo (923–973) prepared for the reconciliation of Hwaeom and Seon, with Hwaeom's accommodating attitude toward the latter. Gyunyeo's works are an important source for modern scholarship in identifying the distinctive nature of Korean Hwaeom. Another important advocate of Seon/Gyo unity was Uicheon. Like most other early Goryeo monks, he began his studies in Buddhism with Hwaeom. He later traveled to China, and upon his return, actively promulgated the *Cheontae* (*Tiantai* in Chinese) teaching, which became recognized as another Seon school.

This period thus came to be described as "five doctrinal and two meditational schools" (*ogyo yangjong*). Uicheon himself, however, alienated too many Seon adherents, and he died at a relatively young age without seeing a Seon-Gyo unity accomplished. The most important figure of Seon in the Goryeo was *Jinul* (1158–1210). In his time, the sangha was in a crisis of external appearance and internal issues of doctrine. Buddhism had gradually become infected by secular tendencies and involvements, such as fortune-telling and the offering of prayers and rituals for success in secular endeavors.

This kind of corruption resulted in the profusion of increasingly larger numbers of monks and nuns with questionable motivations. Therefore, the correction, revival, and improvement of the quality of Buddhism were prominent issues for Buddhist leaders of the period. Jinul sought to establish a new movement within Korean Seon, which he called the *"samâdhi and prajñâ society"*, whose goal was to establish a new community of disciplined, pure-minded practitioners deep in the mountains. He eventually accomplished this mission with the founding of the Songgwangsa monastery at Mt. Jogye.

Jinul's works are characterized by a thorough analysis and reformulation of the methodologies of Seon study and practice. One major issue that had long fermented in Chinese *Chan*, and which received special focus from Jinul, was the relationship between "gradual" and "sudden" methods in practice and enlightenment. Drawing upon various Chinese treatments of this topic, most importantly those by Zongmi (780–841) and Dahui (1089–1163), Jinul created a "sudden enlightenment followed by gradual practice" dictum, which he outlined in a few relatively concise and accessible texts.

From Dahui, Jinul also incorporated the *gwanhwa* method into his practice. This form of meditation is the main method taught in Korean Seon today. Jinul's philosophical resolution of the Seon-Gyo conflict brought a deep and lasting effect on Korean Buddhism. The general trend of Buddhism in the latter half of the Goryeo was a decline due to corruption, and the rise of strong anti-Buddhist political and philosophical sentiment. However, this period of relative decadence would nevertheless produce some of Korea's most renowned Seon masters. Three important monks of this period who figured prominently in charting the future course of Korean Seon were contemporaries and friends: Gyeonghan Baeg'un (1298–1374), Taego Bou (1301–1382) and Naong Hyegeun (1320–1376). All three went to Yuan China to learn the *Linji* (or *Imje* in Korean) *gwanhwa* teaching that had been popularized by Jinul.

All three returned, and established the sharp, confrontational methods of the Imje school in their own teaching. Each of the three was also said to have had hundreds of disciples, such that this new infusion into Korean Seon brought about considerable effect. Despite the Imje influence, which was generally considered to be anti-scholarly in nature, Gyeonghan and Naong, under the influence of Jinul and the traditional *tong bulgyo* tendency, showed an unusual interest in scriptural study, as well as a strong understanding of *Confucianism* and

Taoism, due to the increasing influence of Chinese philosophy as the foundation of official education.

From this time, a marked tendency for Korean Buddhist monks to be "three teachings" exponents appeared. A significant historical event of the Goryeo period is the production of the first woodblock edition of the Tripitaka, called the Tripitaka Koreana.

Two editions were made, the first one completed from 1210 to 1231, and the second one from 1214 to 1259. The first edition was destroyed in a fire, during an attack by Mongol invaders in 1232, but the second edition is still in existence at Haeinsa in Gyeongsang province. This edition of the Tripitaka was of high quality, and served as the standard version of the Tripitaka in East Asia for almost 700 years.

Joseon Dynasty (1392–1910)

The Buddhist establishment at the end of the Goryeo period had become ridden with excesses. There were too many monks and nuns, a large percentage of whom were only in the sangha as a means of escaping taxation and/or government service. There were also far too many temples being supported, and too many elaborate rituals being carried out. The support of Buddhism had become a serious drain on the national economy.

The government itself was suffering from rampant corruption, while also struggling with wars on its northern and eastern borders. Moreover, a new and rapidly growing *Neo-Confucian* ideological movement of stridently anti-Buddhist inclination gained political power. In 1388, an influential general named Yi Seonggye (1380–1400) carried out a coup d'etat, and established himself as the first ruler of the Joseon Dynasty under the reign title of *Taejo* in

1392 with the support of this Neo-Confucian movement. Subsequently, Buddhism was gradually suppressed for the next 500 years. The number of temples was reduced, restrictions on membership in the sangha were installed, and Buddhist monks and nuns were literally chased into the mountains, forbidden to mix with society.

Joseon Buddhism, which had started off under the so-called "five doctrinal and two meditational" schools system of the Goryeo, was first condensed to two schools:Seon and Gyo. Eventually, these were further reduced to the single school of Seon. Despite this strong suppression from the government, and vehement ideological opposition from Korean Neo-Confucianism, Seon Buddhism continued to thrive intellectually. An outstanding thinker was *Giwha* ((Hamheo Deuktong) 1376–1433), who had first studied at a Confucian academy, but then changed his focus to Buddhism, where he was initiated to the *gwanhwa* tradition by *Muhak Jacho* (1327–1405). He wrote many scholarly commentaries, as well as essays and a large body of poetry.

Being well-versed in Confucian and Daoist philosophies, Giwha also wrote an important treatise in defense of Buddhism, from the standpoint of the intrinsic unity of the three teachings, entitled the *Hyeon jeong non*. In the tradition of earlier philosophers, he applied *che-yong* ("essence-function") and *Hwaeom* (*sa-sa mu-ae*, "mutual interpenetration of phenomena"). Common in the works of Joseon scholar-monks are writings on Hwaeom-related texts, as well as the *Awakening of Faith*, *Sutra of Perfect Enlightenment*, *Ůûrangama-sûtra*, *Diamond Sutra* and the *Heart Sutra*.

The Jogye order instituted a set curriculum of scriptural study, including the above-mentioned works, along with other shorter selections from eminent Korean monks, such as Jinul. During the Joseon period, the number of Buddhist monasteries dropped from several hundred to a mere thirty-six. Limits were placed on the number of clergy, land area, and ages for entering the sangha. When the final restrictions were in place, monks and nuns were prohibited from entering the cities. Buddhist funerals, and even begging, were outlawed. However, some rulers occasionally appeared who looked favorably upon Buddhism and did away with some of the more suppressive regulations.

The most noteworthy of these was the Queen Munjeong, who, as a devout Buddhist, took control of the government in the stead of her young son Myeongjong (r. 1545–67), and immediately repealed many anti-Buddhist measures. The queen had deep respect for the brilliant monk *Bou* (1515–1565), and installed him as the head of the Seon school. One of the most important reasons for the restoration of Buddhism to a position of minimal acceptance was the role of Buddhist monks in repelling the Japanese invasions of Korea, which occurred between 1592 and 1598. At that time, the government was weak from internal squabbles, and was not initially able to muster strong resistance to the incursion.

The plight of the country encouraged some leaders of the sangha to organize monks into guerrilla units, which enjoyed some instrumental successes. The "righteous monk" (*uisa*) movement spread during this eight-year war, finally including several thousand monks, led by the aging *Seosan Hyujeong* (1520–1604), a first-rate Seon master and the author of a number of important religious texts. The presence of the monks' army was a critical factor in the eventual expulsion of the Japanese invaders.

Seosan is also known for continuing efforts toward the unification of Buddhist doctrinal study and practice. His efforts were strongly influenced by Wonhyo, Jinul, and Giwha.

He is considered the central figure in the revival of Joseon Buddhism, and most major streams of modern Korean Seon trace their lineages back to him through one of his four main disciples: *Yu Jeong* (1544–1610); *Eongi* (1581–1644), *Taeneung* (1562–1649) and *Ilseon* (1533–1608), all four of whom were lieutenants to Seosan during the war with Japan. The biographies of Seosan and his four major disciples are similar in many respects, and these similarities are emblematic of the typical lifestyle of Seon monks of the late Goryeo and Joseon periods. Most of them began by engaging in Confucian and Daoist studies. Turning to Seon, they pursued a markedly itinerant lifestyle, wandering through the mountain monasteries.

At this stage, they were initiated to the central component of Seon practice, the *gong'an*, or *gwanhwa* meditation. This *gwanhwa* meditation, unlike some Japanese *Zen* traditions, did not consist of contemplation on a lengthy, graduated series of deeper *kôans*. By contrast, the typical Korean approach was that "all *gong'an* are contained in one" and therefore it was, and still is, quite common for the practitioner to remain with one hwadu during his whole meditational career, most often Zhaozhou's *"mu."* Buddhism during the three centuries, from the time of Seosan down to the next Japanese incursion into Korea in the late nineteenth century, remained fairly consistent with the above-described model.

A number of eminent teachers appeared during the centuries after Seosan, but the Buddhism of the late Joseon, while keeping most of the common earlier characteristics, was especially marked by a revival of Hwaeom studies, and occasionally by new interpretations of methodology in Seon study. There was also a revival, during the final two centuries, of the *Pure Land* (*Amitâbha*) faith.

Although the government maintained fairly tight control of the sangha, there was never again the extreme suppression of the early Joseon.

Japanese Occupation (1910–1945)

The Japanese occupation from 1910 to 1945 brought great suffering on the Korean people as a whole, and to the Korean sangha in particular, as it had to comply with an extensive set of Japanese regulations. Japanese Buddhists demanded the right to proselytize in the cities, lifting the five-hundred year ban on monks and nuns entering cities. The formation of new Buddhist sects, such as *Won Buddhism*, and the presence of Christian missionaries during this period led to further turbulence in traditional Korean Buddhism.

The Japanese Buddhist custom of allowing Buddhist priests to marry contradicted the lifestyle of Korean Buddhist monks and nuns, who traditionally lived in celibacy. The Japanese occupational authorities encouraged this practice, appointed their own heads of temples, and had many works of art shipped to Japan. Negotiations for the repatriation of Korean Buddhist artworks are still ongoing.

Buddhism and Westernization (1945–Present)

When Korea was liberated from Japanese occupation in 1945, the celibate monastics of what has become the main sect of Korean Buddhism, Chogye or Jogye, began to take over for the married monks who ran the temples during the occupation. This order sees itself as the primary representative of traditional Korean Buddhism in existence.

South Korea

Starting in the 1950s, Syngman Rhee and others worked to further divide and weaken the Buddhist Sangha in the country. Rhee campaigned in 1954 against the so-called "Japanized Buddhists". Western education and scholarship, and the empowerment of women and the poor, caused divisions among Koreans. Specifically, a deep rift opened between married priests and celibate monks. The differences were so great that fistfights over the control of temples became frequent. Monks, mostly belonging to the celibate Jogye order, threatened to kill themselves.

Many of them were against the Japanized Buddhists. As the Buddhist riots continued, the influence of Buddhism lessened. Buddhism continued to lose followers to Christian missionaries, who were able to capitalize on these weaknesses. President Park Chung-hee unsuccessfully attempted during his rule (1961–1979) to settle the dispute by building a pan-national Buddhist organization. However, he did succeed in allying himself with the celibate faction of the sangha. In the 1980s, President Chun Doo-hwan also used politics and intrigue to attack Buddhism. He sent troops to raid temples, and had hundreds of monks arrested and tortured. During the 1990s, conflicts between the South Korean government and Buddhist leaders, and Christian denominations continued. The government accused Buddhist monks of immorality and some Christians used this to forward their missionary work.

Some religious gatherings have even turned violent, with statues of Buddha and Dangun, the founder of Korea, being vandalized. There was also a rash of temple burnings in the 1980s and 1990s, and attacks on Buddhist artwork have continued. In one instance, a Christian minister used a microphone on a cord as a bolo weapon and smashed temple paintings and a statue. In other instances, red crosses have been painted on temple walls, murals, and statues.

Buddha statues have also been decapitated. Furthermore, students at Buddhist universities report aggressive attempts to convert them to Christianity on campus, especially near campus temples. See Frank Tedesco's "Questions for Buddhist and Christian Cooperation in Korea," *Buddhist-Christian Studies* 17 (1997). On and off, sectarian tensions between Christians and Buddhists occasionally rises due to what was seen by a tendency of the government officials–many of whom are Christians–to tilt the political balance in favour of Christians over Buddhists which has occasionally led to discontent over some quarters.

Of particular note was after Lee Myung-bak's ascendency to Presidency, Buddhists drew flak over the high proportion of Christians favouring over Buddhists in the public sector–particularly the cabinet whereby there were 12 Christian ministers to only one Buddhist minister within his cabinet among other reported incidences.

North Korea

The regime in North Korea actively discourages the practice of religion, including Buddhism. Currently, the country claims to have about 10,000 active adherents of Buddhism. As with other religions in the country, Buddhism came under the close scrutiny of the country's government–including worship at Buddhist temples by monks, through the state-sponsored Korea Buddhist Federation.

Nevertheless, Buddhists in North Korea reportedly fared

better than other religious groups–particularly Christians, who were said to often face persecution by the authorities, and Buddhists were given limited funding by the government to promote the religion, given that Buddhism played an integral role in traditional Korean culture.

Current Situation

The Seon school, which is led by the dominant Jogye order, practices disciplined traditional Seon practice at a number of major mountain monasteries in Korea, often under the direction of highly regarded masters. Modern Seon practice is not far removed in content from the original practice of Jinul, who introduced the integrated combination of the practice of Gwanhwa meditation with the study of selected Buddhist texts.

The Korean sangha life is markedly itinerant: while each monk has a "home" monastery, he will regularly travel throughout the mountains, staying as long as he wishes, studying and teaching in the style of whatever monastery is housing him. The Korean monastic training system has seen a steadily increasing influx of Western practitioner-aspirants in the second half of the twentieth century. Currently, Korean Buddhism is in a state of slow transition. While the reigning theory behind Korean Buddhism was based on Jinul's "sudden enlightenment, gradual cultivation," the modern Korean Seon master, Seongcheol's revival of Hui Neng's "sudden enlightenment, sudden cultivation" has taken Korean Buddhism by storm. Although there is resistance to change within the ranks of the Jogye order, with the last three Supreme Patriarchs' stance that is in accordance with Seongcheol, there has been a gradual change in the atmosphere of Korean Buddhism.

Antagonism with Korean Protestantism

Protestant antagonism against Buddhism is perceived to have increased in recent years. Acts of vandalism against Buddhist amenities and "praying for the destruction of all Buddhist temples" have all drawn attention to this persistent antagonism between the two religions. Some South Korean Buddhists have denounced what they view as discriminatory measures against them and their religion by the administration of President Lee Myung-bak, which they attribute to Lee being a Protestant. The Buddhist Jogye Order has accused the Lee government of discriminating against Buddhism by ignoring certain Buddhist temples in certain public documents. In 2006, according to the *Asia Times*, "Lee also sent a video prayer message to a Christian rally held in the southern city of Busan in which the worship leader prayed feverishly: 'Lord, let the Buddhist temples in this country crumble down!'" Further, according to an article in *Buddhist-Christian Studies*: "Over the course of the last decade a fairly large number of Buddhist temples in South Korea have been destroyed or damaged by fire by misguided Protestant fundamentalists.

More recently, Buddhist statues have been identified as idols, attacked and decapitated. Arrests are hard to effect, as the arsonists and vandals work by stealth of night." A 2008 incident in which police investigated protesters who had been given sanctuary in the Jogye temple in Seoul and searched a car driven by Jigwan, executive chief of the Jogye order, led to protests by some claiming police had treated Jigwan as a criminal.

REFERENCES

1. "Buddhists set to protest against Lee's religious bias". HANKYOREH. August 22, 2008.

2. "Buddhist Temple Being Restored in N. Korea". Los Angeles Times. October 2, 2005.
3. Democratic People's Republic of Korea, U.S. Department of State.
4. Harry L. Wells, *Korean Temple Burnings and Vandalism: The Response of the Society for Buddhist-Christian Studies. Buddhist-Christian Studies*, Vol. 20, 2000, pp. 239-240.
5. Rahn, Kim (July 30, 2008). "President Embarrassed Over Angry Buddhists". *The Korea Times*. Retrieved October 7, 2008.
6. "South Korea Buddhists March Against Christian President, Alleging Religious Discrimination". Fox news. August 27, 2008.
7. "USCIRF Annual Report 2005 - Korea, Democratic Republic of". UNCHR. May 1, 2005.
8. YouTube — S. Korean Christians praying for Buddhist temple to collapse.
9. "Who's Really to Blame for Religious Bias?". *The Chosun Ilbo*. September 1, 2008.

7

Buddhism in South Asia

BUDDHISM IN NEPAL

Current Status

According to 2001 census, the adherents of Buddhism are as follows-

Ethnic Group	*Total Population*	*Total Buddhist*	*Percentage Buddhist*
Tamang	1,282,304	1157461	90.3
Magar			24.5
Gurung			69
Newar	1,242,232	190,629	15.3
Sherpa			92.8
Bhote			60.5
Thakali			65
Chantel			64.2
Jirel			87
Lepcha			88.8
Yehlmo			98.4

Lord Buddha, the founder of Buddhism was born in a kingdom of Nepal. Hence Nepal can be considered as the starting point of Buddhism. Buddha was born in Shakya kingdom which lies in Rupandehi district, Lumbini zone of Nepal. As of now 10.74% of Nepal's population practice Buddhism, consisting mainly of groups of Tibeto-Burman origin. The Kirant tribes, especially the Limbu and the Rai, have also adopted Tibetan Buddhist practises from their Buddhist neighbours. The Jirel, which is considered a Kirata tribe, have also adopted Tibetan Buddhism.

Buddhist influences are evident in the culture of Nepal because Buddha was born in Nepal. It has strong Buddhist background and has played role in spread of Buddhism to Tibet. Nepalese princess Bhrikuti played a significant role in development of Buddhism in Tibet and Far East. Tibetan Buddhist architecture has long been influenced by Nepalese artists and sculptors like Araniko.

The sacred Buddhist texts in Mahayana Buddhism are mainly written in Ranjana script (the script of Newars) or scripts like Lantsa which are derived from Ranjana. Among the Tibeto-Burman tribes, Tibetan Buddhism is the most widely practised form. Newar practice Newar variant of Vajrayana Buddhism and Theravada Buddhism. Many Buddhist groups are also influenced by Hinduism.

Buddhism is the dominant religion of the thinly-populated northern areas, which are inhabited by Tibetan-related peoples, namely the Sherpa, Lopa, Manangi, Thakali, Lhomi, Dolpa and Nyimba. They constitute a small minority of the country's population. Ethnic groups that live in central Nepal, such as Gurung, Lepcha, Tamang, Magar, Newar, Yakkha, Thami and Chepang, are also followers of Buddhism. These ethnic groups have larger populations compared to their northern neighbours. They came under the influence of Hinduism due to their close contacts with the Hindu castes. In turn, many of them eventually adopted

Hinduism and have been largely integrated into the caste system.

Buddha was born in Nepal. He preached in parts of South Asia which lie in modern Nepal.

Shakya clans of Lumbini

Buddha was born in Lumbini (which is now in Nepal). According to Tripitaka, he visited his father's kingdom and converted his family and clan to Buddhism. The Shakya clans later moved to Kathmandu valley and helped establish Buddhism there.

Pre Lichchavi Buddhism

During Kirant era, Buddha is believed to have visited Kathmandu valley during the reign of Kirat king Jitedasti. Emperor Ashoka from India put up a pillar at Lumbini, the birthplace of the Buddha in the 2nd century BC.

After third Buddhist Council, king Ashoka sent dhamma missionaries to Nepal . It is also believed that Ashoka went to Patan and had four stupas built there. It is believed that his daughter Charumati established the village of Chabahi, which is located between Kathmandu and Bodhnath (khasti-in newari language). There is a stupa and monastery in Chabahi that are said to date back to her time.

It is said that upon the expansion of the Mauryan dynasty into the Terai plains in Nepal, Buddhism was adopted by the ancestors of the Tharu and flourished until the resurgent Licchavi repelled its adherents in AD 200.

Buddhism During the Licchavi Period (400-750)

The Licchavi period saw the flourishing of both Hinduism and Buddhism in Nepal. Excellent examples of Buddhist art of the period are the half-sunken Buddha in

Pashupatinath, the sleeping Vishnu in Budhanilkantha, and the statue of Buddha and the various representations of Vishnu in Changu Narayan.

Ancient Buddhist texts claim that Mulasarvasti Vadavinaya (better known as the Shakyas of Kapilvastu, Bhikshu Ananda, and the Baniyas of Sravasti) came to Nepal, then known as Newal, from Tibet. Another Buddhist text, the Manjushrimula Kalpa, mentioned Manadeva as the King of Nepal Mandala. Researchers believe the Mulasarvastivadavinaya was written in the 2nd century CE, and that the Manjushriulakalpa was written during Manadeva's reign.

The Swayambhu Purana, the ancient Buddhist Purana text, and a Licchavi inscription all mentioned Nepal Mandala. Buddhist inscriptions and chronicles and Tibetan sources also record a few tantric Buddhist deities, namely Aksyobhya, Amitabha, Vajrayogini, Vajrabhairava, Usnisavijaya and Samantabhadra. Strong influence from Animist cults resulted in belief in Buddhist deities such as the Pancaraksas.

In fact, religious tolerance and syncretism were stressed during the Licchavi period. King Manadeva paid homage at both Hindu and Buddhist sites. His family subsequently found expression for their beliefs in various different religions. The worship of the Caitya and the Rath Jatra cart festival of Avalokitesvara were introduced around this period. Many ancient sites in the Kathmandu Valley were identified with major Buddhist Caityas, such as Swayambhunath, Boudnanath Stupa, Kathmandu and the four "Ashoka" stupas of Patan, and another two hundred stone caityas dating from the Licchavi Period, were testified to the widespread antiquity of caitya worship. It is possible that this practice, in its earliest incarnation, was related to the worship of stones, which may have originated in the early, rival Kirata inhabitants of the Valley, prior to the Licchavis.

According to one of the earliest Licchavi inscriptions, Caitya worship ordinarily consisted of ritual circumambulation of the caitya and offering standard items such as incense, colored powder, oil lamps and ablutions.

At times, the inscriptions indicate, it could even involve resurfacing an existing Caitya and covering the new surface with many elaborate paintings. Caitya worship was an important factor in bringing more of the proto-Newar tribal inhabitants into the Buddhist fold, as it was a devotional practice designed for the general public. Thus, the masses probably began practicing the cart festival of Avalokitesvara/ Matsyendranath (Bungakya) during the latter half of the seventh century A.D.

This festival was celebrated by hundreds or even thousands of people, who helped to construct and transport a huge, wheeled cart that bore the image of Avalokitesvara for several days or weeks along a specific route. The introduction of this festival must have been an instant success among the majority of the Kathmandu Valley population. This strengthened Buddhism's standing in relation to the other Hindu and Animist faiths of the Valley at the time.

Forty stone inscriptions made some mention of Buddhism throughout the Licchavi period. Most of the references are concerned with monasticism. However, almost nothing is known about the day-to-day life in the Vihara monasteries or how they functioned administratively.

The names of the fifteen Buddhist monasteries are known, and it is clear from the context in which some of these are named that they are among the most important religious sites of that time. It is not known for certain what schools of Buddhism were most prominent at the time. But the strongest early influences (aside from an even earlier probable substratum of Pali Buddhism) probably came from the Mahasanghika, Sammitiya and the Sarvastivada schools. The Makhyamaka and Yogacara schools were thought to be more influential in the later period with the emergence and growth of the Vajrayana school.

Inscriptional evidence also proves that there was a string of traditional methods of making religious gifts. These offerings were used for earning blessing and making merit, and the women of the Buddhist seem to have taken the lead in offering these gifts. Strikingly, parallel points within the Buddhist cave contain inscriptions of Maharastra, which predated the Licchvi Nepal. The references in the Licchavi inscriptions to the Mahayana and Vajrayana will be mentioned below in connection with Buddhist art and notable Buddhist figures of the Licchavi period.

Buddhism During the Licchabi Period (600-1200)

The first Licchabi king, Amsuvarma, married his daughter Bhrikuti to the ruler of Tibet, King Songtsen Gampo. According to legend, she received the begging bowl of the Buddha as part of her wedding dowry. It is believed that she introduced Buddhism into Tibet. she is also believed as a reincarnation of the Green Tara of Tibetan Buddhism, who is seen in many Buddhist Thangkas. Lichhabi period is known as the golden time for Buddhism.

Buddhism During the Malla Dynasty (1200-1769)

The Malla dynasty saw to the golden period of the syncretism of Hindu and Buddhist art forms by the Newar.

The Paubha, the Newari counterpart of the Tibetan Buddhist Thangka, flourished in this period.

During the reign of Jayasthiti Malla, after implementation of Manudharmasastra, celibate monks were banned from practicing in Nepal. This gave way to the decelebate Newar Buddhism. Because of this, Theravada Buddhism was lost in Nepal only to be revitalized in late 19th century.

Buddhism During the Shah Dynasty (1769-1846)

The Shah dynasty saw the decline of Buddhism in Nepal where it eventually merged with Hinduism as the Hindu Gurkha rose to prominence. In the north, the Mustang kingdom ruled by the Buddhist Lopa and the Thakali saw to the flourishing of Vajrayana (Tibetan Buddhism) in the North.

Buddhism During the Rana Dynasty (1846-1951)

Modern Newar Buddhist practises in Nepal have largely been absorbed into mainstream Hinduism, although certain distinct practises, artforms and castes do remain. In the north, people of Tibetan origin continued to be the much-unchanged practises of Tibetan Buddhism, especially in the case of the Nyimba of Northwest Nepal.

On the other hand, the Thakali, who had traditionally played an important role in the Nepali society but yet retained Tibetan Buddhism, have begun to embrace Hinduism as well in the recent years. It is significant to note that during Rana dynasty, several Theravada Buddhists were banished from Nepal for preaching Buddhism.

Also, the rediscovery of Lumbini, the birthplace of Buddha, occurred in this era with contributions from among others, General Khadga Sumsher Rana.

Shah Dynasty (1951-2006)

After the overthrown of Rana dynasty in 1951, Buddhism gradually developed in the country. Theravadin Buddhist played a great significance role for the Buddhist revival campaign in modern Nepal since 1920s. This revival movement has changed Buddhism from ethnic-religion of some ethnic groups and castes into beyond the caste and ethnic religion in Nepal.

Presently, there are three main Buddhist schools; Tibetan Buddhism, Newar Buddhism and Theravada Buddhism. Tourism is another important factor for promoting Nepali Buddhism to the world. Every year, Kathmandu can receive more than 10,000 travellers from all over the world just to visit the Boudhanath and the Swayambhunath stupas.

These are the remarkable and significant architect, which only found in Nepal. Apart from these two main Buddhist monuments there are hundreds of Buddhist monuments every corner of streets of Kathmandu and some other main cities of Nepal.

Nepal became a secular country in 2006. All religion got equal opportunities to propagate according to their belief. Thus, the role the Buddhist tradition played, is playing and will play to smoothly run society, strengthen it and extend it widely from the narrow frontiers is a great thing worth appreciating.

As such, it is obvious from the above discussion that Nepal's socio-religious life is greatly influence by Buddhism.

BUDDHISM IN BHUTAN

It is significant to note that Mahayana Buddhism is the state religion of the Himalayan Kingdom of Bhutan, and Buddhists comprise two-thirds to three-quarters of its population. Although originating in Tibetan Buddhism, the Buddhism practiced in Bhutan differs significantly in its rituals, liturgy, and monastic organization. The state religion has long been supported financially by the government through annual subsidies to monasteries, shrines, monks, and nuns. In the modern era, support of the state religion during the reign of Jigme Dorji Wangchuck includes the manufacture of 10,000 gilded bronze images of the Buddha, publication of elegant calligraphied editions of the 108-volume Kangyur (Collection of the Words of the Buddha) and the 225-volume Tengyur (Collection of Commentaries), and the construction of numerous *chorten* (stupas) throughout the country. Guaranteed representation in the National Assembly and the Royal Advisory Council, Buddhists constitute the majority of society and are assured an influential voice in public policy.

In 1989 some 1,000 monks (*lam*, or *gelong*, novices) belonged to the Central Monastic Body in Thimphu and Punakha, and some 4,000 monks belonged to district monastic bodies. The hierarchy is headed by the Je Khenpo, who was assisted by five *lopons* or masters, each in charge of religious tradition, liturgy, lexicography, or logic and university. The *lonpon*, one of whom, the Dorji Lonpon, normally succeeded the current Je Khenpo, had under them religious administrators and junior monastic officials in charge of art, music, and other areas. Gelugpa monks were celibate, but Nyingmapas consist of not only monks but also householders, allowing them to marry, raise families, and work in secular occupations while performing liturgical functions in temples and homes. In all, there were some 12,000 monks in Bhutan in the late 1980s. There were also active congregations of nuns, but no figures were readily available.

The majority of Bhutan's Buddhists are adherents of the Drukpa subsect of the Kargyupa (literally, oral transmission) school, one of the four major schools of Tibetan Buddhism. Since July 2002, Menjong Chöthün Tshogpa, currently a nationwide non-profit organization in Bhutan, has been formed by the Supreme Dharma King or His Holiness of Bhutan mainly to preserve the indigenous Buddha's Teachings as their age-old culture and tradition. Subsequently Trizin Tsering Rimpoche has been enthroned as the chairman by His Holiness Truku Jigme Chödrag Rinpoche 70th Kyabje Dorjechang (Supreme Dharma King) of Bhutan himself since June 2003.

Remarkably, later in 2004, Trizin Tsering Rimpoche founded the Buddha Dordenma Image Foundation, under the patron of His Holiness of Bhutan, with an aim to fulfill a former prophecy in a terma of Guru Padmasambhava to bestow blessings on world peace and glorious happiness through the currently running Buddha Dordenma Project.

The Shabdrung

Prior to 1907, the highest Buddhist leader in Bhutan was the Shabdrung, a tulku who is seen as the reincarnation of Bhutan's founder. His formal activity to benefit all sentient beings is destined to occur in seven lives, each with his own prophecy.

Monasteries

It is pertinent to note that monasteries and convents are common in Bhutan. Both monks and nuns keep their heads shaved and wear distinguishing maroon robes. Their days are spent in study and meditation but also in the performance of rituals honoring various bodhisattvas, praying for the dead, and seeking the intercession of bodhisattvas on behalf of the ill. Some of their prayers involved chants and singing accompanied by conch shell trumpets, trumpets made from human thighbones, metal horns up to three meters long, large standing drums and cymbals, hand bells, temple bells, gongs, and wooden sticks.

Such monastic music and singing, not normally heard by the general public, has been reported to have "great virility" and to be more melodious than its Tibetan monotone counterparts. Common people do practice the religion in their own ways: day to day works, in their speech, in their thought and visiting the holy place and persons on holy dates (holy dates are the 8, 10, 15, 25, 28 and 30th day in a month in Bhutanese calendar).

To bring Buddhism to the people, numerous symbols and structures are employed. Religious monuments, prayer walls, prayer flags, and sacred mantras carved in stone hillsides are prevalent. Among the religious monuments are chorten, the Bhutanese version of the Indian stupa. They range from simple rectangular "house" chorten to complex edifices with ornate steps, doors, domes, and spires. Some are decorated with the Buddha's eyes that see in all directions simultaneously. These earth, brick, or stone structures commemorate deceased kings, Buddhist saints, venerable monks, and other notables, and sometimes they serve as reliquaries. Prayer walls are made of laid or piled stone and inscribed with Tantric prayers. Prayers printed with woodblocks on cloth are made into tall, narrow, colorful prayer flags, which are then mounted on long poles and placed both at holy sites and at dangerous locations to ward off demons and to benefit the spirits of the dead. To help propagate the faith, itinerant monks travel from village to village carrying portable shrines with many small doors, which open to reveal statues and images of the Buddha, bodhisattavas, and notable lamas.

Before the introduction of Buddhism, Bön religion was prevalent in Bhutan. Imported from Tibet and India, perhaps in the eighth century, Bön doctrine became so strongly reinvigorated by Buddhism that by the eleventh century it reasserted itself as an independent school apart from Buddhism. Bön continues to be practiced in modern Bhutan.

SRI LANKA

It is significant to note that Buddhism in Sri Lanka is primarily of the Theravada school, and constitutes the religious faith of about 70% of the population. According to traditional Sri Lankan chronicles (such as the Dipavamsa), Buddhism was introduced into Sri Lanka in the 2nd century BCE by Venerable Mahinda, the son of the Emperor Ashoka, during the reign of Sri Lanka's King Devanampiyatissa. During this time, a sapling of the Bodhi Tree was brought to Sri Lanka and the first monasteries were established under the sponsorship of the Sri Lankan king.

The Pali Canon, having previously been preserved as an oral tradition, was first committed to writing in Sri Lanka around 30 BCE. Sri Lanka has the longest continuous history of Buddhism of any Buddhist nation, with the Sangha having existed in a largely unbroken lineage since its introduction in the 2nd century. During periods of decline, the Sri Lankan monastic lineage was revived through contact with Myanmar and Thailand. Periods of Mahayana influence, as well as official neglect under colonial rule, created great challenges for Theravada Buddhist institutions in Sri Lanka, but repeated revivals and resurgences- most recently in the 19th century CE- have kept the Theravada tradition alive for over 2000 years.

From the 16th century onward, Christian missionaries

and Portuguese, Dutch and British colonizers of Sri Lanka have attempted to convert the local population to Christianity. In the late 19th century, a national Buddhist movement started, inspired by the American Buddhist Henry Steel Olcott, and empowered by the results of the Panadura debate between a Christian priest and the Buddhist monk Migettuwatte Gunananda Thera.

Divisions in the Buddhist Clergy

The different sects of the Sri Lankan Buddhist clergy are referred to as Nikayas, and three main Nikayas are:

Main Nikayas

- Siam Nikaya, founded in the 18th century by Ven. Upali, a Thai monk who was invited by the King of Kandy Kirti Sri Rajasinghe, and on the initiative of Ven. Weliwita Saranankara.
- Amarapura Nikaya, founded in 1800 with higher ordination obtained from Myanmar (Burma)
- Ramanna Nikaya, founded in 1864 by Ambagahawatte Saranankara.

In fact, within these three main divisions there are numerous other divisions, some of which are caste based. There are no doctrinal differences among any of them.

Mahamevnawa Buddhist Monastery

Mahamevnawa is "an organization of monasteries established for the sake of spiritual development of human beings through the teachings of the Sakyamuni Buddha who was born in 500 B.C. Our only wish is to give you spiritual help in order to make your mind pure which is useful for the realization of Nibbâna: the unbounded liberation." It has 38 branches for dissemination of Dhamma in Sri Lanka. Overseas branches are in Canada, USA, Australia, UK and Germany.

Founder and the chief Buddhist monk in charge of these monasteries is Venerable Kiribathgoda Gnanananda Thero who is engaged in spreading Buddhism in its true form (to both local and international communities), highlighting the aim of Buddhism: putting and end to Dukkha (suffering) or attaining Nibbana.

Buddhism is the doctrine revealed by Sammasambuddha Gauthama, in India, around 5th century BC. Buddhahood is a rare achievement, in which one perfectly understands the true nature of the world (*loka*) through unmatched wisdom (*paññâ*) developed through concentration (*samâdhi*) of mind; and reveals it with pure compassion (*mahâ karunâ*) towards the others.

Message embedded in the Teachings (*Dahmma*) is clear and evident in almost all Suttas. It is that the *samsâra* - one's existence over a boundless succession of births & deaths is abundant with suffering (*dukkha*); and that one should get started, without further delays, with a process that helps cease this suffering. Without just stopping at cautioning, the Buddha discloses desire (*tanhâ*) as the cause of samsâraic existence; highlights the capability of ending it (attaining *Nibbâna*); and shows fully the path one needs to follow to attain it.

"Ye dhammâ hetuppabhavâ tesam hetum tathâgato âha - Tesañca yo nirodho evamvâdi mahâsamano

> Of whatever phenomena arising from a cause, Tathagata - the Great Contemplative explains the cause; He explains its cession as well; this is the Doctrine of the Great Samano."
>
> — Sâriputtamoggallânapabbajjâkathâ

Although present in all life forms, peril of samsâraic existence is somewhat obscured in humans. It is having to be born in worlds of essential suffering, which one cannot unfortunately evade because of selfless (*anatta*) nature of one's existence.

What one gains with birth (*jâthi*) is: aging (*jarâ*), illness (*vyâdhi*), death (*marana*), sorrow (*soka*), lamenting (*parideva*), suffering (*dukkha*), distress (*domanassa*), despair (*upâyâsa*), association with things disliked (*appiyehi sampayogo dukkho*), separation from things liked (*piyehi vippayogo dukkho*) and not getting what one wishes (*yampiccham na labhati, tampi dukkham*). Concisely *pañupâdânakkhandhâ*: the forms (*rupha*), feelings(*vedanâ*), perceptions (*saññâ*), volitional/mental formations (*sankâra*) and consciousness (*viññâna*) that one clings to as oneself is suffering.

> *"Idam kho pana bhikkave dukkham ariyasaccam: jâtipi dukkhâ, jarâpi dukkhâ, vyâdhipi dukkha, maranampi dukkhm appiyehi sampayogo dukkho piyehi vippayogo dukkho yampiccham na labhati tampi dukkham sankhittena pañupâdânakkhandhâ dukkhâ"*
>
> — *Dhammacakkappavattanasuttam*

Unlike some other worlds, humans seem to experience both comfort (*sukha*) and suffering/discomfort. But it is not difficult to perceive if one thinks carefully that

- the life is impermanent (*anithya*)
- therefore subjected to suffering (*dukkha*)
- hence and because it's subjected to change (*vipaprinâma dhamma*) life should not be seen as self (*anatta*)

Dhamma seeks just one goal: putting an end to samsâraic existence or attaining Nibbâna. Path to achieve it is the Nobel Eightfold Path (*Ariya Attangiko Maggo*). And the core of Dhamma is *Vimukti* - becoming free of *tanhâ*.

Ample advice on how to cultivate the Path as virtue (*sila*), concentration of mind (*samâdhi*) and wisdom (*paññâ*) is found in Dhamma.

Practicing Dhamma

According to Lord Buddha's teachings: birth as a human being is a very rare opportunity. Fortunate people who also gets to hear about Dhamma should develop their minds to attain the ultimate goal of Nibbâna.

One can attain Nibbâna only by adhering to the Buddhist doctrine (*Dhamma*); through a process called: Noble Eightfold Path (*Ariya Attangiko Maggo*). Initial levels of spiritual development: e.g. Stream Enter (*Sothâpañña*) & Once Returner (*Sakadâgami*), may be achieved even amidst the chores of one's day-to-day life.

First step towards cession of suffering (achieving *Nibbâna*) is getting to know Buddha's teaching. Mahamevnawa plays an important role in this regard through promotion of teaching, discussing and practicing Dhamma in unaltered form.

Mahamevnawa also facilitates people to practice meditation, one of the key aspects for improving concentration (*Samâdhi*) and wisdom (*Paññâ*), through cultivating mindfulness (*Sathi*) as a component of path to Nibbâna.

A key point highlighted is that: Dhamma not only says that the life is suffering (*Dukkha*), but also shows a proven path to cession of suffering.

Spreading Dhamma

"Tathâgatappavedito dhammavinayo, bhikkhave, vivato virocati, no paticchanno

The Teaching and Discipline declared by the Thus Gone One shine when manifested and not when covered. "

—Paticchannasuttam

"Caratha bhikkhave, cârikam bahujanahitâya bahujanasukhâya lokânukampâya atthâya hitâya sukhâya devamanussânam. Mâ ekena dve agamittha. Desetha, bhikkhave, dhammam âdikalyânam majjhe kalyânam pariyosânakalyânam sâttham sabyañajanam kevalaparipunnam parisuddham brahmacariyam pakâsetha. Santi sattâ apparajakkhajâtikâ, assavanatâ dhammassa parihâyanti. Bhavissanti dhammassa aññâtâro.

Go, bhikkhus, and wander for the benefit of many people, wellbeing of many people, out of compassion for the world, for the good, for the benefit, and for the wellbeing of the divine and men. Let two of you not take the same path. Bhikkhus, preach the Dhamma, which is beautiful in the beginning; beautiful in the middle; beautiful at the end; substantive; immaculately proclaimed; perfect in every way; the pure path to Nibbana. There are beings with less defilements in the hearts; They will wither away, if they do not get the opportunity to Listen to Dhamma. They will realize the Truth and Flourish, if they get to Listen to Dhamma. "

— Mârakathâ

True disciples of Buddha are *Sâmichipatipanno*. In other words, they not only practice Dhamma with the sole aim of relinquishing suffering, but also spread it with compassion towards others. Both lay and clergy associated with Mahamevnawa adhere to this whenever possible.

The way of preaching/ teaching Dhamma adopted by the clergy at Mahamevnawa is what advocated by the Buddha.

""If a monk preaches Dhamma, to help one resolve to let down (*Nibbidhayâ*), loose interest in (*Virâgayâ*), and cease

> (*Nirodhayâ*) forms (*Rupha*), that monk deserves to be called an expounder of the Teaching (*Dhammakathika*)...
>
> If a monk preaches Dhamma, to help one resolve to let down, loose interest in, and cease feelings/sensations (*Vedanâ*), that monk deserves to be called an expounder of the Teaching...
>
> If a monk preaches Dhamma, to help one resolve to let down, loose interest in, and cease perceptions (*Saññâ*), that monk deserves to be denoted an expounder of the Teaching...
>
> If a monk preaches Dhamma, to help one resolve to let down, loose interest in, and cease volitional/mental formations (*Sankâra*), that monk deserves to be called an expounder of the Teaching...
>
> If a monk preaches Dhamma, to help one resolve to let down, loose interest in, and cease consciousness (*Viññâna*), that monk deserves to be called an expounder of the Teaching.. "
>
> — Dhammakathikasuttam

Recorded Sermons & Dhamma text based on original teachings of Buddha that reveal the Truth in life and emphasize the urge of cession of suffering are therefore in circulation among those associated with Mahamevnawa.

Owing to the initial Sri Lankan context, most of the publications are in Sinhalese; but English versions are now being released through *Buddha Vision*.

BUDDHISM IN PAKISTAN

The region that is today known as Pakistan once had a large Buddhist population, with the majority of people in Gandhara (present day North Western Pakistan and Eastern Afghanistan) being Buddhist. Gandhara was largely Mahayana Buddhist, and was also a stronghold of Vajrayana

Buddhism. The Swat Valley, known in antiquity as Uddiyana, was a kingdom tributary to Gandhara. There are many archaeological sites from the Buddhist era in Swat.

The Buddhist sage Padmasambhava is said to have been born in a village near the present day town of Chakdara in Lower Dir District, which was then a part of Uddiyana. Padmasambhava is known as Guru Rinpoche in Tibetan and it is he who introduced Vajrayana Buddhism in Tibet.

Buddhism was also practiced in the Punjab and Sindh regions.

Gandhara remained a largely Buddhist land until around 800 AD, when the Pashtun people invaded the region from Southern Afghanistan and introduced the Islamic religion.

Most Buddhists in Punjab reverted to Hinduism from 600 AD onwards. Buddhism was the faith practiced by the majority of the population of Sindh up to the Arab conquest by the Umayad Caliphate in 710 AD.

There are no significant Buddhist populations in Pakistan proper.

REFERENCES

1. Holy Sites of Buddhism: Lumbini - Buddha's Birthplace.
2. Lumbini, the Birthplace of the Lord Buddha - UNESCO World Heritage Centre.
3. Population Monograph of Nepal, Volume 1, Page 104, Published by Central Bureau of Statistics, 2003 based on census 2001.

8

Buddhism in Myanmar and Thailand

As we know China, South, Southeastern and fareast Asia are the regions where Buddhism is mainly concentrated. Herein this chapter we will give an account of Buddhism in Burma and Thailand.

MYANMAR (BURMA)

It is to be noted that Buddhism in Burma (Myanmar) is predominantly of the Theravada tradition, practised by 89% of the country's population It is the most religious Buddhist country in terms of proportion of monks in the population and proportion of income spent on religion. Adherents are most likely found among the dominant ethnic Bamar (or Burmans), Shan, Rakhine (Arakanese), Mon, Karen, and Chinese who are well integrated into Burmese society.

Among ethnic Bamar, Theravada Buddhism is practised often in conjunction with nat worship. Monks, collectively known as the Sangha, are venerated members of Burmese society.

It is also pertinent to note that the importance of Buddhism in the history of Burma is evident from a landscape dominated by pagodas, which is why the country is often called "the land of pagodas." The Shwedagon Pagoda in Yangon is steeped in myth and legend, and represents the faith of the people who have worshipped there for generations. Every village in Burma has a pagoda and a monastery, the traditional places for worship and education.

Coming to Burmese Buddhism, the history of Buddhism in Burma extends nearly a millennium. The *Sasana Vamsa*, written by Pinyasami in 1834, summarises much of the history of Buddhism in Burma. According to many historians, Sohn Uttar Sthavira (one of the royal monks) to Ashoka the Great came to Burma (Suvarnabhumi or Suvannabhumi) around 228 BC with other monks and sacred texts, including books.

Notably Ari Buddhism era included the worship of Bodhisattas and nagas, and also was known for corrupt monks. King Anawrahta of Bagan was converted by Shin Arahan, a monk from Thaton to Theravada Buddhism. In 1057 AD, Anawrahta sent an army to conquer the Mon city of Thaton in order to obtain the *Tipitaka* Buddhist canon. Mon culture, from that point, came to be largely assimilated into the Bamar culture based in Bagan.

Despite attempts at reform, certain features of Ari Buddhism and traditional nat worship continued, such as reverence of Avalokiteœvara, a Boddhisatta called *Lawka nat* in Burmese. Successive kings of Bagan continued to build large numbers of monuments, temples, and pagodas in honour of Buddhism. Burmese rule at Bagan continued until the invasion of the Mongols in 1287. The Shan, meanwhile, established themselves as rulers throughout the region now known as Burma. Thihathu, a Shan king, established rule in Bagan, by patronising and building many monasteries and pagodas. Bhikkus continued to be influential, particularly in Burmese literature and politics. The Mon kingdoms, often ruled by Shan chieftains, fostered Theravada Buddhism in the 1300s. Wareru, who became king of Mottama (a Mon city kingdom), patronised Buddhism, and established a code of law (*Dhammathat*) compiled by Buddhist monks. King Dhammazedi, formerly a Mon monk, established rule in the late 1400s at Innwa and unified the Sangha in Mon territories.

He also standardised ordination of monks set out in the Kalyani Inscriptions. Dhammazedi moved the capital back to Hanthawaddy (Bago). His mother-in-law Queen Shin Sawbu of Pegu was also a great patron of Buddhism. She is credited for expanding and gilding the Shwedagon Pagoda giving her own weight in gold.

Notably, the Bamar, who had fled to Taungoo before the invading Shan, established a kingdom there under the reigns of Tabinshwehti and Bayinnaung who conquered and unified most of modern Burma. These monarchs also embraced Mon culture and patronised Theravada Buddhism. In the reigns of succeeding kings, the Taungoo kingdom became increasingly volatile and was overthrown by the Mon. In the mid- 1700s, King Alaungpaya defeated the Mon, expanded the Bamar kingdoms, and established the Konbaung dynasty. Under the rule of King Bodawpaya, a son of Alaungpaya, a unified sect of monks (Thudhamma) was created within the kingdom. Bodawpaya restored ties with Sri Lanka started by Anawrahta, allowing for mutual influence in religious affairs. In the reigns of the Konbaung kings that followed, both secular and religious literary works were created.

King Mindon Min moved his capital to Mandalay. After Lower Burma had been conquered by the British, Christianity began to gain acceptance. Many monks from Lower Burma had resettled in Mandalay, but by decree of Mindon Min, they returned to serve the Buddhist laypeople. However, schisms arose among the Sangha, which were resolved during the Fifth Buddhist Synod, held in Mandalay in 1871. From 1860 to 1868, the Tipitaka was engraved on 729 marble slabs and assembled in the Kuthodaw Pagoda. In 1871, a new *hti* (the gold umbrella that crowns a stupa) encrusted with jewels from the crown was also donated by Mindon Min for the Shwedagon now in British Burma. During the British administration of Lower and Upper Burma, also known as Burma Proper, government policies were secular which meant monks were not protected by law. Nor was Buddhism patronised by the colonial government.

This resulted in tensions between the colonised Buddhists and their European rulers. There was much opposition to the efforts by Christian missionaries to convert the Burmese people, Bamar, Shan, Mon, Rakhine and plains Karen, with one exception - the hill tribes.

Today, Christianity is most commonly practised by the Chin, Kachin, and the Kayin. Notwithstanding traditional avoidance of political activity, monks often participated in politics and in the struggle for independence. Since 1948 when the country gained its independence from Great Britain, both civil and military governments have supported Theravada Buddhism. The 1947 Constitution states, "The State recognizes the special position of Buddhism as the faith professed by the great majority of the citizens of the Union."

The Ministry of Religious Affairs, created in 1948, was responsible for continuing Buddhism in Burma. In 1954, the prime minister, U Nu, convened the Sixth Buddhist Synod in Rangoon (Yangon), which was attended by 2,500 monks, and the World Buddhist University was established. During the military rule of Ne Win (1962–1988), he attempted to reform Burma under the Burmese Way to Socialism which contained elements of Buddhism. In the 8888 Uprising, many monks participated and were killed by Tatmadaw soldiers.

The current military regime, the State Peace and Development Council (SPDC) patronises Buddhism, although persecution of persons of other religions, namely Islam and Christianity, continues.

Traditions

The culture of Burma is deemed synonymous with its Buddhism. There are many Burmese festivals all through the year, most of them related to Buddhism. The Burmese New Year, *Thingyan*, also known as the water festival, has its origins in Hindu tradition, but it is also a time when many Burmese boys celebrate *shinbyu* , a special rite of passage by which a boy enters the monastery for a short time as a novice monk.

Shinbyu

It is the most important duty of all Burmese parents to make sure their sons are admitted to the Buddhist *Sangha* by performing a shinbyu ceremony once they have reached the age of seven or older. A symbolic procession and ceremony of exchanging princely attire with that of an ascetic follows the example of the historical Buddha.

He was born a royal prince called Siddartha Gautama, but left his palace on horse-back followed by his groom *Maung San* or Chanda, in search of the Four Noble Truths and to attain *Nirvana*, after he found out that life is made up of suffering (*dukkha*) and the notion of self is merely an illusion (*anatta* or non-self) when one day he saw the 'Four Great Signs' (*Nameit Lei Ba*) - the old, the sick, the dead, and the ascetic - in the royal gardens. All Buddhists are required to keep the basic Five Precepts (*ngaba thila*), and novices are expected to keep the Ten Precepts (*seba thila*).

Parents would expect them to stay at the monastery immersed in the teachings of the Buddha as members of the Sangha for a few weeks or longer, at least for the duration of Thingyan. They will have another opportunity to join the Sangha at the age of 20, taking the *upasampada* ordination, to become a fully fledged monk, keeping the 220 precepts of the full monastic rules (*Patimokkha*), and perhaps remain a monk for life.

Buddhist Holidays

Thingyan usually falls in mid-April and tops the list of public holidays in Burma. The full moon in May (*Kason*) is however the most sacred of all as the Buddha was born, became the Enlightened One, and entered *Parinirvana* (died) on the same day, celebrated by watering the Bodhi tree.

Pagoda festivals (*Paya pwè*) held throughout the country also usually fall on full moon days and most of them will be on the full moon of Tabaung (February/March) including the Shwedagon pagoda. They attract not only crowds of pilgrims from near and far, often in caravans of bullock carts, but they also double as great market fairs where both local and itinerant traders set up their stalls and shops among food stalls, restaurants,and free open-air stage performances as well as theatre halls.

The three monsoon months from mid-July to mid-October coincide with the Buddhist Lent or *Wa-dwin*, a time when people are busy tilling their land and planting the paddyfields, and monks will not travel but stay at their monasteries (*Wa-kup* or the rains retreat). *Waso* robes are offered at the beginning of lent, the end of which is marked by the *Thadingyut* Light Festival.

The harvest is now in and robes (*thingahn*) are again offered at the *Kathina* Festival usually held during October and November. *Uposatha* or sabbath days are observed keeping the Eight Precepts by most during Thingyan and Lent, and by devout Buddhists all the year round. Parents and elders also receive obeisance from younger members of the family at the beginning as well as the end of lent, after the tradition established by the Buddha himself. It was during lent that he ascended to the *Tavatimsa* Heaven in order to preach a sermon, as an act of gratitude, to his mother who had become a celestial being, and he was welcomed back to earth with a great festival of lights. Teachers receive the same obeisance, a tradition started by National Schools founded in defiance of the colonial administration and continued after independence by state schools. Wedding ceremonies - nothing to do with religion and not conducted by the Sangha - are not held during the three months of lent, a custom which has resulted in a spate of weddings after Thadingyut or *Wa-kyut*, awaited impatiently by couples wanting to tie the knot.

Buddhist Education

Burmese also send their children to the monastery to receive a Buddhist education, learning the Pali Canon, *Buddhawin* (the lifestory of the Gautama Buddha), *Nga-ya nga-ze nipattaw* (the 550 Jataka tales) - most importantly *Zatkyi sebwè* (the Ten Great Incarnations), and *Thonze shihpya mingala* (the 38 Buddhist Beatitudes) as soon as they have a good grounding of the three Rs.

Monks were the traditional teachers of the young and old alike until secular and missionary schools came into being during the British colonial administration. The Burmese word *kyaung* for school is derived from *Hpongyi kyaung* (monastery). There has been a revival of monastic schools since the 1990s with the deepening economic crisis. Children from poor families that can ill afford fees, uniforms and books have renewed the demand for a free monastic education, and ethnic minorities such as the Shan, Pa-O, Pałaung, Lahu and Wa are benefitting from this revival.

Monasticism

Buddhist monks, who are venerated throughout Burmese society, are approximately 400,000 strong. Nuns form an additional 75,000. Monks belong to one of two primary monastic orders or *gaing:* Thudhamma Nikaya (88% of Buddhist monks) and the more orthodox Shwegyin Nikaya (7% of Buddhist monks). It is important to note that Burmese monastic orders do not differ in doctrine, but in monastic practice, lineage and organizational structure. There are also a number of esoteric Buddhist sects that are not recognized by any authority and incorporate non-Buddhist elements like alchemy, magic and occultism.

Politics

Burmese nationalism first began with the formation of the Young Men's Buddhist Associations (YMBA) - modelled on the YMCA - which started to appear all over the country at the turn of the century. Buddhist monks along with students had been in the forefront of the struggle for independence and later for democracy, the best known leaders in history being U Ottama and U Seinda in Rakhine

State, and U Wisara who died after a protracted hunger strike in Yangon prison.

A major thoroughfare in Yangon is named after U Wisara. The League of Young Monks (*Yahanpyo*) based in Mandalay is a well known activist organisation. The Burmese word for boycott is *thabeik hmauk* which literally means to turn the monk's alms bowl upside down - declining to accept alms in protest. Civilian governments, after the country gained independence, patronised Buddhism donating large sums to fund the upkeep and building of Buddhist monuments. In addition, leaders of political parties and parliamentarians, in particular U Nu, passed legislation influenced by Buddhism. He declared Buddhism the state religion which alienated minority groups, especially the Kachin.

This added yet another group to the growing number of ethnic insurgencies. The present military government has been so keen to be seen as patrons of Buddhism that it has become a joke- "Burmese TV has only two colours, green and yellow" - describing the military green uniforms and monk's yellow robes or golden pagodas which dominate the screen. Shwedagon Pagoda has been an important venue for large public meetings where both Aung San and his daughter Aung San Suu Kyi had made their famous speeches.

During the second university strike in history of 1936 the students camped out on the Shwedagon terraces. Aung San Suu Kyi returned from London to lead the National League for Democracy which was founded during the 1988 popular uprising, but was placed under house arrest in 1989; since she is a devout Buddhist and leader of the opposition, she is considered a socially engaged Buddhist.

In September 2007, Buddhists again took to the streets in mass protest against the military government. Thousand of junta military and police forces poured into Yangon to try to control the situation, which rapidly deteriorated. A curfew was imposed and on the 25th of September troops surrounded Sule Pagoda.

The protest continued to grow with regular citizens joining to support and defend the Buddhists. Over night junta forces invaded all the Buddhist monasteries in the country and imprisoned thousands of monks. Also, it was reported that Nobel prize winning human rights activist and Buddhist Aung San Suu Kyi was removed from her home where she has languished under house arrest and moved to the infamous Insein Prison. Mass protests erupted over this and junta troops began firing on monks, civilians, and demonstrators in the largest clash since 1988, which left thousands injured and hundreds dead. Images of the brutality were aired worldwide. Leaders around the world condemned the junta's actions and many nations imposed economic sanctions on Burma in protest. President of the United States George W. Bush addressed the United Nations, stating, "Every civilized nation has a responsibility to stand up for people suffering under a brutal military regime like the one that has ruled Burma for so long."

BUDDHISM IN THAILAND

It is pertinent to note that Buddhism in Thailand is largely of the Theravada school. Nearly 95% of Thailand's population is Buddhist of the Theravada school, though Buddhism in this country has become integrated with folk beliefs as well as Chinese religions from the large Thai-Chinese population. Buddhist temples in Thailand are characterized by tall golden stupas, and the Buddhist architecture of Thailand is similar to that in other Southeast Asian countries, particularly Cambodia and Laos, with which Thailand shares cultural and historical heritage.

Thai Buddhism was based on the religious movement founded in the sixth century B.C. by Siddhartha, later known as the Buddha, who urged the world to relinquish the extremes of sensuality and self-mortification and follow the enlightened Middle Way.

The focus of this religion is on man, not gods; the assumption is that life is pain or suffering, which is a consequence of craving, and that suffering can end only if desire ceases. The end of suffering is the achievement of nirvana (in Theravada Buddhist scriptures, nibbana), often defined as the absence of craving and therefore of suffering, sometimes as enlightenment or bliss. By the third century B.C., Buddhism had spread widely in Asia, and divergent interpretations of the Buddha's teachings had led to the establishment of several sects. The teachings that reached Ceylon (present-day Sri Lanka) were given in a final written form in Pali (an Indo-Aryan language closely related to Sanskrit) to religious centers there in the first century A.D. and provided the Tipitaka (the scriptures or "three baskets"; in Sanskrit, Tripitaka) of Theravada Buddhism.

This form of Buddhism reached what is now Thailand around the sixth century A.D. Theravada Buddhism was made the state religion only with the establishment of the Thai kingdom of Sukhothai in the thirteenth century A.D..According to many historians around 228 BC Sohn Uttar Sthavira (one of the royal monks)to when Ashoka the Great came to Thailand (Suvarnabhumi or Suvannabhumi) with other monks and sacred books.

In fact, the details of the history of Buddhism in Thailand

from the thirteenth to the nineteenth century are obscure, in part because few historical records or religious texts survived the Burmese destruction of Ayutthaya, the capital city of the kingdom, in 1767. The anthropologist-historian S.J. Tambiah, however, has suggested a general pattern for that era, at least with respect to the relations between Buddhism and the sangha on the one hand and the king on the other hand.

In Thailand, as in other Theravada Buddhist kingdoms, the king was in principle thought of as patron and protector of the religion (sasana) and the sangha, while sasana and the sangha were considered in turn the treasures of the polity and the signs of its legitimacy. Religion and polity, however, remained separate domains, and in ordinary times the organizational links between the sangha and the king were not close. Among the chief characteristics of Thai kingdoms and principalities in the centuries before 1800 were the tendency to expand and contract, problems of succession, and the changing scope of the king's authority. In effect, some Thai kings had greater power over larger territories, others less, and almost invariably a king who sought successfully to expand his power also exercised greater control over the sangha.

That control was coupled with greater support and patronage of the ecclesiastical hierarchy. When a king was weak, however, protection and supervision of the sangha also weakened, and the sangha declined. This fluctuating pattern appears to have continued until the emergence of the Chakkri Dynasty in the last quarter of the eighteenth century.

Modern Era

By the nineteenth century, and especially with the

coming to power in 1851 of King Mongkut, who had been a monk himself for twenty-seven years, the sangha, like the kingdom, became steadily more centralized and hierarchical in nature and its links to the state more institutionalized. As a monk, Mongkut was a distinguished scholar of Pali Buddhist scripture. Moreover, at that time the immigration of numbers of monks from Burma was introducing the more rigorous discipline characteristic of the Mon sangha. Influenced by the Mon and guided by his own understanding of the Tipitaka, Mongkut began a reform movement that later became the basis for the Dhammayuttika order of monks. Under the reform, all practices having no authority other than custom were to be abandoned, canonical regulations were to be followed not mechanically but in spirit, and acts intended to improve an individual's standing on the road to nirvana but having no social value were rejected. This more rigorous discipline was adopted in its entirety by only a small minority of monasteries and monks. The Mahanikaya order, perhaps somewhat influenced by Mongkut's reforms but with a less exacting discipline than the Dhammayuttika order, comprised about 95 percent of all monks in 1970 and probably about the same percentage in the late 1980s. In any case, Mongkut was in a position to regularize and tighten the relations between monarchy and sangha at a time when the monarchy was expanding its control over the country in general and developing the kind of bureaucracy necessary to such control.

The administrative and sangha reforms that Mongkut started were continued by his successor. In 1902 King Chulalongkorn (Rama V, 1868-1910) made the new sangha hierarchy formal and permanent through the Sangha Law of 1902, which remained the foundation of sangha administration in modern Thailand.

Three major forces have influenced the development of Buddhism in Thailand. The most visible influence is that of the Theravada school of Buddhism, imported from Sri Lanka. While there are significant local and regional variations, the Theravada school provides most of the major themes of Thai Buddhism. By tradition, Pâli is the language of religion in Thailand.

Scriptures are recorded in Pâli, using either the modern Thai script or the older Khom and Tham scripts. Pâli is also used in religious liturgy, despite the fact that most Thais understand very little of this ancient language. The Pâli Tipitaka is the primary religious text of Thailand, though many local texts have been composed in order to summarise the vast number of teachings found in the Tipitaka.

The monastic code (Patimokkha) followed by Thai monks is taken from the Pâli Theravada—something that has provided a point of controversy during recent attempts to resurrect the bhikkhuni lineage in Thailand.

Further, the second major influence on Thai Buddhism is Hindu beliefs received from Cambodia, particularly during the Sukhothai period. Vedic Hinduism played a strong role in the early Thai institution of kingship, just as it did in Cambodia, and exerted influence in the creation of laws and order for Thai society as well as Thai religion. Certain rituals practiced in modern Thailand, either by monks or by Hindu ritual specialists, are either explicitly identified as Hindu in origin, or are easily seen to be derived from Hindu practices.

While the visibility of Hinduism in Thai society has been diminished substantially during the Chakri dynasty, Hindu influences, particularly shrines to the god Brahma, continue to be seen in and around Buddhist institutions and ceremonies. Folk religion—attempts to propitiate and attract the favor of local spirits known as *phi*—forms the third major influence on Thai Buddhism. While Western observers (as well as urbane and Western-educated Thais) have often drawn a clear line between Thai Buddhism and folk religious practices, this distinction is rarely observed in more rural locales. Spiritual power derived from the observance of Buddhist precepts and rituals is employed in attempting to appease local nature spirits.

Many restrictions observed by rural Buddhist monks are derived not from the orthodox Vinaya, but from taboos derived from the practice of folk magic. Astrology, numerology, and the creation of talismans and charms also play a prominent role in Buddhism as practiced by the average Thai—topics that are, if not proscribed, at least marginalized in Buddhist texts. Additional, more minor influences can be observed stemming from contact with Mahayana Buddhism. Early Buddhism in Thailand is thought to have been derived from an unknown Mahayana tradition. While Mahayana Buddhism was gradually eclipsed in Thailand, certain features of Thai Buddhism—such as the appearance of the bodhisattva Lokesvara in some Thai religious architecture, and the belief that the king of Thailand is a bodhisattva himself—reveal the influence of Mahayana concepts. The only other bodhisattva prominent in Thai religion is Maitreya, often depicted in Budai form, and often confused with. Images of one or both can be found in mant Thai Buddhist temples, and on amulets as well.

Thai may pray to be reborn during the time of Maitreya, or dedicate merit from worship activities to that end. In modern times, additional Mahayana influence has stemmed from the presence of Chinese immigrants in Thai society. While some Chinese have "converted" to Thai-style Theravada

Buddhism, many others maintain their own separate temples in the East Asian Mahayana tradition. The growing popularity of the goddess Kuan Yin in Thailand (a form of Avalokitesvara) may be attributed to the Chinese Mahayanist presence in Thailand.

While Thailand is currently a constitutional monarchy, it inherited a strong Southeast Asian tradition of Buddhist kingship that tied the legitimacy of the state to its protection and support for Buddhist institutions. This connection has been maintained into the modern era, with Buddhist institutions and clergy being granted special benefits by the government, as well as being subjected to a certain amount of government oversight. In addition to the ecclesiastic leadership of the *sangha*, a secular government ministry supervises Buddhist temples and monks. The legal status of Buddhist sects and reform movements has been an issue of contention in some cases, particularly in the case of Santi Asoke, which was legally forbidden from calling itself a Buddhist denomination, and in the case of the ordination of women- monks attempting to revive the Theravada bhikkhuni lineage have been prosecuted as though attempting to impersonate members of the clergy. To obtain a passport for travel abroad, a monk must have an official letter from Sangha Supreme Council granting the applicant permission to travel abroad; Buddhist monk identification card; a copy of House/Temple Registration; and submit any previous Thai Passport or a certified copy thereof.

In addition to state support and recognition—-in the form of formal gifts to monasteries made by government officials and the royal family (for example, Kathin)—-a number of special rights are conferred upon Buddhist monks. They are granted free passage on public transportation, and most train stations and airports have special seating sections reserved for members of the clergy. Conversely, ordained monastics are forbidden from standing for office or voting in elections.

In 2007, calls were made by some Thais for Buddhism to be recognized in the new national constitution as a state religion. This suggestion was initially rejected by the committee charged with drafting the new constitution. This move prompted a number of protests from supporters of the initiative, including a number of marches on the capital and a hunger strike by twelve Buddhist monks. Some critics of the plan, including scholar and social critic Sulak Sivaraksa, have claimed that the movement to declare Buddhism a national religion is motivated by political gain, and may be being manipulated by supporters of ousted Prime Minister Thaksin Sinawatra. The Constitution Drafting Committee later voted against the special status of Buddhism, provoking the religious groups. The groups condemned the Committee and the constitution draft.

On August 11, Sirikit, the Queen of Thailand, expressed her concern over the issue. According to her birthday speech, Buddhism is beyond politics. Some Buddhist organizations announced the break of the campaigns a day after.

Ordination and Clergy

Remarkably, like in most other Theravada nations, Buddhism in Thailand is represented primarily by the presence of Buddhist monks, who serve as officiants on ceremonial occasions, as well as being responsible for preserving and conveying the teachings of the Buddha.

Notably, in the latter half of the 20th century, most monks in Thailand began their careers by serving as *dek wat* (literally, 'child[ren] of the wat'). *Dek wat* are traditionally no younger than eight, and do minor housework around the temple. The primary reason for becoming a *dek wat* is to gain a basic education, particularly in basic reading and writing and the memorization of the scriptures chanted on ritual occasions. Prior to the creation of state-run primary schools in Thailand, village temples served as the primary form of education for most Thai boys.

Service in a temple as a *dek wat* was a necessary prerequisite for attaining any higher education, and was the only learning available to most Thai peasants. Since the creation of a government-run educational apparatus in Thailand, the number of children living as *dek wat* has declined significantly. However, many government-run schools continue to operate on the premise of the local village temple. After serving (typically for four years or more) as a *dek wat*, a future monk typically ordains as a novice (*samana* in Pâli, or *samanen*, but often shortened to *nen*. Novices live according to the Ten Precepts, as do monks, but are not formally required to follow the full range of monastic rules found in the Patimokkha (Buddhist monastic code). There are a few other significant differences between novices and monks. Novices often are in closer contact with their families, spending more time in the homes of their parents than monks.

Novices do not participate in the recitation of the monastic code (and the confessions of violations) that take place on the uposatha days. Novices technically do not eat with the monks in their temple, but this typically only amounts to a gap in seating, rather than the separation observed between monks and the laity. Young men typically do not live as a novice for longer than one or two years. At the age of 20, they become eligible to receive upasampada, the higher ordination that establishes them as a full bhikkhu.

A novice is technically sponsored by his parents in his ordination, but in practice in rural villages the entire village participates by providing the robes, alms bowl, and other requisites that will be required by the monk in his monastic life. Temporary ordination is the norm among Thai Buddhists. Most young men traditionally ordain for the term of a single rainy season (known in Pâli as *vassa*, and in Thai as *phansa*).

Those who remain monks beyond their first *vassa* typically remain monks for between one and three years, officiating at religious ceremonies in surrounding villages and possibly receiving further education in reading and writing (possibly including the Kham or Tham scripts traditionally used in recording religious texts). After this period of one to three years, most young monks return to lay life, going on to marry and begin a family. Young men in Thailand who have undergone ordination are seen as being more suitable partners for marriage; unordained men are euphemistically called 'raw', while those who have been ordained are said to be 'cooked'.

A period as a monk is a prerequisite for many positions of leadership within the village hierarchy. Most village elders or headmen were once monks, as were most traditional doctors, spirit priests, and some astrologists and fortune tellers. Monks who do not return to lay life typically specialize in either scholarship or meditation. Those who specialize in scholarship typically travel to regional education centers to begin further instruction in the Pâli language and the scriptures, and may then continue on to the major monastic universities located in Bangkok.

The route of scholarship is also taken by monks who desire to rise in the ecclesiastic hierarchy, as promotions within the government-run system is contingent on passing examinations in Pâli and Dhamma studies. Monks who specialize in meditation typically seek out a known master in the meditation tradition, under whom they will study for a period of years.

'Meditation monks' are particularly revered in Thai society as possessing great virtue and as potential sources of supernatural powers. Ironically, monks of the Thai Forest Tradition often find themselves struggling to find time and privacy to meditate in the face of enthusiastic supporters seeking their blessings and attention.

Reform Movements

- Thammayut Nikaya literally "Those adhering strictly to the monastic discipline", an order of Theravada Buddhist monks founded in the 19th century by King Mongkut, son of King Rama II as a reform movement that later became an independent denomination recognized by the Thai Sangha.
- Dhammakâya Movement founded in Thailand in the 1970s. It was criticized to be a cult of personality rather than a legit Buddhist movement, and was investigated by Thai government in the 1990s.
- Santi Asoke literally Peaceful Asoke established by Phra Bodhirak after he "declared independence from the Ecclesiastical Council (Sangha) in 1975"

Position of Women

Unlike in Myanmar (Burma) and Sri Lanka, the female Theravada bhikkhuni lineage was never established in Thailand. As a result, there is a widespread perception among Thais that women are not meant to play an active role in monastic life; instead, they are expected to live as lay followers, making merit in the hopes of being born in a different role in their next life. As a result, lay women primarily participate in religious life either as lay participants in collective merit-making rituals, or by doing domestic work around temples. A small number of women choose to become Mae Ji, non-ordained religious specialists who permanently observe either the eight or ten precepts. Mae Ji do not generally receive the level of support given to ordained monks, and their position in Thai society is the subject of some discussion.

Recently, there have been efforts to attempt to introduce a bhikkhuni lineage in Sri Lanka as a step towards improving the position of women in Thai Buddhism. Unlike similar efforts in Sri Lanka, these efforts have been extremely controversial in Thailand. Women attempting to ordain have been accused of attempting to impersonate monks (a civil offense in Thailand), and their actions have been denounced by many members of the ecclesiastic hierarchy. Most objections to the reintroduction of a female monastic role hinge on the fact that the monastic rules require that both five ordained monks and five ordained bhikkhunis be present for any new bhikkhuni ordination. Without such a quorum, critics say that it is not possible to ordain any new Theravada bhikkhuni.

The Thai hierarchy refuses to recognize ordinations in the Taiwanese tradition (the only currently existing bhikkhuni ordination lineage) as valid Theravada ordinations, citing differences in philosophical teachings, and (more critically) monastic discipline.

Buddha Images in Thailand

A Buddha image in Thailand typically refers to three dimensional stone, wood, clay, or metal cast images of the Buddha. While there are such figures in all regions where Buddhism is commonly practiced, the appearance, composition and position of the images vary greatly from country to country.

Dvaravati Period

During the Dvaravati period (seventh through eleventh centuries), there were two factions of Buddhism practiced in the region that now encompasses present day Thailand, namely Mahayana and Theravada. The types of images constructed during this era reflects the distinction. Much of the basis for the Buddhist artwork of the Dvaravati period was influence from Buddhist art in India, including the Amaravati and Gupta styles, although there was also local and Khmer influence. Such images include the following classical archetypes:

- Buddha in the Tribhanga (leaning) position with somewhat Indian facial features and no aureole. The right hand is typically free, while the left is depicted grasping the Buddha's robe.
- Buddha in the Amaravati style with loosely folded legs and a lotus shaped aureole. Such statues have a continuous eye-brow, a flat nose and thick lips.
- Square faced cleft chin Buddha with some Khmer features. Legs are typically fully folded. The Buddha sits on a lotus base.

Sri Vijaya Images

Sri Vijaya images are found in southern Thailand. They were constructed between the eighth and thirteenth centuries. Typically, they reflect the teachings of the Mahayana school of Buddhism. Unlike other Thai Buddha images, Sri Vijaya images were generally made of clay, with less emphasis on durability, as their purpose was to benefit the deceased, rather than perpetuate the teachings of the Buddha.

Lopburi Images

Lopburi images date back to the eleventh century. They are typically found in Northeast Thailand, and their style is essentially similar to Cambodian Buddha images. Such images typically have a cone-shaped cranial protuberance in the form of tiers of lotus petals. The hair depicted in the images is considerably more realistic than the hair of the Dvaravati images, and may be either straight or curly. The face of the Buddha typically has a small smile, while the earlobes are in unusually large proportion relative to the rest of the face, often hanging down nearly to the image's shoulders. A second Lopburi style is the Naga Protected Buddha with the heads of Naga forming a protective taper around the Buddha's head.

Chiang Saen and Lanna Images

Chiang Saen and Lanna images were created in northern Thailand between the tenth and thirteenth centuries. Early images were similar to the Pala style Buddha images of India, with lotus bud or orb shaped hair curls, round faces, narrow lips and prominent chests. Such images were usually in the subduing Mara position, cross-legged, with the soles of the Buddha's feet visible. Many later Chiang Saen and Lanna images began to be constructed from crystals and gemstones.

U Thong Images

There are three categories of U Thong images from the twelfth through fifteenth century in central Thailand. The first such style was a fusion of the Dvaravati and Khmer style images. They would typically adorn a lotus bud aureole and Khmer facial features. The second style was similar to the Lopburi images. The third and most recent U Thong style had considerable influence from the Sukhothai images, but often had hair bands unique to U Thong images.

Ayutthaya Period

Ayutthaya images were created between the tenth and eighteenth centuries. They had a unique hair frame and tell-tale narrow carvings above the lips and eyes. Early Ayutthaya images were carved in stone with heavy influence from the Lopburi images. Middle Ayutthaya images were similar to the Sukhothai images, and were in similar poses. During this period, the images were often cast in Bronze, and the size of the images were often large. In the late Ayutthaya period, the images typically depicted the Buddha in royal attire, and the bases of the images bore ornate design.

Modern Thai Buddha Images

In modern times, Buddha images are often replicas of images from the Sukhothai and other early periods, often more ornately and elaborately adorned. Faces in new innovative depictions are typically more realistic and human-like. An elongated flame aureole is popular. Robes depicted in modern images often depict floral designs. The Indian Gandhara style, as well as western art have also influenced many of the modern images.

Bunleua Sulilat's concrete sculpture gardens (Buddha Park and Sala Keoku) give an example of contemporary highly creative and unconventional artistic treatment of Buddhist subjects. See also Wat Rong Khun and Sanctuary of Truth.

REFERENCES

1. Aung Zaw. "Burmese Monks in Revolt". *The Irrawaddy* September 11, 2007. http://www.irrawaddy.org/article.php?art_id=8581. Retrieved 2007-09-11.

1. Aung Zaw. "The Power Behind the Robe". *The Irrawaddy* October 5, 2007. http://www.irrawaddy.org/article.php?art_id=8908. Retrieved 2007-10-07.

3. Bischoff, Roger (1995) (PDF). *Buddhism in Myanmar-A Short History*. Buddhist Publication Society. ISBN 955-24-0127-5. http://www.buddhanet.net/pdf_file/bud-myanmar.pdf. Retrieved 2006-08-26.

4. Buckley, Sarah (2007-09-26). "Who are Burma's monks?". BBC News 26 September 2007.

5. "Burma—International Religious Freedom Report 2009". U.S. Department of State. 2009-10-26.

6. Cone & Gombrich, *Perfect Generosity of Prince Vessantara*, Oxford University Press, 1977, page xxii

7. Hlaing, Maung Myint (August 1981). *The Great Disciples of Buddha*. Zeyar Hlaing Literature House. pp. 66–68.

8. Htet Aung. "Save Our Schools". *Irrawaddy* May 30, 2007. http://www.irrawaddy.org/article.php?art_id=7329. Retrieved 2007-06-03.

9. http://web.ukonline.co.uk/buddhism/rdhamma4.htm

10. http://philtar.ucsm.ac.uk/encyclopedia/seasia/shwegyin.html

11. Kabilsingh, Chatsumarn (1991). *Thai Women in Buddhism*. Parallax Press.

12. Keown, Damien; Stephen Hodge, Paola Tinti (2003). *A Dictionary of Buddhism*. Oxford UP.

13. Spiro, Melford (1982). *Buddhism and society: a great tradition and its Burmese vicissitudes*. University of California Press.

14. Tambiah, Stanley (1970). *Buddhism and the Spirit Cults in North-East Thailand*. Cambridge University Press.

15. Terwiel, B.J. (May 1976). "A Model for the Study of Thai Buddhism". *Journal of Asian Studies* 35: 391–403.

9

Some Southeast Asian Countries

BUDDHISM IN CAMBODIA

It is remarkable that Buddhism has existed in Cambodia since at least the 5th century CE, with some sources placing its origin as early as the 3rd century BCE. Theravada Buddhism has been the Cambodian state religion since the 13th century CE (excepting the Khmer Rouge period), and is currently estimated to be the faith of 95% of the population. The history of Buddhism in Cambodia spans nearly two thousand years, across a number of successive kingdoms and empires. Buddhism entered Cambodia through two different streams. The earliest forms of Buddhism, along with Hindu influences, entered the Funan kingdom with Hindu merchants.

In later history, a second stream of Buddhism entered Khmer culture during the Angkor empire when Cambodia absorbed the various Buddhist traditions of the Mon kingdoms of Dvaravati and Haripunchai. For the first thousand years of Khmer history, Cambodia was ruled by a series of Hindu kings with an occasional Buddhist king, such as Jayavarman of Funan, and Suryavarman I. A variety of Buddhist traditions co-existed peacefully throughout

Cambodian lands, under the tolerant auspices of Hindu kings and the neighboring Mon-Theravada kingdoms.

Unconfirmed Singhalese sources assert that missionaries of King Ashoka introduced Buddhism into Southeast Asia in the 3rd century B.C. Various Buddhist sects competed with Brahamanism and indigenous animistic religions over approximately the next millennium; during this period, Indian culture was highly influential.

The Funan Kingdom that flourished between 100 B.C. and 500 A.D. kingdom was Hindu, with the kings of Funan sponsoring the worship of Vishnu and Shiva. Buddhism was already present in Funan as a secondary religion in this era. Buddhism began to assert its presence from about year 450 A.D. onward, and was observed by the Chinese traveler I Ching toward the close of the seventh century. The Kingdom of Chenla replaced Funan and endured from 500-700 A.D. Buddhism was weakened in the Chenla period, but survived, as seen in the inscriptions of Sambor Prei Kuk (626 A.D.) and those of Siem Reap dealing with the erection of statues of Avalokitesvara (791 A.D.). Some pre-Angkorean statuary in the Mekong Delta region indicate the existence of Sanskrit-based Sarvastivada Buddhism. Khmer-style Buddha images are abundant from the period of 600-800 A.D.

Many Mahayana bodhisattva images also date from this period, often found alongside the predominantly Hindu images of Shiva and Vishnu. An inscription from Ta Prohm temple in Bali province, dated about 625 A.D., states, that the Buddha, Dharma and Sangha are flourishing. The transition from Hindu god-king to Mahayana Buddha-king was probably gradual and imperceptible. The prevailing Vaishnavite and Shaivite faith traditions gave way to the worship of the Gautama Buddha and the Bodhisattva Avalokitesvara.

In fact, the Buddhist Sailendra kingdom exercised suzerainty over Cambodia as a vassal state during the end of the eighth and the beginning of the ninth centuries. King Jayavarman II (802-869), the first real Khmer king of the Angkor Empire, proclaimed himself god-king and identified himself with Shiva. Nevertheless, he was increasingly friendly to and supportive of Mahayana Buddhist influence throughout his kingdom. Mahayana Buddhism became increasingly established in his empire. The form of Mahayana Buddhism that was propagated in the Srivijaya lands was similar to the Pala Dynasty Buddhism of Bengal, and of the Nalanda University in northern India. "The Bengal University of Nalanda in Megadha (now Behar) was the theological center of Mahayana Buddhism under the protection of the Pala Dynasty [750-1060]. Shivaist interpretations of Buddhism, tinged with Tantric mysticism (that may have revived portions of pre-Aryan northeastern Indian faith traditions) were worked out in Megadha and then were exported throughout insular and peninsular Southeast Asia, particularly to Java. Yashovarman I (889-910), who ruled from the vicinity of Rolous in the late ninth century, seems to have been a Shivite Buddhist influenced by Nalanda syncretism. His successors (notably Jayavarman IV) dedicated themselves to Vishnu and Brahma, as well as to Shiva, with whom they continued to be identified by hereditary families of priests. Rajendravarman II studied Buddhism intensely."

The Sailendra dynasty also built the fantastic Mahayana Buddhist temple Borobudur (750-850) in Java. Borobudur appears to have been the inspiration for the later fabulous Angkor building projects in Cambodia, particularly Angkor

Wat and Angkor Thom. The primary form of Buddhism practiced in Cambodia during Angkor times was Mahayana Buddhism, strongly influenced with Tantric tendencies.

"The prevalence of Tantrayana in Java, Sumatra and Kamboja [Cambodia], a fact now definitely established by modern researches into the character of Mahayana Buddhism and Sivaism in these parts of the Indian Orient. Already in Kamboja inscription of the 9th century there is definite evidence of the teaching of Tantric texts at the court of Jayavarman II. In a Kamboja record of the 11th century there is a reference to the 'Tantras of the Paramis'; and images of Hevajra, definitely a tantric divinity, have been recovered from amidst the ruins of Angkor Thom. A number of Kamboja inscriptions refer to several kings who were initiated into the Great Secret (Vran Guhya) by their Brahmanical gurus; the Saiva records make obvious records to Tantric doctrines that had crept into Sivaism."

"But it was in Java and Sumatra that Tantrayana seems to have attained greater importance. There Mahayana Buddhism and Shaivism, both deeply imbued with tantric influences, are to be seen often blending with one another during this period. The Sang Hyang Kamahayanikan, consisting of Sanskrit versus explained by an Old Javanese commentary, professed to teach the Mahayana and Mantrayana."

The presence and growing influence of Buddhism continued as the Angkor empire increased in power. King Yosavarman built many Buddhist temples in 887-889, representing the mandala of Mount Meru, the mythical axis of the world. The largest of these temples is Phnom Kandal or "Central Mountain" which lies near the heart of the Angkor complex. King Rajendravarman II (944-968) "studied Buddhism intensely. Although he decided to remain a Shivaist, he appointed a Buddhist, Kavindrarimathana, chief minister. Kavindrarimathana built shrines to Buddha and Shiva. Jayavarman V (son of Rajendravarman) also remained a devote of Shiva. He, too, permitted his own chief minister, Kirtipandita, to foster Mahayana Buddhist learning and divination."

Suryavarman I

Suryavarman I (1002-1050) is considered the greatest of the Buddhist kings, excepting only Jayavarman VII.

Surayvarman was from present-day southern Thailand in the kingdom of Sri Dhammarat. He was a Tamil-Malay (Srivijaya) "usurper" to the Khmer throne, who claimed legitimate succession to the throne through his Khmer mother. His father was king of the Buddhist kingdom of Tambralingam on the Malay peninsula. He publicly venerated Shiva or Rama according to his official traditions, but was also a devout Mahayana Buddhist king.

A strong proponent of Mahayana Buddhism, he did not interfere or obstruct the growing presence and dissemination of Theravada Buddhism during his reign. "Indeed, inscriptions indicate he sought wisdom from wise Mahayanists and Hinayanists and at least somewhat disestablished the Sivakaivalya family's hereditary claims to being chief priests (purohitar). Surayvarman's posthumous title of Nirvanapada, 'the king who has gone to Nirvana' is the strongest evidence that he was a Buddhist."

Jayavarman VII

Jayavarman VII (1181-1215), the most significant Khmer Buddhist king, worked tirelessly to establish Buddhism as the state religion of Angkor. Jayavarman VII was a

Mahayana Buddhist, and he regarded himself to be a Dharma-king, a bodhisattva, whose duty was to "save the people" through service and merit-making, liberating himself in the process. Jayavarman withdrew his devotion from the old gods and began to identify more openly with Buddhist traditions. His regime marked a clear dividing line with the old Hindu past. Before 1200, art in the temples mostly portrayed scenes from the Hindu pantheon; after 1200, Buddhist scenes began to appear as standard motifs.

During Jayavarman VII's reign, there was a shift away from the concept of devaraja god-king, toward the concept of the Sangha, the concept of monks. In former times, great effort and resources were invested into building temples for elite brahman priests and god-kings. Under Jayavarman, these resources were redirected to building libraries, monastic dwellings, public works, and more "earthly" projects accessible to the common people.

While Jayavarman VII himself was Mahayana Buddhist, the presence of Theravada Buddhism was increasingly evident. "This Singhalese-based Theravada Buddhist orthodoxy was first propagated in Southeast Asia by Taling (Mon) monks in the 11th century and together with Islam in the 13th century in southern insular reaches of the region, spread as a popularly-based movement among the people. Apart from inscriptions, such as one of Lopburi, there were other signs that the religious venue of Suvannabhumi were changing. Tamalinda, the Khmer monk believed to be the son of Jayavarman VII, took part in an 1180 Burmese-led mission to Sri Lanka to study the Pali canon and on his return in 1190 had adepts of the Sinhala doctrine in his court. Chou Ta-Laun, who led a Chinese mission in to Angkor in 1296-97 confirms the significant presence of Pali Theravada monks in the Khmer Capital."

Decline of Angkor & the Emergence of a Theravada Kingdom

After the 13th century Theravada Buddhism became the state religion of Cambodia.

King Jayavarman VII had sent his son Tamilinda to Sri Lanka to be ordained as a Buddhist monk and study Theravada Buddhism according to the Pali scriptural traditions. Tamalinda then returned to Cambodia and promoted Buddhist traditions according to the Theravada training he had received, galvanizing and energizing the long standing Theravada presence that had existed throughout the Angkor empire for centuries. During the time Tamalinda studied at the famous Mahavihara Monastery in Sri Lanka (1180-1190), a new dynamic type of Theravada Buddhism was being preached as the "true faith" in Sri Lanka.

This form of Buddhism was somewhat militant and highly disciplined in reaction to the wars with the Tamil that nearly destroyed Buddhism in Sri Lanka in the 9th and 10th centuries. As Theravada Buddhism struggled for survival in Sri Lanka, it developed a resiliency that generated a renaissance throughout the Buddhist world, and would eventually spread across Burma, Chang Mai, the Mon kingdoms, Lana, Sukothai, Laos, and Cambodia. In the 13th century, wandering missionaries from the Mon-Khmer-speaking parts of Siam, Burma, Cambodia, and Sri Lanka played an important part in this process.

When Prince Tamalinda returned after ten years of ordination, he was a Thera, a senior monk, capable of administering ordination into this vigorous Theravada lineage, which insisted on orthodoxy and rejected Mahayana "innovations" such as tantric practices. The mass conversion of Khmer society to Theravada Buddhism amounted to a nonviolent revolution every all level of society. All monumental building projects that had characterized the Angkor empire came to a sudden end. Scholars struggle to account for this sudden and inexplicable transformation of Khmer civilization. Theravada Buddhism succeeded because it was inclusive and universal in its outreach, recruiting the disciples and monks from not only the elites and court, but also in the villages and among the peasants, enhancing its popularity among the Khmer folk. .

"The post-Angkor period saw the dramatic rise of the Pali Theravada tradition in Southeast Asia and concomitant decline of the Brahmanic and Mahayana Buddhist religious traditions. A 1423 Thai account of a mission to Sri Lanka mentions eight Khmer monks who again brought orthodox Mahavihara sect of Singhalese order to Kampuchea. This particular event belied, however, the profound societal shift that was taking place from priestly class structure to a village-based monastic system in Theravada lands. While adhering to the monastic discipline, monks developed their wats, or temple-monasteries, not only into moral religious but also education, social-service, and cultural centers for the people. Wats became the main source of learning and popular education. Early western explorers, settlers, and missionaries reported widespread literacy among the male populations of Burma, Thailand, Kampuchea, Laos, and Vietnam. Until the 19th century, literacy rates exceeded those of Europe in most if not all Theravada lands. In Kampuchea, Buddhism became the transmitter of Khmer language and culture."

The Theravada revolution was therefor a grassroots movement of the Khmer people rejecting the oppressive burden of maintaining the god-king religion of Hinduism and Mahayana Buddhism. The monumental temples that had countless thousands of slaves attached to them were gradually abandoned to the jungles.

With the rise of Siam in the west and Vietnam in the east, the classical Angkor empire disappeared and the beginning of present day Cambodia began. Cambodia became from this time forward a Theravada Buddhist nation.

Buddhist Middle Ages

The Jinakalamali gives an account of the cultural connections between Cambodia and Sri Lanka in the fifteenth century. It states that 1967 years after the Mahaparinibbana of the Buddha, eight monks headed by Mahananasiddhi from Cambodia with 25 monks from Nabbispura in Thailand came to Sri Lanka to receive the umpasampada ordination at the hands of the Sinhalese Mahatheras. As Angkor collapsed under the advancing jungles, the center of power of the Theravada Cambodia moved south toward present day Phnom Penh. Phnom Penh was originally a small riverside market center where the Mekong River and the Tonle Sap River converge.

Phnom Penh was founded when Lady Penh found a "four-faced Buddha" floating down the river on a Koki tree during the flooding season. She retrieved the Buddha image and had the Wat Phnom constructed to house the image.

The four-faced Buddha [Buddha facing the four directions] is important in Khmer Buddhist iconography, signifying the establishment of the kingdom of the Buddha of the Future, Maitreya, who is often identified with the

Buddha-king of Cambodia. After 1431 when the Cambodian kings permanently abandoned Angkor due to a Siamese invasion, the royal court was located on Udon Mountain, a few miles north of Phnom Penh. Siamese incursions from the west and Vietnamese invasions from the east weakened the Khmer empire. The Vietnamese invaders attempted to suppress Theravada Buddhism and force the Khmer people to practice Mahayana Buddhism.

The Siamese, on the other hand, would periodically invade Cambodia and attempt to drive out the "unbelievers" in an attempt to protect the Theravada religion. This power-struggle between the two ascendant powers continued until the arrival of the Europeans in the 16th century.

Colonial Era

Buddhism continued to flourish in Cambodia in the sixteenth century. King Ang Chan (1516-1566), a relative of King Dhammaraja, was a devout Buddhist. He built pagodas in his capital and many Buddhist shrines in different parts of Cambodia. In order to popularize Buddhism, King Satha (1576-1549), son and successor of King Barom Reachea, restored the great towers of the Angkor Wat, which had become a Buddhist shrine by the sixteenth century. Each successive wave of European influence was accompanied by Catholic missionaries, but Theravada Buddhism proved surprisingly resistant to foreign attempts to convert the Khmer people.

During the colonial period, the peace was periodically breached by outbreaks of religiously-motivated violence including periodic millenarian revolts. During the seventeenth, eighteenth, and nineteenth centuries, Thailand's involvement in Cambodian politics extended Thai influence into religious matters as well. On King

Norodom's invitation, monks from the Thai Dhammayuttika Nikaya established a Dhammayuttika presence in Cambodia.

The newly-formed Thommayut order benefited from royal patronage, but frequently came into conflict with the existing Mohanikay (Mahanikaya) lineage. The Thommayut were sometimes accused of holding loyalty to the Thai court, rather than to the Khmer nation. During the era of French rule, convulsions of violence, led by Buddhist holy men, would periodically break out against the French.

Significant advances were made in the education of Cambodian monks, both in specifically Buddhist topics and more general studies. Primary education of Cambodian children continued to take place at temple schools. Monks were also encouraged to become involved in community development projects.

Khmer Rouge Era

In 1975 when the communist Khmer Rouge took control of Cambodia, they tried to completely destroy Buddhism and very nearly succeeded. By the time of the Vietnamese invasion in 1979, nearly every monk and religious intellectual had been either murdered or driven into exile, and nearly every temple and Buddhist temple and library had been destroyed. The Khmer Rouge policies towards Buddhism-which included the forcible disrobing of monks, the destruction of monasteries, and, ultimately, the execution of uncooperative monks effectively destroyed Cambodia's Buddhist institutions.

Monks who did not flee and avoided execution lived among the laity, sometimes secretly performing Buddhist rituals for the sick or afflicted. Estimates vary regarding the number of monks in Cambodia prior to the ascension of the Khmer Rouge, ranging between 65,000 and 80,000. By the time of the Buddhist restoration in the early 1980s, the number of Cambodian monks worldwide was estimated to be less than 3,000. The patriarchs of both Cambodian nikayas perished sometime during the period 1975-78, though the cause of their deaths is not known. Due to their association with the Thai monarchy, monks of the Thommayut order may have been particularly targeted for persecution.

Post-Khmer Rouge Era

Today Buddhism is struggling to re-establish itself as the lack of Buddhist scholars and leaders and the continuing political instability makes the task difficult. Following the defeat of the Khmer Rouge by forces of the Vietnamese government, Buddhism initially remained officially suppressed within Cambodia. Following challenges to the legitimacy of the Vietnamese-backed People's Republic of Kampuchea, policies towards Buddhism began to liberalize starting in the summer of 1979.

A group of monks who had been exiled and re-ordained in Vietnam during the Khmer Rouge period were sent to Cambodia, and in 1981 one of their number, Venerable Tep Vong, was elected the first sangharaja of a new unified Cambodia sangha, officially abolishing the division between the Thommayut order and the Mohanikay. The ordination of new monks was sponsored by the government as a public show of piety and lifted restrictions on ordination. Following the withdrawal of the Vietnamese military, the newly-renamed Cambodian People's Party sought to align itself with the Buddhist sangha, declaring Buddhism to be Cambodia's 'state religion' in a 1991 policy statement In 1991, King Sihanouk returned from exile and appointed a new sangharaja for each of the Thommayut and Mohanikay orders, effectively marking the end of the unified system created under Vietnamese rule in 1981.

The Cambodian Sangha

Since 1855, the Buddhist monastic community in Cambodia has been split into two divisions, excepting a brief period of unification between 1981 and 1991: the Maha Nikaya and the Dhammayuttika Nikaya. The Maha Nikaya is by far the larger of the two monastic fraternities, claiming the allegiance of a large majority of Cambodian monks.

The Dhammayuttika Nikaya, despite royal patronage, remains a small minority, isolated somewhat by its strict discipline and connection with Thailand. The Maha Nikaya monastic hieı archy- headed by the *sanghreach* (sangharaja)- has been closely connected with the Cambodian government since its re-establishment in the early 1980s High-ranking officials of the Maha Nikaya have often spoken out against criticism of the government and in favor of government policies, including calling for the arrest of monks espousing opposition positions.

Officials from the Maha Nikaya hierarchy appoint members to lay committees to oversee the running of temples, who also act to ensure that temples do not become organizing points for anti-government activity by monks or lay supporters Nevertheless, divisions within the Maha Nikaya fraternity do exist.

Modernists and Traditionalists

Divisions within the sangha between "modernists" and "traditionalists" were recorded in Cambodia as early as 1918. Broadly speaking, "modernists" have attempted to respond to Western criticism of Buddhist institutions by reinterpreting Buddhist teachings- particularly those related to philosophy and meditation- in light of both modern secular knowledge and the textual source of Theravada teachings- the Pali Canon. "Traditionalist", on the other hand, prefer to stick to the practices and teachings handed down through the monastic oral tradition, which have traditionally centered on the performance of merit-making ceremonies and the attainment of "heightened states" through concentration meditation. Traditionalists have tended to reject modern interest in vipassana meditation as a foreign affectation, and have focused on the rote memorization and recitation of Pali passages rather than attempts to study, translate, and interpret the contents of the Pali tripitaka. For many years, Maha Ghosananda remained the most visible and recognizable figure of the Maha Nikaya modernists. Through his Dhammayatra program and other attempts to use the influence of the sangha to effect social change in Cambodian society, Maha Goshananda brought to Cambodia a form of Engaged Buddhism not previously seen among Cambodian religious institutions.

This form of modernist, Engaged Buddhism has proved very popular with Western Buddhists and NGO's, who have lent their support and funding to efforts by Maha Goshananda and other modernist leaders. High officials of the Cambodian government, by contrast, have tended to support the most conservative of the Maha Nikaya monks, particular the members of a segment known as the *boran*, an ultra-conservative movement that touts the worldly efficacy of the rote recitation of various Pali and Khmer prayers and discourses.

Monks in the *boran* movement do not typically possess a significant knowledge of Pali, instead focusing on the rote memorization and recitation of certain verses and scriptures considered powerful. *Boran* monks maintain that by sponsoring recitations of these verses, lay supporters can accrue great merit that will result in immediate, worldly benefits, such as financial or career success. A large number of senior Cambodian officials (including Hun Sen) have patronized *boran* temples, providing for extensive expansions and rich decoration of the most popular temples.

Boran monks also teach the efficacy of 'group repentance' rituals, where through the recitation of Pali texts the karmic fruit of earlier misdeeds can be avoided or moderated. These rituals, which developed from New Years repentance ceremonies, have become very popular among certain segments of Cambodian society, and have been conducted by the current Maha Nikaya sangharaja, Tep Vong. The Dhammayuttika order in Cambodia seems to occupy a middle position between the Maha Nikaya modernists and traditionalists. Like the Dhammayuttika order in Thailand, they place a higher premium on scriptural study and knowledge of the Pali language than the monks of the traditionalist camp.

At the same time, they have not embraced the modernist/ Engaged notion of monks as agents of social development, preferring instead to stick closely to traditional monastic roles of study, meditation, and providing merit-making opportunities for lay supporters.

"Young Monks" Movement

Another division in the Cambodian sangha can be seen in what has been called the "young monks" movement, a small group of politically active monks (primarily Maha Nikaya) voicing public opposition to the current government. The "young monks" are primarily junior members of the clergy, drawn from temples in and around Phnom Penh.

Unlike the Engaged modernists, their interest is not in using the authority of the sangha to aide social development programs, but rather to express direct opposition to government policies and corruption.

Since the 1993 UN-monitored elections, monks have been permitted to vote in Cambodia (a move opposed by some senior monks). While this has not resulted in any large-scale mobilization of the sangha as a political force, it has drawn some young monks farther into participation in parliamentary politics. Many of these young monks are associated with opposition figure Sam Rainsy and his political party, the SRP. Members of the young monks movement have participated in and organized public demonstrations in Phnom Penh, aimed at drawing attention to perceived government misdeeds. The Maha Nikaya hierarchy has condemned this form of political activism, calling for the arrest of some monks and defrocking others.

Khmer Nationalism and Buddhism

Cambodian Buddhism was instrumental in fomenting Khmer national identity and the independence movement in the 20th century, leading to Cambodian independence as a sovereign state. In their attempt to separate the Khmer people from their cultural allegiance to the neighboring Theravada kingdom of Siam, the French "protectors" nurtured a sense of Khmer identity by emphasizing Khmer-language studies and Khmer Buddhist studies. They established Pali schools within Cambodia to keep the Cambodian monks from traveling to Siam for higher education. These Khmer-language study centers became the birthplace of Cambodian nationalism.

Cambodian Buddhism has no formal administrative ties with other Buddhist bodies, although Theravada monks from other countries, especially Thailand, Laos, Burma, and Sri Lanka, may participate in religious ceremonies in order to make up the requisite number of clergy. Cambodian Buddhism is organized nationally in accordance with regulations formulated in 1943 and modified in 1948. During the monarchical period, the king led the Buddhist clergy. Prince Sihanouk continued in this role even after he had abdicated and was governing as head of state. He appointed both the heads of the monastic orders and other high-ranking clergy.

After the overthrow of Sihanouk in 1970, the new head of state, Lon Nol, appointed these leaders. Two monastic orders constituted the clergy in Cambodia. The larger group, to which more than 90 percent of the clergy belonged, was the Mohanikay. The Thommayut order was far smaller. The Thommayut was introduced into the ruling circles of Cambodia from Thailand in 1864; it gained prestige because of its adoption by royalty and by the aristocracy, but its adherents were confined geographically to the Phnom Penh area.

Among the few differences between the two orders is stricter observance by the Thommayut bhikkhus (monks) of the rules governing the clergy. In 1961 the Mohanikay had more than 52,000 ordained monks in some 2,700 wats, whereas the Thommayut order had 1,460 monks in just over 100 wats.

In 1967 more than 2,800 Mohanikay wats and 320 Thommayut wats were in existence in Cambodia. After Phnom Penh, the largest number of Thommayut wats were found in Batdambang, Stoeng Treng, Prey Veng, Kampot, and Kampong Thum provinces. Each order has its own superior and is organized into a hierarchy of eleven levels. The seven lower levels are known collectively as the thananukram; the four higher levels together are called the rajagana.

The Mohanikay order has thirty-five monks in the rajagana; the Thommayut has twentyone . Each monk must serve for at least twenty years to be named to these highest levels.

The cornerstones of Cambodian Buddhism are the Buddhist bhikkhu and the wat. Traditionally, each village has a spiritual center—a wat—where from five to more than seventy bhikkhus reside. A typical wat in rural Cambodia consists of a walled enclosure containing a sanctuary, several residences for bhikkhus, a hall, a kitchen, quarters for nuns, and a pond.

The number of monks varies according to the size of the local population. The sanctuary, which contains an altar with statues of the Buddha and, in rare cases, a religious relic, is reserved for major ceremonies and usually only for the use of bhikkhus. Other ceremonies, classes for monks and for laity, and meals take place in the hall. Stupas containing the ashes of extended family members are constructed near the sanctuary. Fruit trees and vegetable gardens tended by local children are also part of the local wat. The main entrance, usually only for ceremonial use, faces east; other entrances are located at other points around the wall. There are no gates. Steinberg notes the striking ratio of bhikkhus to the total population of Cambodia. In the late 1950s, an estimated 100,000 bhikkhus (including about 40,000 novices) served a population of about 5 million.

This high proportion undoubtedly was caused in large part by the ease with which one could enter and leave the sangha. Becoming a bhikkhu and leaving the sangha are matters of individual choice although, in theory, nearly all

Cambodian males over sixteen serve terms as bhikkhus. Most young men do not intend to become fully ordained bhikkhus (bhikkhu), and they remain as monks for less than a year. Even a son's temporary ordination as a bhikkhu brings great merit to his parents, however, and is considered so important that arrangements are made at a parent's funeral if the son has not undergone the process while the parent was living. There are two classes of bhikkhus at a wat—the novices (samani or nen) and the bhikkhu. Ordination is held from mid-April to mid-July, during the rainy season. Buddhist monks do not take perpetual vows to remain monks, although, in fact, some become monks permanently. Traditionally, they became monks early in life. It is possible to become a novice at as young an age as seven, but in practice thirteen is the earliest age for novices. A bhikkhu must be at least twenty. The monk's life is regulated by Buddhist law, and life in the wat adheres to a rigid routine. A bhikkhu follows 227 rules of monastic discipline as well as the 10 basic precepts. These include the five precepts that all Buddhists should follow.

The five precepts for monastic asceticism prohibit eating after noon, participating in any entertainment (singing, dancing, and watching movies or television), using any personal adornments, sleeping on a luxurious bed, and handling money. In addition, a monk also is expected to be celibate. Furthermore, monks supposedly avoid all involvement in political affairs. They are not eligible to vote or to hold any political office, and they may not witness a legal document or give testimony in court. Since the person of a monk is considered sacred, he is considered to be outside the normal civil laws and public duties that affect lay people.

Some of these practices have changed in the modern

period, however, and in the 1980s Buddhist monks have been active even in the PRK government. Women are not ordained, but older women, especially widows, can become nuns. They live in wat and play an important role in the everyday life of the temple. Nuns shave their heads and eyebrows and generally follow the same precepts as monks. They may prepare the altars and do some of the housekeeping chores.

Buddhist monks traditionally were called upon to perform a number of functions in Cambodian life. They participated in all formal village festivals, ceremonies, marriages, and funerals. They also might have participated in ceremonies to name infants and in other minor ceremonies or rites of passage. Monks did not lead the ceremonies, however, because that role was given to the achar, or master of ceremonies; the monk's major function was to say prayers of blessing.

They were often healers and, in traditional Khmer culture, they were the practitioners whose role was closest to that of modern psychiatrists. They might also have been skilled in astrology. The monk traditionally occupied a unique position in the transmission of Khmer culture and values. By his way of life, he provided a living model of the most meritorious behavior a Buddhist could follow. He also provided the laity with many opportunities for gaining merit.

For centuries monks were the only literate people residing in rural communities; they acted as teachers to temple servants, to novices, and to newly ordained monks. Until the 1970s, most literate Cambodian males gained literacy solely through the instruction of the sangha. After independence from France, young Cambodian intellectuals changed their attitude toward the clergy. In describing a general shift away from Buddhism in the late 1950s and the early 1960s, Vickery cites the early work of anthropologist May Mayko Ebihara and his own observations. He suggests that the Khmer Rouge was able to instill antireligious feelings in younger males because the latter were losing interest in becoming monks even during their teenage years, the traditional temporary period of service.

The monks themselves had abandoned some of their traditional restrictions and had become involved in politics. At intervals during the colonial period, some monks had demonstrated or had rebelled against French rule, and in the 1970s monks joined pro- government demonstrations against the communists. Anticlerical feelings reached their highest point among the Khmer Rouge, who at first attempted to indoctrinate monks and to force them to pass anticlerical ideas on to the laity. Under the Khmer Rouge regime, monks were expelled forcibly from the wats and were compelled to do manual labor. Article 20 of the 1976 Constitution of Democratic Kampuchea permitted freedom of religion but banned all reactionary religions, that were "detrimental to the country." The minister of culture stated that Buddhism was incompatible with the revolution and was an instrument of exploitation. Under this regime, to quote the Finnish Inquiry Commission, "The practice of religion was forbidden and the pagodas were systematically destroyed."

Observers estimated that 50,000 monks died during the Khmer Rouge regime. The status of Buddhism and of religion in general after the Vietnamese invasion was at least partially similar to its status in pre-Khmer Rouge times. According to Michael Vickery, who has written positively about the PRK, public observance of Buddhism and of

Islam has been reestablished, and government policies allow Cambodians freedom to believe or not to believe in Buddhism. Vickery cites some differences in this reestablished Buddhism. Religious affairs are overseen by the PRK's Kampuchean (or Khmer) United Front for National Construction and Defense, the mass organization that supports the state by organizing women, youths, workers, and religious groups. In 1987 there was only a single Buddhist order because the Thommayut order had not been revived. The organization of the clergy also had been simplified. The sangharaja (primate of the Buddhist clergy) had been replaced by a prathean (chairman). Communities that wanted a wats had to apply to a local front committee for permission. The wat were administered by a committee of the local laity. Private funds paid for the restoration of the wats damaged during the war and the Khmer Rouge era, and they supported the restored wats.

Monks were ordained by a hierarchy that has been reconstituted since an initial ordination in September 1979 by a delegation from the Buddhist community in Vietnam. The validity of this ordination continues to be questioned. In general, there are only two to four monks per wat, which is fewer than before 1975. In 1981 about 4,930 monks served in 740 wats in Cambodia.

The Buddhist General Assembly reported 7,000 monks in 1,821 active wats a year later. In 1969 by contrast, observers estimated that 53,400 monks and 40,000 novice monks served in more than 3,000 wats. Vickery sums up his observations on the subject by noting that, "The government has kept its promise to allow freedom for traditional Buddhism, but does not actively encourage it." Martin offers another, more pessimistic, view of the religious situation in the late 1980s. In a 1986 study, she asserts that the PRK showed outsiders only certain aspects of religious freedom; she also states that the few wats that were restored had only two or three old monks in residence and that public attendance was low.

The monks were allowed to leave the wats only for an hour in the mornings, to collect their food, or during holy days. Lay people who practiced their faith were about the same ages as the monks, and they were allowed to visit the wats only in the evenings. A government circular had also instructed civil servants to stop celebrating the traditional New Year Festival.

Some traditional Buddhist festivals still were tolerated, but the state collected a 50 percent tithe on donations. Martin believes that Buddhism was threatened externally by state repression and by nonsupport and internally by invalid clergy. She noted that the two Buddhist superiors, Venerable Long Chhim and Venerable Tep Vong, were both believed to be from Vietnam. Venerable Tep Vong was concurrently the superior of the Buddhist clergy, vice president of the PRK's Khmer National Assembly, and vice president of the KUFNCD National Council.

She quoted a refugee from Batdambang as having said, "During the meetings, the Khmer administrative authorities, accompanied by the Vietnamese experts, tell you, `Religion is like poison, it's like opium; it's better to give the money to the military, so they can fight'." In fact, Buddhism is still strong among the various Cambodian refugee groups throughout the world, although some younger monks, faced with the distractions of a foreign culture, have chosen to leave the clergy and have become laicized. In the United States in 1984, there were twelve Cambodian wats with about twenty-one monks. In the 1980s, a Cambodian Buddhist wat was constructed near Washington,

D.C., financed by a massive outpouring of donations from Cambodian Buddhists throughout North America.

This wat is one of the few outside Southeast Asia that has the consecrated boundary within which ordinations may be performed. Most of the major Cambodian annual festivals are connected with Buddhist observances. The chol chnam (New Year Festival) takes place in mid-April; it was one of the few festivals allowed under the Khmer Rouge regime. The phchun ben, celebrated in September or in October, is a memorial day for deceased ancestors and for close friends. Meak bochea, in January or February, commemorates the last sermon of the Buddha. Vissakh bochea, in April or in May, is the triple anniversary of the birth, death, and enlightenment of the Buddha. The chol vossa takes place in June or in July; it marks the beginning of a penitential season during which the monks must remain within the temple compounds. The kathen marks the end of this season; celebrated in September, it features offerings, especially of robes, to the monks. The kathen was still celebrated in the PRK in the late 1980s. Cambodian Buddhism exists side-by-side with, and to some extent intermingles with, pre-Buddhist animism and Brahman practices. Most Cambodians, whether or not they profess to be Buddhists (or Muslims), believe in a rich supernatural world. When ill, or at other times of crisis, or to seek supernatural help, Cambodians may enlist the aid of a practitioner who is believed to be able to propitiate or obtain help from various spirits.

Local spirits are believed to inhabit a variety of objects, and shrines to them may be found in houses, in Buddhist temples, along roads, and in forests. Several types of supernatural entities are believed to exist; they make themselves known by means of inexplicable sounds or happenings. Among these phenomena are khmoc (ghosts), pret and besach (particularly nasty demons, the spirits of people who have died violent, untimely, or unnatural deaths), arak (evil spirits, usually female), neak ta (tutelary spirits residing in inanimate objects), mneang phteah (guardians of the house), meba (ancestral spirits), and mrenh kongveal (elf-like guardians of animals). All spirits must be shown proper respect, and, with the exception of the mneang phteah and mrenh kongveal, they can cause trouble ranging from mischief to serious life-threatening illnesses.

An important way for living people to show respect for the spirits of the dead is to provide food for the spirits. If this food is not provided, the spirit can cause trouble for the offending person. For example, if a child does not provide food for the spirit of its dead mother, that spirit can cause misfortunes to happen to the child. Aid in dealing with the spirit world may be obtained from a kru (shaman or spirit practitioner), an achar (ritualist), thmup (witch, sorcerer or sorceress), or a rup arak (medium, usually male).

The kru is a kind of sorcerer who prepares charms and amulets to protect the wearer from harm. He can cure illnesses, find lost objects, and prepare magic potions. Traditionally, Cambodians have held strong beliefs about protective charms. Amulets are worn routinely by soldiers to ward off bullets, for example. The kru are believed to have the power to prepare an amulet and to establish a supernatural link between it and the owner. A kru may acquire considerable local prestige and power.

Many kru are former Buddhist monks. Another kind of magical practitioner is the achar, a specialist in ritual. He may function as a kind of master of ceremonies at a wat and as a specialist in conducting spirit worship rituals connected with life-cycle ceremonies. Rup arak are mediums who can be possessed by supernatural beings and communicate with the spirit world. The thmup are sorcerers who cause illnesses.

Fortunetellers and astrologers—haor teay—are important in Cambodian life. They are consulted about important decisions such as marriages, building a new house, or going on a long journey. They are believed to be able to foretell future events and to determine lucky or unlucky days for various activities. Villagers are sensitive to the power and to the needs of the spirit world. According to observations by an American missionary in the early 1970s, villagers consulted the local guardian spirit to find out what the coming year would bring, a new province chief held a ceremony to ask the protection of the spirits over the province, and soldiers obtained magic cloths and amulets from mediums and shamans to protect them from the bullets of the enemy. Before embarking on a mission against enemy forces, a province chief might burn incense and call on a spirit for aid in defeating the enemy.

BUDDHISM IN LAOS

It is remarkable that Buddhism is the primary religion of Laos. The Buddhism practiced in Laos is of the Theravada tradition. Lao Buddhism is a unique version of Theravada Buddhism and is at the basis of Lao culture. Buddhism in Laos is often closely tied to animist beliefs and belief in ancestral spirits, particularly in rural areas. The percentage of the population that adheres to Buddhism in modern Laos is variously reported, the CIA World Factbook estimates 65% of the total population have taken refuge in the Three Jewels. The creation of accurate estimates of the number of Buddhists in Laos is complicated by the paucity of information made available by the Laotian government, and the close connection between Buddhist and animist practices in Laos could make the numbers of nominal adherents of both Buddhism-Animism as much higher as over 90% because these traditions have influenced on mostly Lao people. It is still exclusive significant numbers of Chinese or Vietnamese Mahayana Buddhists.

Theravada Buddhism is believed to have first reached Laos during the 7th - 8th Centuries CE, via the kingdom of Dvaravati. During the 7th Century, tantric Buddhism was also introduced to Laos from the kingdom of Nan-chao, an ethnically Thai kingdom centered in modern day Yunnan, China. The Nan-chao kingdom also likely introduced the political ideology of the king as defender and protector of Buddhism, an important ideological tie between the monarchy and the *sangha* in much of Southeast Asia.

During the 11th & 12th Century, Khmer rulers took control of Muang Sua, the historical region of the kingdom of Luang Prabang in northern Laos. During this period, Mahayana Buddhism replaced Theravada Buddhism as the dominant religious ideology of the ruling classes.

Historically, the Lao state is regarded as beginning in 1353 CE with the coronation of Fa Ngum at Luang Prabang. Fa Ngum brought his Khmer Theravada teacher with him to act as adviser and head priest of the new kingdom. This Khmer monk named Phramaha Pasaman also brought to the kingdom a revered image of the Buddha that became known as the Phra Bang, the namesake of the city of Luang Prabang and the symbol of the Lao kingdom. Subsequent alliances with Burma and Thailand helped cement the primacy of Theravada Buddhism in the Laotian kingdom.

Faced with rugged, isolating geography and the absence of a strong central government, Theravada Buddhism became one of the primary unifying features of Lao culture. During the 1920s, the administration of Buddhism in Laos was reorganized by Prince Phetsarath, who established a system of schools for providing instruction to the Lao clergy.

In contrast with the brutal repression of the *sangha* undertaken in Cambodia, the communist government of Laos has not sought to oppose or suppress Buddhism in Laos to any great degree. Rather, since the early days of the Pathet Lao, communist officials have sought to use the influence and respect afforded to Buddhist clergy to achieve political goals, while discouraging religious practices seen as detrimental to Marxist aims.

Starting as early as the late 1950s, members of the Pathet Lao sought to encourage support for the Communist cause by aligning members of the Lao *sangha* with the Communist opposition. Though resisted by the Royal Lao Government, these efforts were fairly successful, and resulted in increased support for the Pathet Lao, particularly in rural communities. Following the Pathet Lao's ascension to control of the government in 1975, efforts to link Buddhism and Communism in the popular imagination continued, with the government stressing the fundamental similarities of Buddhist and Communist views with regard to equality and material possessions, while simultaneously discouraging religious practices seen as wasteful or otherwise at odds with Communist doctrine- such as the donation of large sums to monastic institutions.

Traditional donations of food to monks were curtailed, and replaced with a government rice ration. In response to this and other government policies limiting the traditional role of Buddhist monks in village life, the number of monks in Laos declined during the late 1970s as new ordinations declined, combined by an exodus of monks either fleeing to neighboring Thailand or leaving the *sangha* and returning to lay life. Senior clergy, such as the sangharaja, were forbidden by the government to preach. Lower clergy were allowed to preach to the public, but their sermons were often taped or otherwise monitored by government officials to ensure that they didn't use their position as a platform for agitating against the government.

As a result, in 1979, the Sangharaja of Laos, Venerable Thammayano, fled to Thailand by floating across the Mekong on a raft of inflated car inner tubes. After 1979, government policy regarding Buddhism began to liberalize, resulting in a gradual resurgence of Buddhist institutions and practices. Party officials are no longer barred from participation in religious services, and may even undergo temporary ordination. Buddhist schools in urban areas continued to teach Buddhist doctrine to monks and laity, albeit with a political bent to their doctrine. Ordinations- both temporary and permanent- have increased, primarily in Vientiene and the Mekong River region. Lao monks are required to do productive work, with most working as teachers and physicians.

The curriculum they teach- which includes basic literacy and Lao history- as well as the medicine they practice (Western medicine and traditional herbal remedies have replaced the sale of blessed amulets and other spiritualist cures) are controlled by the government. Communist reform of the Lao *sangha* has been variously praised and criticized by outside observers, with supporters seeing it as a significant achievement in modernizing and reforming a traditional institution, and opponents criticizing the co-opting of Buddhist clergy to serve political ends.

Lao Buddhist are very devout and almost every Lao man joins a monastery, or temple, for at least a short period of time. Many men also become monks for the rest of their lives. Most people donate food to the monks to gain merit and improve their karma. The temples of Laos were once seen as "Universities" for monks. Lao monks are highly respected and revered in Lao communities.

The Pha That Luang, Wat Sisakhet, Wat Xieng Thong, and That Dam are all Buddhist structures in Laos. Lao Buddhism is also famous for images of the Buddha performing uniquely Lao mudras, or gestures, such as calling for rain, and striking uniquely Lao poses such as showing the Buddha lying down and welcoming death, after which he would achieve Nirvana.

BUDDHISM IN INDONESIA

Buddhism in Indonesia has a long history, with a considerable range of relics from its earlier years in Indonesia.

During the New Order era the five official religions of Indonesia, according to the state ideology of Pancasila included Buddhism. The national leader of the time Suharto, had considered Buddhism and Hinduism as Indonesia's classical religions. Early Buddhism in Indonesia is noted in the ninth century with Buddhist temples on Java such as Borobudur. The Buddhist pilgrim I-tsing visited Srivijaya in Sumatra on his voyage to India. Other Buddhist monks that visited Indonesia were Atisa, Dharmapala, a professor of Nalanda, and the South Indian Buddhist Vajrabodhi.

Two important Buddhist Javanese texts are the *Sang hyang Kamahaanikan* and the *Kamahayanan Mantranaya.*

The *Lalitavistara Sutra* was known to the Mantranaya stonemasons of Borobodur, refer: The birth of Buddha (Lalitavistara). 'Mantranaya' is not a corruption or misspelling of 'mantrayana' even though it is largely synonymous. Mantranaya is the term for the esoteric tradition on mantra, a particular lineage of Vajrayana and Tantra, in Indonesia. The clearly Sanskrit sounding 'Mantranaya' is evident in Old Javanese tantric literature, particularly as documented in the oldest esoteric Buddhist tantric text in Old Javanese, the *Sang Kyang Kamahayanan Mantranaya* refer Kazuko Ishii (1992).

Buddhism is mainly followed by the Chinese and some indigenous groups of Indonesia, with 1% (Buddhism only) to 2.3% (including Taoism and Confucianism) of Indonesia's population of Buddhists.

BUDDHISM IN MALAYSIA

It is significant to note that Buddhism is the second largest religion in Malaysia, after Islam, with 19.2% of Malaysia's population being Buddhist. Buddhism in Malaysia is mainly practised by the ethnic Malaysian Chinese.

Buddhism was introduced to the Malays and also to the people of the Malay Archipelago as early as 200 BCE. Chinese written sources indicated that some 30 small Indianised states rose and fell in the Malay Peninsula. Malay-Buddhism began when Indian traders and priests traveling the maritime routes and brought with them Indian concepts of religion, government, and the arts.

For many centuries the peoples of the region, especially the royal courts, synthesised Indian and indigenous ideas including Hinduism and Mahayana Buddhism and that shaped their political and cultural patterns. However, the

Malay Kedah Kingdom denounced Indian religion after the king of Chola from Tamil attack them in the early 11th century, the king of Kedah, Phra Ong Mahawangsa was the first Malay ruler to denounce the traditional Indian religion, he converted to Islam, and in the 1400s, during the golden age of Malacca Sultanate, majority of the Malays converted to Islam.

The last of the pre-Islamic-Malay king move to what is now Bali. Today, the Malays living in Malaysia are obliged to profess Islam, and the number of Malays denouncing Islam is almost nil. According the Malaysian constitution, the majority ethnic group, the Malays, are legally defined as Muslim. They constitute 60% of the population, with the remainder consisting mostly of Chinese, who are generally Buddhists or Christians, and to the lesser extent Indians, who are generally Hindus.

There are also smaller numbers of other indigenous and immigrants; among the latter are Malaysians of Sinhalese, Thai, and Eurasian origin. Many of these immigrant peoples also profess the Christian faith, but there are also Buddhists among the Sinhalese and Thai. Nearly all of the Buddhists in Malaysia live in urban areas, since they are mostly engaged in business or employed in various professions. The general climate of religious freedom in Malaysia indicates that Buddhism may have the opportunity to expand in the future.

However, Buddhism has often been described as a gentle religion which does not carry out an active program to seek converts. Recently, a number of Malaysian Buddhist leaders have responded to the decline in religious participation by the children of Buddhist families, have attempted to reformulate their message to address modern life more directly. Groups involved in these education efforts include such as the Buddhist Missionary Society.

Missionary Society leaders have argued that, while many educated youths seek an intellectual approach to Buddhism, an equally large number of people prefer to approach the religion through the tradition of ceremony and symbolism. In response to these needs, religious practices are carried out, but in a way that is simple and dignified, removing what can be seen as superstition. Efforts are made to explain why sutras are chanted, lamps lit, flowers offered, and so on.

As a religion without a supreme head to direct its development, Buddhism is practised in various forms, which, although rarely in open conflict, can sometimes lead to confusion among Buddhists. In Malaysia, some ecumenical moves have been made to coordinate the activities of different types of Buddhists.

One example is the formation of the Joint Wesak Celebrations Committee of the temples in Kuala Lumpur and Selangor, which coordinates the celebration of Wesak, a holiday commemorating the birth of the Buddha. An initiative has also begun to form a Malaysian Buddhist Council, representing the various sects of Buddhism in the country to extend the work of the development of Buddhism, especially in giving contemporary relevance to the practise of the religion, as well as to promote solidarity among Buddhists in general.

HONG KONG

Buddhism, often practiced with Taoism, is the majority religion of Hong Kong. 90% of the population of Hong Kong are thought to practice an eclectic mixture of the two, sometimes combined with other practices.). The numbers of Buddhists are approximately 700 thousand. There are more than 600 temples in the HKSAR (Government of the Hong Kong Special Administrative Region). The history of some of these temples can be traced back to more than 700 years ago, while some others have been built in recent years. Notable temples include the Wong Tai Sin Temple located in the Wong Tai Sin District in Kowloon. This popular temple is dedicated to the Taoist deity, Wong Tai Sin. The Chi Lin Nunnery in Diamond Hill is a group of temple structures in Tang Dynasty's architectural style. It is now open to the public following the completion of its redevelopment in 2000.

The Po Lin Monastery on Lantau Island is famous for the outdoor bronze statue, Tian Tan Buddha, which attracts a large number of visitors during the weekends and holidays. It is now linked to the city's latest tourist attraction Ngong Ping 360. The cable car and park complex is built around a Buddhism theme, featuring sites of the Wisdom Path and the Po Lin Monastery. Buddhists' organizations and temples in Hong Kong have long been involved in social welfare and education in the city. The Buddhist's Association of Hong Kong operates a dozen primary and secondary schools, hospices and elderly homes as well as centres for youth and children in Hong Kong

The leadership of mainstream buddhists organizations have aligned themselves with the establishment in Hong Kong. For example, high-ranking Buddhist Association's executives have openly endorsed the re-election of the city's Chief Executive Donald Tsang. Several of the association's members were on the drafting committee of the Basic Law of Hong Kong's mini constitution]. Under the leadership of the former Chief Executive Tung Chee

Hwa, the SAR government formally recognized the influence of Buddhism in Hong Kong. In 1997 the SAR government designated one public holiday in May or June to mark Buddha's birthday, which replaced the Queen's birthday. This year Buddha's birthday is on May 24th. Tung himself is a Buddhist and participated in major, widely publicised Buddhist activities in Hong Kong and China.

Academic studies and research of Buddhism in Hong Kong have thrived over the past 10 years. The University of Hong Kong has a Centre of Buddhist Studies. The Chinese University of Hong Kong also has a Centre for the Study of Humanistic Buddhism.

VIETNAM

In fact, Buddhism came to Vietnam as early as the second century CE through the North from central Asia and via Southern routes from India. Buddhism in Vietnam as practiced by the ethnic Vietnamese is mainly of the Mahayana school, although some ethnic minorities (such as the Khmer Krom) adhere to the Theravada school. Buddhism in Vietnam has had a symbiotic relationship with Taoism, Chinese spirituality, and the indigenous Vietnamese religion. The majority of Buddhist practitioners focus on devotional rituals rather than meditation. Buddhism is not practiced the same as in other Asian countries and does not contain the institutional structures, hierarchy, or sanghas that exist in other traditional Buddhist settings. Due to this observation the estimate that 80% of the Vietnamese population is Buddhist is questionable, but does however show that many Vietnamese define their spiritual needs using a Buddhist worldview.

By the end of the second century, Vietnam developed a major Buddhist centre (probably Mahayana) in the region, commonly known as the Luy Lâu centre, now in the B¯c Ninh province, north of the present day Hanoi city. Luy Lâu was the capital of Giao ChÉ, (the former name of Vietnam), and was a popular place visited by many Indian Buddhist missionary monks to China. The monks followed the sea route from the Indian sub-continent to China used by Indian traders. A number of Mahayana sutras and the Agamas were translated into Chinese script at that centre, including the Sutra of Forty-Two Chapters and the Anapanasati. Over the next 18 centuries Vietnam and China shared many common features of cultural, philosophical and religious heritage. This was due to geographical proximity to one another and Vietnam being annexed twice by the Chinese. Vietnamese Buddhism has been greatly influenced by the development of Mahayana Buddhism in China, with the dominant traditions of Pure Land and Ch'an/Zen. Theravada Buddhism would become incorporated through the annexation of the Khmer land and khmer people.

During the Đinh Dynasty (968-980) Buddhism was recognized by the state as an official religion (~971) suggesting that the current kings at the time held Buddhism in high regard. The Early Lê Dynasty (980-1009) would follow a similar path. Reasons for growth of Buddhism during this time is contributed to an influx of educated monks, a newly independent state needing an ideological basis on which to build a country and the development of Confucianism. Buddhism became more prominent during the Lý Dynasty (1009-1225) beginning with the founder Lý Thái TÕ who was raised in a pagoda (Buddhist temple). All of the kings during the Ly Dynasty supported Buddhism as a state religion and this continued into the Tr§n Dynasty (1225-1400) where Buddhism later developed in combination with Confucianism. Buddhism fell out of favor during the

Later Lê Dynasty and would grow under the NguyÅn Dynasty.

A Buddhist revival (Chan Hung Phat Giao) started in 1920 in an effort to reform and develop institutional Buddhism, which continues today. Under Communist rule many religious practices in Vietnam Buddhism were suppressed. However a government sanctioned and approved United Buddhist Church was created in the North. In the South, The Unified Buddhist Church was created and opposed the communist government.

Since ĐÕi MÛi (1986) many reforms have allowed Buddhism to be practiced further. It was not until 2007 that Pure Land Buddhism, the largest type of Buddhism practiced in Vietnam, was officially recognized as a religion by the government.

Practice

Although some people believe that the differing schools of Buddhism are incompatible and cannot practice together, within Vietnam followers practice differing traditions without any problem or without contradiction. Although Vietnamese Buddhism does not have a strong centralized structure, the practice is similar throughout the country at almost any temple. Gaining merit is the most common and essential practice in Vietnamese Buddhism with a belief that liberation takes place with the help of Buddhas and bodhisattvas. Buddhist monks commonly chant sutras, recite Buddhas' names (Amitabha most notably, doing repentance and praying for rebirth in the Pure Land). Meditation is not always a common daily practice.

The Lotus Sutra and Amitabha Sutra are the most commonly used sutras. Most sutras and texts have come from China and have been translated into Sino-Vietnamese

(Han –Viet) rather than the vernacular making them largely incomprehensible to most practitioners.

Three services are practiced regularly at dawn, noon, and dusk. They include sutras (mainly devotional), reciting dharanis and Buddha's name, and circumambulation (walking meditation). Laypeople at times join the services at the temple and some devout Buddhist practice the services at home. Special services such as Sam Nguyen / Sam Hoi (confession / repentance) takes place on the full moon and new moon each month. Chanting the name of Buddha is one way of repenting and purifying bad karma.

Pure Land

Pure Land Buddhism is the most widespread form of Buddhism within Vietnam. It is common for practitioners to recite sutras, chants and dharanis looking to gain protection from bodhisattvas or Dharma-Protectors. It is a devotional practice where those practicing put their faith into Amitabha Buddha. Followers believe they will gain rebirth in the Pure Land by chanting Amitabha's name. The Pure Land is where one can more easily gain enlightenment since suffering does not exist. Many religious organizations have not been recognized by the government however in 2007, with 1.5 million followers, The Vietnamese Pure Land Buddhism Association received official recognition as an independent and legal religious organization.

Zen in Vietnam

ThiÁn Buddhism is the Vietnamese name for the school of Zen Buddhism. Thien is ultimately derived from Chan Zong, itself a derivative of the Sanskrit "Dhyâna".

The traditional account is that in 580, when an Indian monk named Vinitaruci traveled to Vietnam after completing his studies with Jianzhi Sengcan, the third patriarch of Chinese Zen. This would be the first appearance of Vietnamese Zen, or Thien (thiÁn) Buddhism. The sect that Vinitaruci and his lone Vietnamese disciple founded would become known as the oldest branch of Thien. After a period of obscurity, the Vinitaruci School became one of the most influential Buddhist groups in Vietnam by the 10th century.

A new school was founded by King Tr§n Nhân Tông (1258–1308); called Trúc Lâm (Bamboo Grove) school, which evinced a deep influence from Confucian and Taoist philosophy. Nevertheless, Trúc Lâm's prestige waned over the following centuries as Confucianism became dominant in the royal court. In the 17th century, a group of Chinese monks led by Nguyên ThiÁu introduced the Ling school.

Controversy over Zen

Some scholars argue that the importance and prevalence of Zen in Vietnam has been greatly overstated and that Zen has played more of an elite rhetorical role than a role of practice.

The Outstanding Figures in the Vietnamese Zen Community has been the dominant text used to legitimize the Zen Buddhist lineage and history within Vietnam. However Cuong Tu Nguyen's "Zen in Medieval Vietnam: A Study and Translation of the Thien Tap Anh" (1997) gives a critical review of how the text has been used to create a history of Zen Buddhism that that is "fraught with discontinuity". Current day Buddhist practices are not reflective of a Zen past is that in modern day Vietnam the common practices are more focused on ritual and devotion than the Zen focus on meditation. Nonetheless, we are seeing an increased population in Zen today. Two figures who have been responsible for this increased interest in

Thien is Thich Nhat Hanh, currently residing in France, and Thich Thanh Tu, who lives in Da Lat.

Theravada

In the 1920s and 1930s, there were a number of movements in Vietnam for the revival and modernization of Buddhist activities. Together with the re-organization of Mahayana establishments, there developed a growing interest in Theravadin meditation as well as the Pali Canon. These were then available in French. He was born in the South, received higher education in Hanoi, and after graduation, was sent to Phnom Penh, Cambodia, to work for the French government.

During that time he became especially interested in Theravada Buddhist practice. Subsequently, he decided to ordain and took the Dhamma name of HÙ-Tông (Vansarakkhita). In 1940, upon an invitation from a group of lay Buddhists led by Mr. NguyÅn Vãn HiÃu, he went back to Vietnam in order to help establish the first Theravada temple for Vietnamese Buddhists, at Gò Dýa, (now a district of HÓ Chí Minh City). The temple was named Bíu Quang (Ratana Ramsyarama). The temple was destroyed by French troops in 1947, and was later rebuilt in 1951. At Bíu Quang temple, together with a group of Vietnamese bhikkhus (monks), who had received training in Cambodia, such as Venerables ThiÇn Lu-t, Bíu Chõn, Kim Quang and GiÛi Nghiêm, Venerable HÙ Tông began teaching the Dhamma in their native Vietnamese. He also translated many Buddhist materials from the Pali Canon, and Theravada became part of Vietnamese Buddhist activity in the country.

In 1949-1950, Venerable HÙ Tông together with Mr NguyÅn Vãn HiÃu and supporters built a new temple in Saigon (now HÓ Chí Minh City), named Kó Viên Tñ

(Jetavana Vihara). This temple became the centre of Theravada activities in Vietnam, which continued to attract increasing interest among the Vietnamese Buddhists. In 1957, the Vietnamese Theravada Buddhist Sangha Congregation was formally established and recognised by the government, and the Theravada Sangha elected Venerable HÙ Tông as its first President, or Sangharaja.

From Saigon, the Theravada movement spread to other provinces, and soon, a number of Theravada temples for ethnic Viet Buddhists were established in many areas in the South and Central parts of Vietnam.

Buddhism in Vietnam Today

After the fall of South Vietnam to communism in 1975 at the end of the Vietnam War, the first major Buddhist community appeared in North America. Since this time the North American Vietnamese Buddhist community has grown to 160 temples and centers, however Vietnamese Buddhism is one of the least popular forms of Buddhism among Buddhists of European descent. Two reasons for this are a lack of meditation within the practice (which is generally favored by Western Buddhists), not much proselytizing being carried out by the Vietnamese Buddhists and the fact that Vietnamese monks do not tend to use English to reach out to Buddhists who are not of Vietnamese descent. The most famous practitioner of synchronized ThiÁn Buddhism in the West is Thích Nh¥t H¡nh who has authored dozens of books and founded Dharma center Plum Village in France together with his colleague, Bhiksuni and Zen Master Chân Không. According to Nguyen and Barber, Thich Nhat Hanh's fame in the Western world as a proponent of engaged Buddhism and a new zen style has "no affinity with or any foundation in traditional Vietnamese Buddhist practices" and according to Alexander Soucy (2007) his style of Zen Buddhism is not reflective of actual Vietnamese Buddhism. (Yet Thích Nh¥t H¡nh often recounts about his early Zen practices in Vietnam in his Dharma talks saying that he continued and developed this practice in the West which has a distinctive Vietnamese Thien flavor.)

Thich Nhat Hanh's Buddhist teachings have started to return to a Vietnam where the Buddhist landscape is now being shaped by the combined Vietnamese & Westernized Buddhism that is focused more on the meditative practices.

REFERENCES

1. Bapat, P.V.; Takasaki, J.N. (1959), "Progress of Buddhist Studies in Ceylon, Burma, Thailand, Cambodia, Laos, Vietnam, China and Japan", in Bapat, V.P., *2500 Years of Buddhism*, Delhi: Ministry of Information and Broadcasting, Government of India, pp. 370–83. http://www.buddhismtoday.com/english/world/figure/005-progress.htm, retrieved 2007-06-29
2. "CIA World Factbook- Laos". https://www.cia.gov/library/publications/the-world-factbook/geos/la.html. Retrieved 2007-04-10.
3. Harris, Ian (2005), *Cambodian Buddhism*, University of Hawai'i Press.
4. Harris, Ian (August 2001), "Sangha Groupings in Cambodia", *Buddhist Studies Review* (UK Association for Buddhist Studies) 18 (I): 65–72
5. International Religious Freedom Report 2007 - Laos
6. Nguyen Tai Thu. The History of Buddhism in Vietnam. 2008.
7. Nguyen, Cuong Tu & A.W. Barber. "Vietnamese Buddhism in North America: Tradition and Acculturation". in Charles S. Prebish and Kenneth K. Tanaka (eds) .The Faces of Buddhism in America. Berkeley: University of California Press, 1998.
8. Nguyen, Cuong Tu. Zen in Medieval Vietnam: A Study of the ThiÃn UyÃn T-p Anh. Honolulu: University of Hawaii Press, 1997.

9. Rajavaramuni, Phra Prayudh Payutto (1984), "A Doubtful Fate of Laotian and Cambodian Buddhism", *Thai Buddhism in the Buddhist World*, Bangkok: Mahachulalongkorn Buddhist University, pp. 78–82, http://www.buddhismtoday.com/english/world/country/013-lao.htm
10. Rawson, Philip (1990), *The Art of Southeast Asia*, Thames & Hudson.
11. Reat, Noble Ross. " "Buddhism in Laos". http://www.buddhanet.net/e-learning/buddhistworld/laos-txt.htm". Retrieved 2007-04-12.
12. Savada, Andrea Matles (1994). *Laos: A Country Study*. Washington, D.C.: GPO for the Library of Congress. http://countrystudies.us/laos/.
13. Soucy, Alexander. "Nationalism, Globalism and the Re-establishment of the Truc Lam Thien Sect in Northern Vietnam." Philip Taylor (ed). Modernity and Re-enchantment: Religion in Post-revolutionary Vietnam. Institute of Southeast Asian Studies: Singapore, 2007.
14. Wyatt, David (2003), *Thailand: A Short History*, New Haven: Yale University Press.

10

Tibetan Buddhism

Tibet is the hub of Buddhism and land of monasteries.

In fact, Tibetan Buddhism is the body of Buddhist religious doctrine and institutions characteristic of Tibet and certain regions of the Himalayas, including northern Nepal, Bhutan, and India (particularly in Arunachal Pradesh, Ladakh, Dharamsala, Lahaul and Spiti in Himachal Pradesh, and Sikkim). It is the state religion of Bhutan. It is also practiced in Mongolia and parts of Russia (Kalmykia, Buryatia, and Tuva) and Northeast China.

Texts recognized as scripture and commentary are contained in the Tibetan Buddhist canon, such that Tibetan is a spiritual language of these areas. In the wake of the 1959 Tibetan uprising, a Tibetan diaspora has made Tibetan Buddhism more widely accessible to the rest of the world. It has since spread to many Western countries, where the tradition has gained popularity. Among its prominent exponents is the 14th Dalai Lama of Tibet. The number of its adherents is estimated to be between ten and twenty million.

Tibetan Buddhism comprises the teachings of the three vehicles of Buddhism: the Foundational Vehicle, Mahâyâna, and Vajrayâna. The Mahâyâna goal of spiritual development is to achieve the enlightenment of Buddhahood in order to most efficiently help all other sentient beings attain this state. The motivation in it is the bodhicitta mind of enlightenment — an altruistic intention to become enlightened for the sake of all sentient beings. Bodhisattvas are revered beings who have conceived the will and vow to dedicate their lives with bodhicitta for the sake of all beings. Tibetan Buddhism teaches methods for achieving Buddahood more quickly by including the Vajrayâna path in Mahâyâna.

Notably, Buddhahood is defined as a state free of the obstructions to liberation as well as those to omniscience. When, in Buddhahood, one is freed from all mental obscurations, one is said to attain a state of continuous bliss mixed with a simultaneous cognition of emptiness, the true nature of reality. In this state, all limitations on one's ability to help other living beings are removed.

It is said that there are countless beings who have attained Buddhahood. Buddhas spontaneously, naturally and continuously perform activities to benefit all sentient beings. However it is believed that sentient beings' karmas limit the ability of the Buddhas to help them. Thus, although Buddhas possess no limitation from their side on their ability to help others, sentient beings continue to experience suffering as a result of the limitations of their own former negative actions.

Introspection as the mark of a Buddhist is embodied in the Tibetan term for Buddhist: literally, "internalist".

More precisely, Tibetans specify two alternative criteria for being Buddhist - a) formal: having taken refuge and b) in belief: acceptance of the four marks of existence.

General Methods of Practice

Remarkably, emphasis on oral transmission as more

important than the printed word derives from the earliest period of Indian Buddhism, when it allowed teachings to be kept from those who should not hear them. Hearing a teaching (transmission) readies the hearer for realisation based on it. The person from whom one hears the teaching should have heard it as one link in a succession of listeners going back to the original speaker: the Buddha in the case of a sutra or the author in the case of a book.

Then the hearing constitutes an authentic lineage of transmission. Authenticity of the oral lineage is a prerequisite for realisation, hence the importance of lineages. Merely reading about a teaching is helpful but no substitute for receiving a transmission on it. Listening to a text recited aloud by someone who holds the lineage for transmission of that text makes oneself also a holder of that lineage and the more ready for realization of the teaching in it.

Oral transmissions by lineage holders traditionally can take place in small groups or mass gatherings of listeners and may last for seconds (in the case of a mantra, for example) or months (as in the case of a section of the canon). A transmission can even occur without actually hearing, as in Asanga's visions of Maitreya.

Spontaneous realisation on the basis of transmission is possible but rare. Normally an intermediate step is needed in the form of analytic meditation, i.e., thinking about what one has heard. As part of this process, entertaining doubts and engaging in internal debate over them is encouraged in some traditions. Analytic meditation is just one of two general methods of meditation. When it achieves the quality of realisation, one is encouraged to switch to "focused" or "fixation" meditation. In this the mind is stabilised on that realisation for periods long enough to gradually habituate it to it.

A person's capacity for analytic meditation can be trained with logic. The capacity for successful focused meditation can be trained through calm abiding. A meditation routine may involve alternating sessions of analytic meditation to achieve deeper levels of realization, and focused meditation to consolidate them. The deepest level of realization is Buddhahood itself.

It is pertinent to note that two characteristic aspects of Tibetan Buddhism are skepticism and devotion to the guru which have led it into conflict with Chinese socialism and so invited the destruction of the Tibetan intelligentsia under Mao. An attitude of critical skepticism is encouraged to promote abilities in analytic meditation.

However, as in other Buddhist traditions, an attitude of reverence for the teacher is also highly prized. In favour of skepticism towards Buddhist doctrines in general, Tibetans are fond of quoting sutra to the effect that one should test the Buddha's words as one would the quality of gold. On the other hand, at the beginning of a public teaching, a lama will do prostrations to the throne on which he will teach due to its symbolism, or to an image of the Buddha behind that throne, then students will do prostrations to the lama after he is seated. Merit accrues when one's interactions with the teacher are imbued with such reverence in the form of guru devotion, a code of practices governing them that derives from Indian sources.

By such things as avoiding disturbance to the peace of mind of one's teacher, and wholeheartedly following his prescriptions, much merit accrues and this can significantly help improve one's practice. There is a general sense in which any Tibetan Buddhist teacher is called a lama. A student may have taken teachings from many authorities and revere them all as lamas in this general sense. However, he will typically have one held in special esteem as his own root guru and is encouraged to view the other teachers who are less dear to him, however more exalted their status, as embodied in and subsumed by the root guru.

Often the teacher the student sees as root guru is simply the one who first introduced him to Buddhism, but a student may also change his personal view of which particular teacher is his root guru any number of times. The opposing principles of skepticism and guru devotion are reconciled with the Tibetan injunction to scrutinise a prospective guru thoroughly before finally adopting him as such without reservation. A Buddhist may study with a lama for decades before finally accepting him as his own guru.

Tibetan Approach to Vajrayâna

It is apt to mention that Vajrayâna is said to be the fastest method for attaining Buddhahood but for unqualified practitioners it can be dangerous. To engage in it one must receive an appropriate initiation (also known as an "empowerment") from a lama who is fully qualified to give it. From the time one has resolved to accept such an initiation, the utmost sustained effort in guru devotion is essential. The aim of preliminary practices (*ngöndro*) is to start the student on the correct path for such higher teachings. Just as Sutrayâna preceded Vajrayâna historically in India, so sutra practices constitute those that are preliminary to tantric ones.

Preliminary practices include all *Sutrayâna* activities that yield merit like hearing teachings, prostrations, offerings, prayers and acts of kindness and compassion, but chief among the preliminary practices are realizations through meditation on the three principle stages of the path: renunciation, the altruistic bodhicitta wish to attain enlightenment and the wisdom realizing emptiness.

For a person without the basis of these three in particular to practice Vajrayâna can be like a small child trying to ride an unbroken horse. While the practices of Vajrayâna are not known in Sutrayâna, all Sutrayâna practices are common to Vajrayâna. Without training in the preliminary practices, the ubiquity of allusions to them in Vajrayâna is meaningless and even successful Vajrayâna initiation becomes impossible.

In fact, the merit acquired in the preliminary practices facilitates progress in Vajrayâna. While many Buddhists may spend a lifetime exclusively on sutra practices, however, an amalgam of the two to some degree is common. For, example, in order to train in calm abiding, one might use a tantric visualisation as the meditation object.

Esotericism

In Vajrayâna particularly, Tibetan Buddhists subscribe to a voluntary code of self-censorship, whereby the uninitiated do not seek and are not provided with information about it. This self-censorship may be applied more or less strictly depending on circumstances such as the material involved. A depiction of a mandala may be less public than that of a deity.

That of a higher tantric deity may be less public than that of a lower. The degree to which information on Vajrayâna is now public in western languages is controversial among Tibetan Buddhists. Buddhism has always had a taste for esotericism since its earliest period in India. Tibetans today maintain greater or lesser degrees of confidentiality also with information on the *vinaya* and emptiness specifically. In Buddhist teachings generally, too, there is caution about revealing information to people who may be unready for it. Esoteric values in Buddhism have made it at odds with the values of Christian missionary activity, for example in contemporary Mongolia.

Some commentators have emphasised Tibetan innovations such as the system of incarnate lamas, but such genuine innovations have been few. True to its roots in the *Pâla* system of North India, however, Tibetan Buddhism carried on a tradition of eclectic accumulation and systematisation of diverse Buddhist elements, and pursued their synthesis. Prominent among these achievements are the Stages of the Path and motivational training.

Tibetan Buddhists practice one or more understandings of the true nature of reality, the emptiness of inherent existence of all things. Emptiness is propounded according to four classical Indian schools of philosophical tenets.

Two belong to the older path of the Foundation Vehicle:

- Vaibhacika (Tib. *bye-brag smra-ba*)
- Sautrântika (Tib. *mdo-sde-pa*)

The primary source for the former is the Abhidharma-koœa by Vasubandhu and its commentaries. The Abhidharmakoúa is also an important source for the Sautrântikas. Dignâga and Dharmakîrti are the most prominent exponents.

The other two are Mahayana (Skt. *Greater Vehicle*) (Tib. *theg-chen*):

- Yogâcâra, also called Cittamâtra (Tib. *sems-tsam-pa*), *Mind-Only*
- Madhyamaka (Tib. *dbu-ma-pa*)

Yogacârins base their views on texts from Maitreya, Asanga and Vasubandhu, Madhyamakas on Nâgârjuna and Âryadeva. There is a further classification of Madhyamaka into Svatantrika-Madhyamaka and Prasangika-Madhyamaka. The former stems from Bhavaviveka, Sântarakcita and Kamalaúîla, and the latter from Buddhapâlita and Candrakîrti.

In fact, the tenet system is used in the monasteries and colleges to teach Buddhist philosophy in a systematic and progressive fashion, each philosophical view being more subtle than its predecessor. Therefore the four schools can be seen as a gradual path from a rather easy-to-grasp, "realistic" philosophical point of view, to more and more complex and subtle views on the ultimate nature of reality, that is on emptiness and dependent arising, culminating in the philosophy of the Mâdhyamikas, which is widely believed to present the most sophisticated point of view.

According to a Tibetan legendary tradition, Buddhist scriptures including the Kâran avyûhasûtra and relics including the *cintamani* arrived in southern Tibet in the fifth century during the reign of Lha Thothori Nyantsen, the 28th king of Tibet. The tale is miraculous: the objects fell from the sky on the roof of the king's palace, but it may have a historical background in the form of the arrival of Buddhist missionaries.

The earliest well-documented influence of Buddhism in Tibet dates from the reign of king Songtsän Gampo, who died in 650. He married a Chinese Tang Dynasty Buddhist princess, Wencheng, who came to Tibet with a statue of Shakyamuni Buddha.

According to a Tibetan legendary tradition, Songtsän Gampo also married a Nepalese Buddhist princess, Bhrikuti;

but Bhrikuti, who bears the name of a goddess, is not mentioned in reliable sources. Songtsän Gampo founded the first Buddhist temples. By the second half of the 8th century he was already regarded as an embodiment of the bodhisattva Avalokiteœvara. The successors of Songtsän Gampo were less enthusiastic about the propagation of Buddhism but in the 8th century, King Trisong Detsen (755-797) established it as the official religion of the state.

He invited Indian Buddhist scholars to his court. In his age the famous tantric mystic Padmasambhâva arrived in Tibet according to the Tibetan tradition. In addition to writing a number of important scriptures, some of which he hid for future *tertons* to find, Padmasambhâva, along with Sântarakcita, established the Nyingma school. The outlines of the history of Buddhism in Tibet from this time are well-known. At this early time also, from the south came the influence of scholars under the Pâla dynasty in the Indian state of Magadha.

They had achieved a blend of Mahayana and Vajrayana that has come to characterize all forms of Tibetan Buddhism. Their teaching in sutra centred on the *Abhisamayâlankâra*, a fourth century Yogacârin text, but prominent among them were the Mâdhyamika scholars Sântarakcita and Kamalasîla. A third influence was that of the Sarvâstivâdins from Kashmir in the south west and Khotan in the north west. Although they did not succeed in maintaining a presence in Tibet, their texts found their way into the Tibetan Buddhist canon, providing the Tibetans with almost all of their primary sources about the Foundation Vehicle.

A subsect of this school, Mûlasarvâstivâda was the source of the Tibetan vinaya. A fourth influence from China in the east came in the form of Chan.

Transmission of Chan to the Nyingmapa

According to A.W. Barber, Chan Buddhism was introduced to the Nyingmapa in three principal streams: the teachings of Master Kim, Kim Ho-shang, (Chin ho shang) transmitted by *Sang Shi* in ca. 750 CE; the lineage of Master Wu Chu of the Pao T'ang School was transmitted within Tibet by Ye-shes Wangpo; and the teaching from Mo Ho Yen, (Tibetan: *Hwa shang Mahayana*) that were a synthesis of the Northern School of Chan and the Pao T'ang School. Tibetan king *Khri srong lde btsan* (742–797) invited the Ch'an master Mo-ho-yen (whose name consists of the same Chinese characters used to transliterate "Mahayana") to transmit the Dharma at Samye Monastery. Mo-ho-yen had been disseminating Dharma in the Tun-huang locale, but, according to Tibetan sources, lost an important philosophical debate on the nature of emptiness with the Indian master Kamalasîla, and the king declared Kamalasîla's philosophy should form the basis for Tibetan Buddhism. However, a Chinese source says their side won, and some scholars conclude that the entire episode is fictitious. Pioneering Buddhologist Giuseppe Tucci speculated that Hwashang's ideas were preserved by the Nyingmapas in the form of dzogchen teachings. Whichever may be the case, Tibetan Buddhists today trace their spiritual roots from Indian masters such as Padmasambhâva, Atisa, Tilopa, Naropa and their later Tibetan students.

From the outset Buddhism was opposed by the native shamanistic Bön religion, which had the support of the aristocracy, but with royal patronage it thrived to a peak under King Rälpachän (817-836). Terminology in translation was standardised around 825, enabling a translation methodology that was highly literal. Despite a reversal in Buddhist influence which began under King Langdarma

(836-842), the following centuries saw a colossal effort in collecting available Indian sources, many of which are now extant only in Tibetan translation. Tibetan Buddhism exerted a strong influence from the 11th century CE among the peoples of Central Asia, especially in Mongolia and Manchuria. It was adopted as an official state religion by the Mongol Yuan dynasty and the Manchu Qing dynasty that ruled China. Coinciding with the early discoveries of "hidden treasures" (*terma*), the 11th century saw a revival of Buddhist influence originating in the far east and far west of Tibet.

In the west, Rinchen Zangpo (958-1055) was active as a translator and founded temples and monasteries. Prominent scholars and teachers were again invited from India. In 1042 Atiœa arrived in Tibet at the invitation of a west Tibetan king. This renowned exponent of the Pâla form of Buddhism from the Indian university of Vikramaúîla later moved to central Tibet. There his chief disciple, Dromtonpa founded the Kadampa school of Tibetan Buddhism, under whose influence the New Translation schools of today evolved.

Schools

Tibetan Buddhism has four main traditions:

- Nyingma(pa), "the Ancient Ones". This is the oldest, the original order founded by Padmasambhâva and Úântarakcita. Whereas other schools categorize their teachings into the three vehicles: The Foundation Vehicle, Mahâyâna and Vajrayâna, the Nyingma tradition classifies its into nine vehicles, among the highest of which is that known as *Atiyoga* or Dzogchen ("Great Perfection"). Hidden treasures (*terma*) are of particular significance to this tradition.
- Kagyu(pa), "Lineage of the (Buddha's) Word". This

is an oral tradition which is very much concerned with the experiential dimension of meditation. Its most famous exponent was Milarepa, an eleventh century mystic. It contains one major and one minor subsect. The first, the Dagpo Kagyu, encompasses those Kagyu schools that trace back to the Indian master Naropa via Marpa, Milarepa and Gampopa and consists of four major sub-sects: the Karma Kagyu, headed by a Karmapa, the Tsalpa Kagyu, the Barom Kagyu, and Pagtru Kagyu.

There are further eight minor sub-sects, all of which trace their root to Pagtru Kagyu and the most notable of which are the Drikung Kagyu and the Drukpa Kagyu. The once-obscure Shangpa Kagyu, which was famously represented by the 20th century teacher Kalu Rinpoche, traces its history back to the Indian master Naropa via Niguma, Sukhasiddhi and Kyungpo Neljor.

- Sakya(pa), "Grey Earth". This school very much represents the scholarly tradition. Headed by the Sakya Trizin, this tradition was founded by Khon Konchog Gyalpo, a disciple of the great translator Drokmi Lotsawa and traces it's lineage to the Indian master Virupa. A renowned exponent, Sakya Pandita 1182–1251CE was the great grandson of Khon Konchog Gyalpo.
- Gelug(pa), "Way of Virtue". Originally a reformist movement, this tradition is particularly known for its emphasis on logic and debate. Its spiritual head is the Ganden Tripa and its temporal one the Dalai Lama. The Dalai Lama is regarded as the embodiment of the Bodhisattva of Compassion Successive Dalai Lamas ruled Tibet from the mid-17th to mid-20th

centuries. The order was founded in the 14th to 15th century by Je Tsongkhapa, renowned for both his scholasticism and his virtue.

Monasticism

Although there were many householder-yogis in Tibet, monasticism was the foundation of Buddhism in Tibet. There were over 6,000 monasteries in Tibet, but nearly all were ransacked and destroyed by Red Guards during the Cultural Revolution. Most of the major ones have been at least partially re-established but many still remain in ruins.

In Mongolia during the 1920s, approximately one third of the male population were monks, though many lived outside monasteries. By the beginning of the 20th century about 750 monasteries were functioning in Mongolia. These monasteries were largely dismantled during Communist rule, but many have been reestablished during the Buddhist revival in Mongolia which followed the fall of Communism.

Monasteries generally adhere to one particular school. Some of the major centers in each tradition are as follows:

Nyingma

The Nyingma lineage is said to have "six mother monasteries," although the composition of the six has changed over time:

(a) Dorje Drak

(b) Dzogchen Monastery

(c) Kathok

(d) Mindroling

(e) Palyul

(f) Shechen

Also of note is

(g) Samye — the first monastery in Tibet, established by Padmasambhâva and Úântarakcita

Kagyu

Many Kagyu monasteries are in Kham, eastern Tibet. Tsurphu, one of the most important, is in central Tibet, as is Ralung and Drikung.

- Palpung Monastery — the seat of the Taì Situpa and Jamgon Kongtrul
- Ralung Monastery — the seat of the Gyalwang Drukpa
- Surmang Monastery — the seat of the Trungpa tülkus
- Tsurphu Monastery — the seat of H.H. the Gyalwa Karmapa

Sakya

- Sakya Monastery — the seat of H.H. the Sakya Trizin

Gelug

The three most important centers of the Gelugpa lineage are Ganden, Sera and Drepung Monasteries, near Lhasa:

- Ganden Monastery — the seat of the Ganden Tripa
- Drepung Monastery — the home monastery of the Dalai Lama
- Sera Monastery

Three other monasteries have particularly important regional influence:

- Tashilhunpo Monastery in Shigatse — founded by

the first Dalai Lama, this monastery is now the seat of the Panchen Lama

- Labrang Monastery in eastern Amdo
- Kumbum Jampaling in central Amdo

Great spiritual and historical importance is also placed on:

- The Jokhang Temple in Lhasa — said to have been built by King Songtsen Gampo in 647 AD, a major pilgrimage site

Today, Tibetan Buddhism is adhered to widely in the Tibetan Plateau, Nepal, Bhutan, Mongolia, Kalmykia (on the north-west shore of the Caspian), Siberia (central Russia, specifically Buryatia and Chita Oblast), and the Russian Far East (concentrated in Tuva). The Indian regions of Sikkim and Ladakh, both formerly independent kingdoms, are also home to significant Tibetan Buddhist populations. In the wake of the Tibetan diaspora, Tibetan Buddhism has gained adherents in the West and throughout the world.

REFERENCES

1. Coleman, Graham, ed. (1993). *A Handbook of Tibetan Culture*. Boston: Shambhala Publications, Inc..
2. Conze, Edward (1993). *A Short History of Buddhism* (2nd ed.). Oneworld.
3. Dhargyey, Geshe Ngawang; ed. Alexander Berzin, based on oral trans. by Sharpa Tulku (3rd edn, 1978). *Tibetan Tradition of Mental Development*. Dharmsala: Library of Tibetan Works and Archives.
4. Dhargyey, Geshe Ngawang; ed. Alexander Berzin, based on oral trans. by Sharpa Tulku (1982). *An Anthology of Well-Spoken Advice on the Graded Paths of the Mind, Vol. I.* Dharmsala: Library of Tibetan Works and Archives.

5. Hopkins, Jeffrey (1996). *Meditation on Emptiness*. Boston: Wisdom.
6. Lati Rinpoche; trans. & ed.: Elizabeth Napper (1980). *Mind in Tibetan Buddhism: Oral Commentary on Ge-shay Jam-bel-sam-pel's "Presentation of Awareness and Knowledge Composite of All the Important Points Opener of the Eye of New Intelligence*. Valois, NY: Snow Lion.
7. Mullin, Glenn H. (1998). *Living in the Face of Death: The Tibetan Tradition*. 2008 reprint: Snow Lion Publications, Ithica, New York.
8. Nyanaponika Thera (1965). *The Heart of Buddhist Meditation*. Boston: Weiser.
9. Pabongka Rinpoche; Ed. Trijang Rinpoche, transl. Michael Richards (3rd edn. 2006). *Liberation in the Palm of Your Hand, A Concise Discourse on the Path to Enlightenment*. Somerville, MA: Wisdom.
10. Powers, John. *History as Propaganda: Tibetan Exiles versus the People's Republic of China* (2004) Oxford University Press.
11. Ringu Tulku. *The Ri-Me Philosophy of Jamgon Kongtrul the Great: A Study of the Buddhist Lineages of Tibet*. Shambhala.
12. Smith, E. Gene (2001). *Among Tibetan Texts: History and Literature of the Himalayan Plateau*. Boston: Wisdom Publications.
13. Sopa, Geshe Lhundup; Jeffrey Hopkins (1977). *Practice and Theory of Tibetan Buddhism*. New Delhi: B.I. Publications.
14. Tsong-kha-pa; the Lamrim Chenmo Translation Committee; Joshua Cutler, ed. in chief; Guy Newland, ed. (2002). *The Great Treatise on the Stages of the Path to Enlightenment, Volume II*. Canada: Snow Lion.

11

Buddhism in Japan

Chronology

- **654:** Dosho introduces the Hosso (Faxiang) school to Japan.
- **736:** Bodhisena introduces the Kegon (Huayan) school to Japan.
- **753:** Ganjin introduces the Ritsu (Lü, Vinaya) school to Japan.
- **807:** Saichô introduces the Tendai (Tientai) school to Japan.
- **816:** Kûkai founds the Shingon school.
- **1175:** Hônen introduces the Jodo (Pure Land) school to Japan.
- **1191:** Eisai introduces the Rinzai (Linji) school to Japan.
- **1227:** Dogen introduces the Soto (Caodung) school to Japan.
- **1253:** Nichiren founds the Nichiren school.
- **1282:** Nichiren school begins to split into several schools.
- **1654:** Ingen introduces the Obaku (Huangbo) school to Japan.

In 467 AD, according to the Chinese historic treatise Liang

Shu, five monks from Gandhara traveled to the country of Fusang (Chinese:, Jp: *Fusô*: "The country of the extreme East" beyond the sea, probably eastern Japan), where they introduced Buddhism:

> Fusang is located to the east of China, 20,000 *li* (1,500 kilometers) east of the state of *Da Han* (itself east of the state of *Wa* in modern Kyûshû, Japan). (....) In former times, the people of Fusang knew nothing of the Buddhist religion, but in the second year of Da Ming of the Song Dynasty (467 AD), five monks from Kipin [Kabul region of Gandhara] travelled by ship to Fusang. They propagated Buddhist doctrine, circulated scriptures and drawings, and advised the people to relinquish worldly attachments. As a result the customs of Fusang changed.
>
> —Liang Shu, 7th century CE

It is remarkable that the history of Buddhism in Japan can be roughly divided into three periods, namely the Nara period (710 - 794), the Heian period (794–1185) and the post-Heian period (1185 onwards). Each period saw the introduction of new doctrines and upheavals in existing schools.

In modern times, the main paths of Buddhism are Amidist (Pure Land) schools, Nichiren Buddhism, Shingon Buddhism and Zen Buddhism. The root of the Japanese word for Buddhism, *bukkyô*comes from(*butsu*, "buddha") + (*kyô*, "teaching").

Arrival along the Silk Road

The arrival of Buddhism in Japan is ultimately consequence of the first contacts between China and Central Asia which occurred with the opening of the Silk Road in the 2nd century BC, following the travels of Zhang Qian between 138 and 126 BC, which culminated with the official introduction of Buddhism in China in 67 AD.

Historians generally agree that by the middle of the 1st century, the religion had penetrated to areas north of the Huai River.

The initial period saw the introduction of the six great Chinese schools on the Japanese Archipelago including the *Huayan* and *Lü*, that became respectively the *Kegon* and *Ritsu* in Japanese. In terms of geography, the six sects were centered around the capital city of Nara, where great temples such as the Tôdai-ji and Hokki-ji were erected. However, the Buddhism of this early period – later known as the Nara period – was not a practical religion, being more the domain of learned priests whose official function was to pray for the peace and prosperity of the state and imperial house.

This kind of Buddhism had little to offer the illiterate and uneducated masses, and led to the growth of "people's priests" who were not ordained and had no formal Buddhist training. Their practice was a combination of Buddhist and Taoist elements, and the incorporation of shamanistic features of the indigenous religion. These figures became immensely popular, and were a source of criticism towards the sophisticated academic and bureaucratic Buddhism of the capital.

Nara Period

It is pertinent to note that introduction of Buddhism to Japan is securely dated to 552 in *Nihon Shoki*, when Seong of Baekje sent monks from Korea to Nara to introduce the eight doctrinal schools. The powerful Soga clan played a key role in the early spread of Buddhism in the country. Initial uptake of the new faith was slow, and Buddhism only started to spread some years later when Empress Suiko openly encouraged the acceptance of Buddhism among all Japanese people. In 607, in order to obtain copies of Sutras, an imperial envoy was dispatched to the Sui dynasty China. As time progressed and the number of Buddhist clergy increased, the offices of *Sojo* (archbishop) and *Sozu* (bishop) were created. By 627, there were 46 Buddhist temples, 816 Buddhist priests, and 569 Buddhist nuns in Japan. There were traditionally six schools of Buddhism in Nara Japan: *Ritsu* (Vinaya), *Jojitsu* (Satyasiddhi), *Kusha* (Abhidharma) *Sanron* (Madhyamika), *Hosso* (Yogacara), and *Kegon* (Hua-yen).

However they were not exclusive schools, and temples were apt to have scholars versed in several of the schools. It has been suggested that they can best be thought of as "study groups".

Different Schools

Ritsu

Founded by Dàoxuân, China, c. 650 CE first introduction to Japan, 753 CE. The Ritsu school specialized in the Vinaya (the monastic rules in the Tripitaka). They used the Dharmagupta version of the vinaya which is known in Japanese as *Shibunritsu.*

Jojitsu

The Satyasiddhi school is considered to be an offshoot of the Sautrantika school, one of the Nikaya schools of Indian Buddhism (see early Buddhist schools). They were distinguished by a rejection of the Abhidharma as not being the "word of the Buddha". The name means literally, "Ends with the Sutras", which refers to the traditional order of texts in the Tripitaka—vinaya, sutra, abhidharma.

Kusha

This school was introduced into Japan from China

during the Nara period (710–784). The school takes its name from its authoritative text, the Abidatsuma-kusha-ron(Abhidharma-kosa), by the 4th- or 5th-century Indian philosopher Vasubandhu. The Kusha school is considered to be an offshoot of the Indian Sarvastivada school.

Sanron

Three-Discourse School; a Madhyamika school which developed in China based on two discourses by Nagarjuna and one by Aryadeva. This school was transmitted to Japan in the 7th century. Madhyamika is one of the two most important Mahayana philosophies, and reemphasizes the original Buddhist teachings that phenomena are neither truly existent or absolutely non-existent, but are characterized by impermanence and insubstantially.

Hosso

The Yogacara (*Yugagyouha*) schools are based on early Indian Buddhist thought by masters such as Vasubandhu, and are also known as "consciousness only" since they teach a form of idealism which posits that all phenomena are phenomena of the mind. The Hosso school was founded by Xuanzang (Jp. *Genjo*), China, c. 630 CE, and introduced to Japan in 654 CE. The *Discourse on the Theory of Consciousness-Only* (Jo yuishikiron is an important text for the Hosso school.

Kegon

Also known by its Chinese name Huayen, the Kegon school was founded by Dushun (*Dojun*), China, c. 600 CE, and introduced to Japan by Bodhisena in 736 CE. The Avatamsaka Sutra (*Kegonkyô* is the central text for the Kegon school. The Shin'yaku Kegonkyô Ongi Shiki is an early Japanese annotation of this sûtra.

Heian Period

The Late Nara period saw the introduction of Esoteric Buddhism (Jp. *mikkyo*) to Japan from China, by Kûkai and Saichô, who founded the Shingon and Tendai schools. The later Heian period saw the formation of the first truly Japanese school of Buddhism, that of Nichiren.

Main Schools

Tendai

Known as Tiantai in China, the Tendai school was founded by Zhiyi (Jp *Chigi*) in China, c. 550 CE. In 804 Saichô traveled to China to study at the Tiantai teachings, at Mount Tiantai. However before his return he also studied, and was initiated into the practice of the Vajrayana - with emphasis on the Mahavairocana Sutra. The primary text of Tiantai is Lotus Sutra (*Hokkekyo*, but when Saichô established his school in Japan he incorporated the study and practice of Vajrayana as well.

Shingon

Kûkai traveled to China in 804 as part of the same expedition as Saichô. In the T'ang capital he studied esoteric Buddhism, Sanskrit and received initiation from Huikuo. On returning to Japan Kûkai eventually managed to establish Shingon as a school in its own right. Kûkai received two lineages of teaching—one based on the Mahavairocana Sutra (*Dainichikyo*, and the other based on the Vajrashekhara.

Kamakura, Muromachi to Modern Period

The Kamakura period saw the introduction of the two schools that had perhaps the greatest impact on the country: (1) the Amidist Pure Land schools, promulgated by evangelists such as Genshin and articulated by monks such as Hônen, which emphasize salvation through faith in Amitabha and remain the largest Buddhist sect in Japan (and throughout Asia); and (2) the more philosophical Zen schools, promulgated by monks such as Eisai and Dogen, which emphasize liberation through the insight of meditation, which were equally rapidly adopted by the upper classes and had a profound impact on Japanese culture.

In Muromachi period, the Zen school, particularly Rinzai, obtained help of the Muromachi shogunate and the Emperor, and accomplished considerable development. With the Meiji Restoration in 1868, the new government adopted a strong anti-Buddhist attitude, and a movement to eradicate Buddhism and bring Shinto to ascendancy arose throughout the country.

Japan has seen a minor decline in Buddhist practice in the 21st century, with roughly 100 temples a year closing. However 70% of Japanese people still follow Buddhism in some form, and 90% of Japanese funerals are conducted according to Buddhist rites.

Nichiren Buddhism

The schools of Nichiren Buddhism trace themselves to the monk Nichiren ("Sun-Lotus") and the proclamation of his teachings in CE 1253. Doctrinally the schools focus on the Lotus Sutra *Myoho Renge Kyô*; abbrev. *Hokkekyô*), but practice centers on the mantra *Nam(u) Myôhô Renge Kyô*. Nichiren Buddhism split into several denominations after the death of Nichiren, typically represented by tradition-oriented schools such as Nichiren Shu and Nichiren Shoshu and "new religions" such as Soka Gakkai, Rissho Kosei Kai, and Reiyukai. See Nichiren Buddhism for a more complete list.

In Japan, Buddhist art started to develop as the country

converted to Buddhism in 548 CE. Some tiles from the Asuka period (shown above), the first period following the conversion of the country to Buddhism, display a strikingly classical style, with ample Hellenistic dress and realistically-rendered body shape characteristic of Greco-Buddhist art.

Buddhist became extremely varied in its expression. Many elements of Greco-Buddhist art remain to this day however, such as the Hercules inspiration behind the Nio guardian deities in front of Japanese Buddhist temples, or representations of the Buddha reminiscent of Greek art such as the Buddha in Kamakura.

Deities

Various other Greco-Buddhist artistic influences can be found in the Japanese Buddhist pantheon, the most striking of which being that of the Japanese wind god Fujin. In consistency with Greek iconography for the wind god Boreas, the Japanese wind god holds above his head with his two hands a draping or "wind bag" in the same general attitude. The abundance of hair have been kept in the Japanese rendering, as well as exaggerated facial features.

Another Buddhist deity, named Shukongoshin, one of the wrath-filled protector deities of Buddhist temples in Japan, is also an interesting case of transmission of the image of the famous Greek god Herakles to the Far-East along the Silk Road. Herakles was used in Greco-Buddhist art to represent Vajrapani, the protector of the Buddha, and his representation was then used in China and Japan to depict the protector gods of Buddhist temples.

The artistic inspiration from Greek floral scrolls is found quite literally in the decoration of Japanese roof tiles, one of the only remaining element of wooden architecture throughout centuries. The clearest one are from 7th century Nara temple building tiles, some of them exactly depicting vines and grapes. These motifs have evolved towards more symbolic representations, but essentially remain to this day in many Japanese traditional buildings.

REFERENCES

1. Asakawa, K., and Henry Cabot Lodge (Ed.). *Japan From the Japanese Government History*.
2. Eliot, Sir Charles. *Japanese Buddhism*. London: Kegan Paul International, 2005.
3. Hoffman, Michael, "Buddhism's arrival, Shinto's endurance", *Japan Times*, March 14, 2010, p. 7.
4. *Kodansha's* furigana *Japanese Dictionary*. Japan: Kodansha Inc.. 1999.
5. Powers, John (2000). "Japanese Buddhism". *A Concise Encyclopedia of Buddhism*. 1. Oxford: Oneworld Publications.

12

Buddhism in the West

It is remarkable that Buddhism is mainly concentrated in South Asia and South eastern and far eastern Asia. Despite that it has reached global dimensions. In the present chapter we will discuss the status of Buddhism in Western countries.

In fact, Buddhism in the West broadly encompasses the knowledge and practice of Buddhism outside of Asia. Occasional intersections between Western civilization and the Buddhist world have been occurring for thousands of years, but it was not until the era of European colonization of Buddhist countries in Asia during the 19th century that detailed knowledge of Buddhism became available to large numbers of people in the west as a result of accompanying scholarly endeavours.

In the latter half of the 19th century, Buddhism came to the attention of Western intellectuals. The first English translation of the *Tibetan Book of the Dead* was published in 1927 the book is said to have attracted many westerners to Tibetan Buddhism.

Remarkably, first Buddhists to arrive in the United States were Chinese and Japanese immigrants who established many temples mainly for their own purposes of worship. Immigrant monks soon began teaching to western audiences, as well. The broader New Age spirituality of the hippie movement proved very receptive to Buddhist themes. In 1959 Suzuki Roshi (a Japanese teacher) arrived in San Francisco. At the time of Suzuki's arrival, Zen had become a hot topic amongst some groups in the United States, especially beatniks. In 1965, monks from Sri Lanka established the Washington Buddhist Vihara in Washington, D.C., the first Theravada monastic community in the United States. Vietnamese Zen monk Nhat Hanh became well known in France and the United States. In the 1970s, interest in Tibetan Buddhism grew dramatically.

Today, Buddhism is practiced by large numbers of people in the Americas, Europe and Oceania. Buddhism has become the fastest-growing religion in Australia and some other Western nations. Many Hollywood movies with Buddhist themes, such as *Kundun*, *Little Buddha* and *Seven Years in Tibet*, have had considerable commercial success.

Greco-Buddhism

Alexander the Great's conquest of much of Central Asia set the stage for contacts between the civilisations of Greece and India. Alexander himself met an Indian sage, who later burned himself. The Hellenistic influence in the area, furthered by Seleucids and the successive Greco-Bactrian and Indo-Greek kingdoms, interacted with Buddhism, as exemplified by the emergence of Greco-Buddhist art.

Greco-Buddhism is the cultural merging between the cultures of Hellenism and Buddhism, which developed over a period of close to eight centuries in Central Asia in the area corresponding to modern-day Afghanistan and Pakistan, between the 4th century BCE and the 5th century CE.

Greco-Buddhism influenced the artistic (and, possibly, conceptual) development of Buddhism, and in particular Mahayana Buddhism, before it was adopted by Central and Northeastern Asia from the 1st century CE, ultimately spreading to China, Korea, Japan, Vietnam, and Mongolia.

Buddhism and the Roman World

Several instances of interaction between Buddhism and the Roman Empire are documented by Classical and early Christian writers. Roman historical accounts describe an embassy sent by the Indian king Pandion (Pandya?), also named Porus, to Augustus around 13 CE. The embassy was travelling with a diplomatic letter in Greek, and one of its members was an Indian religious man (sramana) who burned himself alive in Athens to demonstrate his faith. The event created a sensation and was described by Nicolaus of Damascus, who met the embassy at Antioch, and related by Strabo (XV,1,73 and Dio Cassius.

A tomb was made for the sramana, still visible in the time of Plutarch, which bore the following inscription:

Notably, These accounts at least indicate that Indian religious men (Sramanas, to which the Buddhists belonged, as opposed to Hindu Brahmanas) were visiting Mediterranean countries. However, the term sramana is a general term for Indian religious man in Jainism, Buddhism, and Âjîvika. It is not clear which religious tradition the man belongs to in this case.

In the latter half of the 19th century, Buddhism (along with many other religions and philosophies) came to the attention of Western intellectuals. These included the pessimistic German philosopher Schopenhauer, who encountered Buddhism, and Eastern thought in general, after having devised a philosophical system of considerable compatibility. The American philosopher Henry David Thoreau translated a Buddhist sutra from French into English.

There are frequent comparisons between Buddhism and the German philosopher Friedrich Nietzsche, who praised Buddhism in his 1895 work *The Anti-Christ*, calling it "a hundred times more realistic than Christianity". Theologist David Loy argues that there is "a deep resonance between them" as "both emphasise the centrality of humans in a godless cosmos and neither looks to any external being or power for their respective solutions to the problem of existence".

The first English translation of the *Tibetan Book of the Dead* was published in 1927 and the reprint of 1935 carried a commentary from none other than C.G. Jung. The book is said to have attracted many westerners to Tibetan Buddhism. Western spiritual seekers were attracted to what they saw as the exotic and mystical tone of the Asian traditions, and created esoteric societies such as the Theosophical Society of H.P. Blavatsky. The Buddhist Society, London was founded by Theosophist Christmas Humphreys in 1924. At first Western Buddhology was hampered by poor translations (often translations of translations), but soon Western scholars such as Max Müller began to learn Asian languages and translate Asian texts. During the 20th century the German writer Hermann Hesse showed great interest in Eastern religions, writing a book entitled *Siddhartha*.

Remarkably, American beat generation writer Jack Kerouac became a well-known literary Buddhist, for his roman-a-clef *The Dharma Bums* and other works. Also influential was Alan Watts, who wrote several books on Zen and Buddhism. The cultural re-evaluations of the hippie generation in the late 1960s and early 1970s led to a re-discovery of Buddhism, which seemed to promise a more methodical path to happiness than Christianity and a way out of the perceived spiritual bankruptcy and complexity of Western life.

Buddhists Arrive in the West

The first Buddhists to arrive in the United States were Chinese. Hired as cheap labor for the railroads and other expanding industries, they established temples in their settlements along the rail lines. At about the same time, immigrants from Japan began to arrive as laborers on Hawaiian plantations and central-California farms. In 1899, they established the Buddhist Missions of North America, later renamed the Buddhist Churches of America.

In 1959 a Japanese teacher, Shunryu Suzuki, arrived in San Francisco. At the time of Suzuki's arrival, Zen had become a hot topic amongst some groups in the United States, especially beatniks. Suzuki-roshi's classes were filled with those wanting to learn more about Buddhism, and the presence of a Zen master inspired the students.

In 1965 Philip Kapleau traveled to Rochester, NY with the permission of his teacher, Haku'un Yasutani to form the Rochester Zen Center. At this time there were few if any American citizens that had trained in Japan with ordained Buddhist teachers. Kapleau had spent 13 years (1952-1965) and over 20 sesshin before being allowed to come back and open his own center. During his time in Japan after World War II, Kapleau wrote his seminal work; The Three Pillars of Zen. In 1965, monks from Sri Lanka established the Washington Buddhist Vihara in Washington, D.C., the first Theravada monastic community in the United States. The Vihara was quite accessible to

English-speakers, and Vipassana meditation was part of its activities. However, the direct influence of the Vipassana movement would not reach the U.S. until a group of Americans returned there in the early 1970s after studying with Vipassana masters in Asia.

Notably, the 1970s, interest in Tibetan Buddhism grew dramatically. This was fuelled in part by the 'shangri-la' view of this country and also because Western media agencies are largely sympathetic with the 'Tibetan Cause'. All four of the main Tibetan Buddhist schools became well known. Tibetan lamas such as the Karmapa (Rangjung Rigpe Dorje), Chögyam Trungpa Rinpoche, Geshe Wangyal, Geshe Lhundub Sopa, Dezhung Rinpoche, Sermey Khensur Lobsang Tharchin, Tarthang Tulku, Lama Yeshe and Thubten Zopa Rinpoche all established teaching centers in the West from the 1970s. Perhaps the most widely visible Buddhist teacher in the west is the much-travelled Tenzin Gyatso, the current Dalai Lama, who first visited the United States in 1979. As the exiled political leader of Tibet, he is now a popular cause célèbre in the west. His early life was depicted in glowing terms in Hollywood films such as *Kundun* and *Seven Years in Tibet*. He has attracted celebrity religious followers such as Richard Gere and Adam Yauch.

Besides this a number of Americans who had served in the Korean or Vietnam Wars stayed out in Asia for a period, seeking to understand both the horror they had witnessed and its context. A few of these were eventually ordained as monks in both the Mahayana and Theravadan tradition, and upon returning home became influential meditation teachers establishing such centres as the Insight Meditation Society in America, such as Bill Porter. Another contributing factor in the flowering of Buddhist thought in the West was the popularity of Zen amongst the counter-culture poets and activists of the 60's, due to the writings of Alan Watts, D.T. Suzuki and Philip Kapleau. Historically, Buddhism has absorbed elements of the culture of the countries in which it is practiced. This can be seen in the artistic style of Buddha statues; a Chinese statue looks different from a Thai, which differs from a Sri Lankan, and similarly across most Asian countries. Different local customs are included also, and may influence the form of rituals and ceremonies.

There is a general distinction between Buddhism brought to the West by Asian immigrants, which may be Mahayana or a traditional East Asian mix, and Buddhism as practiced by converts, which is often Zen, Pure Land, Indian Vipassana or Tibetan Buddhism. Some Western Buddhists are actually non-denominational and accept teachings from a variety of different sects, which is far less frequent in Asia. The largest Buddhist temple in the Southern Hemisphere is the Nan Tien Temple (translated as "Southern Paradise Temple"), situated at Wollongong, Australia, while the largest Buddhist temple in the Western Hemisphere is the Hsi Lai Temple (translated as "Coming West Temple"), in California, USA. Both are operated by the Fo Guang Shan Order, founded in Taiwan, and around 2003 the Grand Master, Venerable Hsing Yun, asked for Nan Tien Temple and Buddhist practice there to be operated by native Australians citizens within about thirty years.

Western Buddhism Today

Today, Buddhism is practiced by increasing numbers of people in the Americas, Europe and Oceania. Buddhism has become the fastest growing religion in Australia and some other Western nations.

Tibetan Buddhism in the West has remained largely

traditional, keeping all the doctrine, ritual, faith, devotion, etc. An example of a large Buddhist group established in the West is the Foundation for the Preservation of the Mahayana Tradition (FPMT) is a network of Buddhist centers focusing on what it claims to be traditional Tibetan Buddhism. Founded in 1975 by Lamas Thubten Yeshe and Thubten Zopa Rinpoche, who began teaching Buddhism to Western students in Nepal, the FPMT has grown to encompass more than 142 teaching centers in 32 countries. Like many Tibetan Buddhist groups, the FPMT does not have "members" per se, or elections, but is managed by a self-perpetuating board of trustees chosen by its "spiritual director" (head lama).

Notably, a feature of Buddhism in the West today is the emergence of other groups which, even though they draw on traditional Buddhism, are in fact an attempt at creating a new style of Buddhist practice. Controversial lama Chögyam Trungpa, the founder of the Shambhala meditation movement, claimed in his teachings that his intention was to strip the ethnic baggage away from traditional methods of working with the mind and to deliver the essence of those teachings to his western students. Chögyam Trungpa also founded Naropa University in Boulder, Colorado in 1974. Trungpa's movement has also found particular success in the Canadian province of Nova Scotia, Shambhala International being based out of Halifax. An associated monastery Gampo Abbey was also built near the community of Pleasant Bay. Another example of schools evolving new idioms for the transmission of the dharma are the Friends of the Western Buddhist Order (FWBO), founded by Sangharakshita in 1967, and the Diamond Way Organisation founded by Ole Nydahl, who has founded more than 600 buddhist centers across the world.

Buddhist imagery is increasingly appropriated by modern pop culture and for commercial use. For example, the Dalai Lama's image was used in a campaign celebrating leadership by Apple Computer. Similarly, Tibetan monasteries have been used as backdrops to perfume advertisements in magazines. Hollywood movies such as *Kundun*, *Little Buddha* and *Seven Years in Tibet* have had considerable commercial success.

It is pertinent to note that Buddhist practitioners in the West are catered for by a minor industry providing such items as charm boxes, meditation cushions, and ritual implements. This is akin to the various industries providing ritual items and publishing scripture historically, however T. Shakya has criticized this industry as the publication of Buddhist books uproots small forests and consequently kills thousands of insects.

Here after we shall discuss the status of Buddhism in different western countries individually.

RUSSIA

Historically, Buddhism was incorporated into Russian lands as early as the late 15th century, when Russian explorers travelled to and settled in Siberia and what is now the Russian Far East. It is also believed that Indian King Ashoka had sent monks to spread Buddhism all over the world including Siberia.

The main form of Buddhism in Russia is the Karma Kagyu school of Tibetan Buddhism, the major sub-sect of the greater Vajrayana Buddhism. Although Tibetan Buddhism is most often associated with the peoples of Tibet, in the north the sect spread into southwestern and northern China, Mongolia, and finally Russia. In the south, it took hold in Bhutan and parts of northern India and Nepal. Afterwards, it began to spread into the geographically and culturally adjacent Russian constituent regions known today as: Amur Oblast, Buryatia, Chita Oblast, Tuva Republic, and Khabarovsk Krai. There is also Kalmykia, another constituent republic of Russia that is in fact the only Buddhist region in Europe, perhaps paradoxically located to the north of the Caucasus.

Tibetan Buddhism is primarily practiced by the indigenous peoples in these various regions of central and eastern Russia, except for a few Russian converts based mainly in the larger cities such as St. Petersburg or Moscow, where there is greater access to urban Buddhist centers or facilities of the like.

The other major form of Buddhism found in Russia is the more commonly known Mahayana Buddhism, primary practiced by the Vietnamese or Chinese immigrant communities based mainly in the large cities.

The Russian Federation, and perhaps strangely, Austria are the only two European states today that recognize Buddhism as an "official", though not necessarily "state religion" in their respective countries. On top of that, Russia also recognizes it, along with Islam, Judaism, and of course Orthodox Christianity, as native to Russian soil in the 1993 Constitution of the Russian Federation. All other religious groups are unrecognized, and must officially register and be subject to rejection by the state. There are a few dozen Buddhist university-monasteries throughout Russia, but concentrated in the Russian Far East and Siberia, known in Russian as Datsans. The central body of Russian Buddhism is the Karma Kagyu Buddhist Association of the Russian Federation.

Adherents to Buddhism account for approximately 700,000 in the Russian Federation, about 0.5% of the total population.

UNITED KINGDOM

Buddhism in the United Kingdom has a small but growing number of adherents which, according to a Buddhist organisation, is mainly the result of conversion. In the UK census for 2001, there were about 152,000 people who registered their religion as Buddhism, and about 174,000 who cited religions other than Christianity, Buddhism, Hinduism, Judaism, Islam, Jainism and Sikhism. This latter figure is likely to include some people who follow the traditional Chinese mixture of religions including Buddhism.

At the 2001 Census, 144,453 people in England and Wales ticked the Buddhist box. Of these, the main places of birth were UK 66,522, Far East 59,931 and South Asia 9,847, and the main ethnic groups were white 56,040, Chinese 34,304, Asian 13,919, Mixed 4,647, Black 1,507 and Other 34,036. In Scotland, people were asked both their current religion and that they were brought up in. 6,830 people gave Buddhism as their current religion, and 4,704 said they were brought up in it, with an overlap of 3,146. In Northern Ireland, the published report which listed religions and philosophies in order of size reported 'Buddhist' at 533.

The earliest Buddhist influences were with the Theravada traditions of Burma, Thailand, and Sri Lanka was primarily scholarly, and a tradition of study grew up that eventually resulted in the foundation of the Pali Text Society, which undertook the huge task of translating the Pali Canon of Theravada Buddhist texts into English. The start of interest in Buddhism as a path of practice was pioneered by the Theosophists, Madame Blavatsky and Colonel Olcott, and in 1880 they became the first Westerners to receive the refuges and precepts, the ceremony by which one traditionally becomes a Buddhist. they were also later received into the Hindu religion. Theosophical and Theravadin influences continued throughout the early twentieth century, though the 1950s saw the development of interest in Zen Buddhism. In 1967 Kagyu Samyé Ling Monastery and Tibetan Centre was founded in Eskdalemuir, Scotland, and is the largest Tibetan Buddhist centre in Western Europe. The Manjushri Kadampa Buddhist Centre in Conishead Priory located just outside of Barrow-in-Furness, Cumbria is a large New Kadampa Tradition Tibetan Buddhist centre. The priory established by Geshe Kelsang Gyatso in 1975 claims to be 'the mother centre from which around 1100 Kadampa Buddhist centres have been set up worldwide'.

A Theravada monastery following the Thai Forest Tradition of Ajahn Chah was established at Chithurst Buddhist Monastery in Sussex, and has established branches elsewhere in the country. A lay meditation tradition of Thai origin is represented by the Samatha Trust, with its headquarters cum retreat centre in Wales. Soto Zen has a priory at Throssel Hole Buddhist Abbey in Northumberland.

As well as the Friends of the Western Buddhist Order there are other Buddhism-based new religious movements such as the New Kadampa Tradition and Sôka Gakkai International.

Buddhism in England

Buddhism is quite a recent religion to arrive in England. Despite this, 144,453 people declared themselves to be Buddhist at the 2001 Census.

Theosophical and Theravadin influences grew in England during the early twentieth century, particularly with the foundation in 1924 of London's Buddhist Society and the Theravadin London Buddhist Vihara in Chiswick in 1926. A slow trickle from England travelled to Asia to take monastic ordination, mainly as Theravadin monks. Kapilavaddho Bhikkhu introduced the Dhammakaya tradition to the UK in 1954 in this way and founded the English Sangha Trust in 1955. A few Asian monks came to live in England.

In 1967, Englishman Sangharakshita (1925-), who had spent time in the east as a Theravadin monk founded the Friends of the Western Buddhist Order, the first home-grown Buddhist movement. He was followed by other westerners who had studied in the East, and by Eastern teachers, particularly refugee Tibetan Lamas, and under the influence of these teachers a large and diverse British Buddhist world has emerged. At the 2001 census, 36% of those stating they were Buddhist lived in London and 38% of Buddhists were white.

The Manjushri Kadampa Buddhist Centre in Conishead Priory located just outside of Barrow-in-Furness, Cumbria is a large New Kadampa Tradition Tibetan Buddhist centre. The priory established by Geshe Kelsang Gyatso in 1975 claims to be 'the mother centre from which around 1100 Kadampa Buddhist centres have been set up worldwide'.

A Theravada monastery consisting mainly of Westerners following the Thai Forest Tradition of Ajahn Chah was established at Chithurst Buddhist Monastery in Sussex, and has established branches elsewhere in the country. A lay meditation tradition of Thai origin is represented by the Samatha Trust, with its headquarters cum retreat centre in Wales. Soto Zen has a priory at Throssel Hole Buddhist Abbey in Northumberland.

Wales

Buddhism in Wales has a relatively short history, having only really established a presence in the country in the 20th Century. 5,407 people declared themselves Buddhist in the 2001 census, representing a number of Buddhist traditions. Tibetan Buddhism is particularly well represented with branches of several different traditions and lineages. Zen Buddhism has several groups in Wales and three Soto Zen masters are currently resident and actively teaching. The Samatha Trust, a lay Theravada group, have their headquarters in Wales as does the Tibetan group, Awakened Heart Sangha. The Friends of the Western Buddhist Order have a number of groups and a large Cardiff Buddhist Centre.

The Buddhist Council of Wales has a growing number of Buddhist organisations and groups listed on their website. The Council is active in representing Buddhism and has two delegates on the National Assembly for Wales Faith Communities Forum and two on the Interfaith Council for Wales.

One notable Welsh person to have converted to Buddhism is former rugby star Ricky Evans.

DENMARK

Buddhism is the 4th largest religion in Denmark with approximately 20,000 - 25,000 members.

In the 19th century, knowledge about Buddhism was brought back from expeditions that explored the East and but interest was mainly from authors,Buddhologists and Philologists. In 1921, Dr. Christian F. Melbye founded the first Buddhist Society in Denmark, but it was later dissolved in 1950 before his death in 1953. In the 1950s, there was a revival in interest towards Buddhism, especially Tibetan Buddhism and Hannah and Ole Nydahl, founded the first Karma Kagyu Buddhist centers in Copenhagen. The third wave of Buddhism came in the 1980s, when refugees from Vietnam, Sri Lanka and China came to Denmark. Some Buddhist women, especially those from Thailand, came to Denmark seeking Danish husbands.

Accurate figures for the number of Buddhists in Denmark is not known, as it is illegal to record people's faiths in Denmark. However, according to Jørn Borup (Department of the Study of Religion at the University of Aarhus), are where approximately 18-20,000 Buddhists in Denmark today, of which 80% are Asian immigrants. Of these, 7,000 - 9,000 from Vietnam and 6,000 are from Thailand. There are about 40 different Buddhist groups in Denmark, but only 6 of them have the status of recognized religion by the state. Despite Buddhism being a minority religion, the Dalai Lama is the Danes preferred religious role model.

Schools

Accurate figures for the number of buddhists in each school are not known. But it has been estimated that of the 20,000 Buddhists in Denmark, 3,000 are Tibetan Buddhists, and 1,000 are part of the Japanese Soka Gakkai. There are fifteen different schools of Tibetan Buddhism represented in Denmark.

Theravadan

Theravada Buddhismin Denmark is practised primarily by Thais and Sri Lankans and between 90 and 95% of the 7,700 Danish Thais are Buddhists. Thai Buddhist temples include the Watpa in Copenhagen, Wat Thai Denmark Brahmavihara Buddhist Monastery and the Wat Buddha, Denmark. 900 of the Sri Lankan Tamil refugees are buddhist.

These Buddhist émigrés seem almost invisible in Denmark, partly because Buddhism is generally not a missionary religion, and they rarely take part in the larger social debate, partly because they have low unemployment and crime rates and therefore not very interesting subjects for the media.

Diamond Way

Diamond Way Buddhism was founded in Denmark by Hannah and Ole Nydahl. It is a Tibetan Buddhist group within the Karma Kagyu, one of the major Tibetan schools. The very first center was opened in Copenhagen in 1972 and relocated in 1975 to its current location. To this day Diamond Way Buddhism has increased to nearly 600 centers world wide. This school is the largest Vajrayana school in Denmark, with 1,200 Danish affiliates.

Zen

Zen Buddhism is amongst the smallest schools of Buddhism in Denmark. It has 7 groups and no more than 100 practitioners.

Soka Gakka

The Soka Gakkai group was established in Denmark in 1983 and has approximately 800 members in 54 local groups.

Attempts at Unity

In 1991, the Tibetan-born Lakha Lama tried to establish a trans-sectarian Buddhist umbrella organization called the Buddhist Forum and since 1993 it has been a member of the European Buddhist Union despite having only two hundred paying members. Another Lakha Lama project called *Phendeling* has subsequently taken over its role and now includes some non-Vajrayana Buddhist groups. Two groups, the Diamond Way Buddhism and Sokka Gakkai have not been invited to join the umbrella organizations. In the early 1990s there was a split between Ole Nydahl and the rest of the groups during the Karmapa controversy. One of two candidates was about to be chosen as the one new reincarnation of the 16th Karmapa. Ole Nydahl was supported Trinley Thaye Dorje whilst Urgyen Trinley Dorje was supported by most other Buddhist groups and the Dalai Lama

The exiled Tibetan leader, the Dalai Lama has visited Denmark several times. He first visited in 1973 to help inaugurate the first Karma Kagyu center founded by the Nydahls. He came back in 1996 for an official visit, but was not met by the Danish prime minister at that time Poul Nyrup Rasmussen who said that he was too busy, which he said again when the Dalai Lama re-visited in 2000. However, he did meet him in the airport just before he left.

In 2003, the Dalai Lama returned and was officially welcomed by Rasmussen's successor Anders Fogh Rasmussen with the backing of the entire government, despite protests from China.

FRANCE

Alexandra David-Néel was an important early French Buddhist. She is best known for her 1924 visit to the forbidden (to foreigners) city of Lhasa, capital of Tibet, and wrote more than 30 books about Buddhism, philosophy, and her travels. In 1911 Alexandra traveled to India, to further her study of Buddhism. She was invited to the royal monastery of Sikkim, where she met Maharaj Kumar (crown prince) Sidkeon Tulku. She became Sidkeong's "confidante and spiritual sister" (according to Ruth Middleton), and perhaps his lover (Foster & Foster). She also met the thirteenth Dalai Lama twice in 1912, and had the opportunity to ask him many questions about Buddhism—a feat unprecedented for a European woman at that time. In the late 1960s and early 1970s, Buddhist teachers of various traditions began to visit France.

It is pertinent to note that Buddhism is widely reported to be the third largest religion in France, after Christianity, and Islam.

France has over two hundred Buddhist meditation centers, including about twenty sizable retreat centers in rural areas. The Buddhist population mainly consists of Chinese and Vietnamese immigrants, with a substantial minority of native French converts and "sympathizers." The rising popularity of Buddhism in France has been the subject of considerable discussion in the French media and academy in recent years.

In the early 1990s, the French Buddhist Union (UBF, founded in 1986) estimated there to be 600,000 to 650,000 Buddhists in France, with 150,000 French converts among them. In 1999, sociologist Frédéric Lenoir estimated there are 10,000 converts and up to 5 million "sympathizers," although other researchers have questioned these numbers. A 1997 opinion poll counted as sympathizers young people who feel "an intellectual affinity with Buddhism or expressed a sympathy to a Buddhist worldview."

Zen Buddhist Communities

Taisen Deshimaru was a Japanese Zen Buddhist who founded numerous zendos in France. Thich Nhat Hanh, a Nobel Peace Prize-nominated, Vietnamese-born Zen Buddhist, founded the Unified Buddhist Church (Eglise Bouddhique Unifiée) in France in 1969. Plum Village, a monastery and retreat center in the Dordogne in southern France, is his residence and the headquarters of his international sangha.

Tibetan Buddhist Communities

By the late 1990s, it has been estimated that there are more than 140 Tibetan Buddhist meditation centers in France. The first Tibetan Buddhist communities in France were established in the early 1970s. The highest-ranking head of schools to reside in France, H.E. Phendé Khenchen, established his temple of E Wam Phendé Ling in 1973. He is of the Ngor school of Buddhism. Buddhism in France's growth was catalyzed by visits, in 1973 and 1974 respectively, of the Karmapa and Dalai Lama, two of the highest lamas. In 1975, Dudjom Rinpoche and Dilgo Khyentse Rinpoche, also very high lamas, visited Dordogne, where they established retreat centers with the help of Pema Wangyal Rinpoche. Pema Wangyal Rinpoche is the son of Kangyur Rinpoche, another high lama who was among the first to take western disciples.

Kalu Rinpoche, also a highly esteemed lama, led the first tradition three-year retreat for westerners in France starting in 1976. In the Kagyu lineage such retreats confer the title "lama" on those who complete them. It is estimated that sixty percent of the centers and monasteries in France are affiliated with the Kagyu school.

There are about twenty retreat centres representing all the different schools as well as many town-based centres which are under the direction of great Tibetan Buddhist masters. Dhagpo Kundreul Ling in Auvergne is said to be the biggest Buddhist monastery outside of Asia.

Some of the Larger Retreat Centers are:

- Chanteloube (Songtsen) in Dordogne (founded by Dilgo Khyentse Rinpoche)
- Dashang Kagyu Ling (Temple Des Milles Boudhas) in Bourgogne (founded by Kalu Rinpoche)
- Dechen Chöling in Limousin (founded by Sakyong Mipham Rinpoche)
- Dhagpo Dargye Lin in Archignac (founded by Shamar Rinpoche)
- Dhagpo Dedrol Ling in Plazac (founded by Gendun Rinpoche)
- Dhagpo Kundreul Ling in Auvergne (founded by Gendun Rinpoche)
- Dhagpo Kagyu Ling in Dordogne (founded by Gendun Rinpoche)
- Drukpa Plouray Pel Drukpay Tcheutsok in Brittany (founded by the Gyalwang Drukpa
- Karma Kagyu Tendar Ling in Dordogne ((founded by Karmapa Orgyen Trinley Dorje)
- E Wam Phendé Ling in Normandy (founded by H.E. Phende Kenchen)
- Karma Ling in Savoie (founded by Kalu Rinpoche)
- Karma Mingyur Ling in Isère (Montchardon) (founded by Lama Tonsang)
- Institut Vajra Yogini in the Tarn department (Lavaur)
- Lerab Ling in Languedoc-Roussillon (founded by Sogyal Rinpoche)
- Nalanda Buddhist Monastery (Lavaur, Tarn District), founded by Lama Yeshe and Lama Zopa Rinpoche of the FPMT (the Foundation for the Preservation of the Mahayana Tradition)

- Ogyen Kunzang Chöling in Alpes-de-Haute-Provence (founded by Robert Spatz)
- Orgyen Samye Chöling (Laugeral) in Dordogne (founded by Dudjom Rinpoche)
- Shechen Tennyi Dargyeling (La Sonnerie) in Dordogne (founded by Dilgo Khyentse Rinpoche)

Monasticism has traditionally been the bedrock of Tibetan Buddhism, but there were only a few dozen ordained French monks and nuns until the mid-1990s. However, there are now at least 300, most of whom were trained at the two monasteries in Auvergne. The most famous French monk in the Tibetan Buddhist tradition is Matthieu Ricard, a longtime student of Dilgo Khyenste Rinpoche who is the son of famous philosopher Jean-Francois Revel. He has published books on Buddhism which have contributed to interest in Buddhism and French Buddhists among the intelligentsia.

SWITZERLAND

According to the 2000 census of Switzerland, 21,305 Swiss residents (0.29% of the total population) self-identified as Buddhists. About a third of them were born in Thailand.

In 1978 the Swiss Buddhist Union *(Schweizerische Buddhistische Union / Union Suisse des Bouddhistes / Unione Buddhista Svizzera)* was founded by the Czech Buddhist *Mirko Fryba (Bhikkhu Kusalananda).*

It is pertinent to note that German Buddhist Nyanatiloka was an important early Buddhist in Switzerland and who planned to found a Buddhist monastery there. The writings of Swiss psychologist Carl Gustav Jung have many allusions to Buddhism. Max Ladner founded a Buddhist group in Zurich in 1942. In 1948, Ladner published the Buddhist journal "Die Einsicht". Geshe Rabten Rinpoche founded in 1977 in Mont-Pèlerin a Buddhist monastery and study centre for European monks, nuns and lay people as well. Switzerland also has Tibetan-Buddhist and Zen monasteries, among them the Tibet Institute Rikon located in Zell-Rikon im Tösstal in the Töss Valley in the canton of Zürich. In earlier censuses, Buddhism figured together with other non-Abrahamic traditions (mainly Hinduism) as "other churches and communities". These accounted for 0.12% in 1970, 0.19% in 1980, 0.42% in 1990 and 0.78% in 2000 (0.38% Hinduism, 0.29% Buddhism, 0.11% other).

SCOTLAND

The arrival of Buddhism in Scotland is relatively recent. In Scotland Buddhists represent 0.13% of the population (6,182). People were asked both their current religion and that they were brought up in. 6,830 people gave Buddhism as their current religion, and 4,704 said they were brought up in it, with an overlap of 3,146.

The earliest Buddhist influence on Scotland came through its imperial connections with South East Asia, and as a result the early connections were with the Theravada traditions of Burma, Thailand, and Sri Lanka. To begin with, 150 years ago, this response was primarily scholarly, and a tradition of study grew up that eventually resulted in the foundation of the Pali Text Society, which undertook the huge task of translating the Pali Canon of Theravada Buddhist texts into English.

The rate of growth was slow but steady through the century, and the 1950s saw the development of interest in Zen Buddhism. In 1967 Kagyu Samyé Ling Monastery and Tibetan Centre was founded by Tibetan lamas and refugees Chögyam Trungpa Rinpoche and Akong Rinpoche.

It is in Eskdalemuir, in south west Scotland and is the largest Tibetan Buddhist centre in Western Europe, and part of the Karma Kagyu tradition.

As well there are other Buddhism-based new religious movements such as the New Kadampa Tradition, Friends of the Western Buddhist Order and Sôka Gakkai International. The FWBO maintains a retreat centre at Balquhidder in the Trossachs.

Samyé Ling

Kagyu Samyé Ling Monastery and Tibetan Centre monastery—founded in 1967—includes the largest Buddhist temple in western Europe. There is an associated community on Holy Isle which is owned by Samyé Ling who belong to the Kagyu school of Tibetan Buddhism. The settlements on the island include the *Centre for World Peace and Health* and a retreat centre for nuns. Samyé Ling has also established centres in more than 20 countries, including Belgium, Ireland, Poland, South Africa, Spain and Switzerland.

BUDDHISM IN BELGIUM

It is pertinent to note that Buddhism is a small religion in Belgium but despite lack of official recognition by the Belgian government has grown rapidly in recent years. As of the 1997 estimate, 29,497 Belgian people identified their religion as Buddhist (about 0.29% of the total population)

Belgium has been comparatively slow in the absorption of Buddhism compared with other countries in Europe because there were no Buddhist countries amongst the territories colonized by Belgium. Alexandra David-Néel introduced the Maha Bodhi Society to the Congress of Free Thinkers in Brussels as early as 1910. There was reportedly a group of those interested in Buddhism who met in Brussels in the period between the Wars.

Buddhism came to the attention of Belgians academically in 1944 through the translations of Indologist Étienne Lamotte at the Catholic University of Leuven. Belgium has remained wary of new religions (even though in many cases they are historically much older than Christianity) and the general attitude has been illustrated by the Government publication of a blacklist of 189 organizations (including two Buddhist ones) in its 'witchhunt' for sects of 1997 and in the ongoing attitudes especially in the French-speaking community of Belgium.

Nonetheless, in 1999 there were about thirty active Buddhist organizations and centres in Belgium alone, representing all traditions of Buddhism. A Buddhist Union of Belgium was set up in 1997 bringing together the various centres of Buddhism in Belgium that had been established through charitable and private organizations. The 2001 census estimated that there were 10,000 Buddhists of Belgian nationality - however the numbers of Buddhists, even in the immigrant population exceeded 20,000.

The government was first approached on 10 June 2005 to grant official recognition for Buddhism - a process which is expected to be completed in 2008 Independent sources now estimate the numbers of Buddhists in Belgium at 29,467.

AUSTRIA

Buddhism is a legally recognized religion in Austria and it is followed by more than 10,000 Austrians. Although still small in absolute numbers (10,402 at the 2001 census), Buddhism in Austria enjoys widespread acceptance. A majority of Buddhists in the country are Austrian nationals (some of them naturalized after immigration from Asia, predominantly from the People's Republic of China and Vietnam), while a considerable number of them are foreign nationals.

As in most European countries, different branches and schools of Buddhism are represented by groups of varying sizes. Vienna not only has the largest number of foreign residents, but is also the place with the longest tradition of Buddhism in the country. Most of Austria's Buddhist temples and centres of practice can be found there; some with a specific Chinese, Vietnamese, Tibetan or Japanese appearance. The latest development has been the establishment of a "Buddhist Cemetery" around a stupa-like building for funeral ceremonies at the Vienna Central Cemetery.

Buddhism was officially recognized under Austrian law in 1983. Russia is the only other "European" country to forwardly recognize Buddhism as "native" to its own soil, giving it official status, along with Orthodox Christianity, Islam, and Judaism.

By the late 19th century, due to the influence of Arthur Schopenhauer and Richard Wagner, artists and intellectuals in the capital city of the Austro-Hungarian Empire started to take interest in Buddhism. Karl Eugen Neumann (1865-1915), who had met the composer Wagner in his father's house. took great interest in what he had heard about Buddhism. In 1884 he decided to become a Buddhist and study the original languages to be able 'to see for himself'. He managed to translate large parts of the Pali Canon into German before dying in Vienna at the age of fifty.

In 1913 in Java Arthur Fitz, a man from Graz became

the first recorded Austrian to be ordained as Buddhist monk, taking the name Bhikkhu Sono. 1923 saw the foundation of a "Buddhist Society" in Vienna and Austrians were among the participants at the 2nd International Buddhist Congress in Paris in 1937. The political situation — an alliance between the Fascist regime and the Catholic Church from 1933 to 1938 followed by Hitler's conquest of Austria and the Second World War — was highly unfavourable to the development of Austrian Buddhism.

Notably, in 1949 the "Buddhist Society of Vienna" was founded and interest for Buddhism started to flourish again. Due to personalities like Fritz Hungerleider, who had returned from exile in the People's Republic of China in 1955 to become the society's president, and Dr. Walter Karwath, who had spent years in Asia practicing medicine, Buddhism took a step out of literary and intellectual circles toward the world of daily life. The late 1970s saw the establishment of Dannebergplatz, the first Buddhist Centre in Vienna; the purchase of a rural property intended to become a retreat centre (Buddhist Centre Scheibbs); and the establishment of the first Buddhist Association outside Vienna (the Salzburg Buddhist Association). The latter was founded by Friedrich Fenzl, who had been a student at the Ryukoku University in Kyoto and who invited Kosho Otani, the Patriarch of the Nishi-Honganji branch of Jodo Shinshu to visit Austria. Hemaloka Thero, Geshe Rabten, the 16th Karmapa, the 14th Dalai Lama, and other eminent representatives from different Buddhist traditions visited the country, gave talks, and attracted dharma students.

In 1979, Genro Koudela, who was ordained as a Zen priest in California by Joshu Sasaki, returned to Vienna, his city of origin, and established the "Bodhidharma Zendo" there. The new Buddhist Centre at Fleischmarkt, in the very centre of Vienna, became the home for Zen, Kagyu and Theravada groups.

When official recognition was granted by the government in early 1983 a new era of Austrian Buddhism was ushered in. A widely visible 'Peace Stupa' was opened at the banks of the river Danube and a retreat and study centre, Letzehof, affiliated with the Geluk school of Tibetan Buddhism was opened in the western province of Vorarlberg. Vanja Palmers, a Zen monk of the Japanese Soto school, and Brother David Steindl-Rast, an Austrian-American Benedictine monk, founded a retreat centre high up in the Salzburg alpine region. The first centre in the south of the country, a retreat centre in the Burmese Theravada tradition was established in the early 1990s.

In 1993, Austria hosted an annual general meeting of the European Buddhist Union, which drew participants from a dozen European countries. A series of visits to the city of Graz by the Dalai Lama in 1995, 1998 (for the consecration of a large stupa), and in 2002 (to speak on "Kalachakra for World Peace") became a strong encouragement for Buddhists in Austria.

It is remarkable official recognition also opened the doors for Buddhist religious education at schools. In 1993, the first few groups of Buddhist children were given the chance to hear about the Buddhadharma on a regular basis as part of their syllabus. Twelve years after the project was started in the cities of Vienna, Graz and Salzburg, Buddhist religious education is being made available to school children of all age groups (6 to 19) at different types of schools in all of nine federal provinces of the Republic. A Teachers' Training Academy was founded in 2001 to offer in-service teacher training for the teachers concerned.

GERMANY

In fact, Buddhism in Germany looks back to a history of over 150 years. Arthur Schopenhauer was one of the earliest Germans who were influenced by Buddhism. Schopenhauer got his knowledge of Buddhism from authors like Isaac Jacob Schmidt (1779-1847). German Buddhists or Orientalists like Karl Eugen Neumann, Paul Dahlke, Georg Grimm, Friedrich Zimmermann (Subhadra Bhikschu) and the first German Buddhist monk Nyanatiloka were also influenced by Schopenhauer and his understanding of Buddhism. But also German Indologists like Hermann Oldenberg and his work „Buddha, sein Leben, seine Lehre, seine Gemeinde" had an important influence on German Buddhism.

In 1888 Subhadra Bickshu (Friedrich Zimmermann) published the first edition of the „Buddhistischer Katechismus", a work based on the "Buddhist Catechism" of Henry Steel Olcott.

In 1903 the first German Buddhist organisation was founded by the Indologist Karl Seidenstücker in Leipzig. In 1904 Florus Anton Gueth became the Theravada monk Nyanatiloka. Some important Pali texts were translated into German in the early part of the 20th century by scholars like Karl Eugen Neumann (1865-1915), Nyantiloka and others.

In 1922 Hermann Hesse published his famous work "Siddhartha", which has been translated into many languages.

In 1924 Dr. Paul Dahlke established the first German Buddhist monastery, the "Buddhistische Haus" in Berlin.

The German Dharmaduta Society, initially known as the Lanka Dhammaduta Society and dedicated to spreading the message of the Buddha in Germany and other Western countries, was founded in 1952.

In 1957 The German Dharmaduta Society purchased the premises of "Das Buddhistische Haus" from the heirs of Dr. Dahlke. It is now a Centre for the spread of Theravada Buddhism in Europe. As the oldest Buddhist institution in Europe, German authorities have designated it a National Heritage site.

According to the Deutsche Buddhistische Union (German Buddhist Union), an umbrella organisation of the Buddhist groups in Germany, there are about 245,000 active Buddhists in Germany (as of 2005), 50% of them are immigrated Asians. They are organized in about 600 groups. In 1977 there were just 15 Buddhist groups.

REFERENCES

1. A. Peel Shitoku *Vroege geschiedenis van het Boeddhisme in België* (A Brief History of Buddhism in Belgium) EKO no.s 74 (September 1997), 75 (December 1997) & 76 (March 1998)
2. ABC - Why so many South Australian's are choosing Buddhism
3. Asian Tribune - Buddhism fastest growing religion in West
4. "Buddhism in France is booming," World Wide Religion Network".
5. Buddhism & meditation in the English Lake District.
6. Buddhism and Ethnicity in Britain: The 2001 Census Data.
7. Buddhist Channel - Seed of Buddhism now growing in UK.
8. BuddhistChannel - Allure of Buddhism growing in the UK.
9. *Census 2001: National Report for England and Wales*, Office for National Statistics, London, TSO, 2003, page 184.
10. *Census 2001: National Report for England and Wales*, part 2, Office for National Statistics, London, TSO, 2004, page 33.
11. Curren, Erik D. (2008)*Buddha's Not Smiling, Uncovering the*

Corruption at the Heart of Tibetan Buddhism Today Alaya Press.

12. David R. Loy, "Review of Nietzsche and Buddhism: A Study in Nihilism and Ironic Affinities by R.G. Morrison".
13. Department of Justice: List of Buddhist faith-societies in Denmark
14. "DR (Danish state news-agency), article about the History of Buddhism ("In Danish")". Dr.dk. 2006-08-10.
15. E.L. Mullen, "Orientalist commercializations: Tibetan Buddhism in American popular film"
16. Fields, Rick, *How the Swans came to the Lake - A Narrative History of Buddhism in America.* (Third edition, 1992).
17. In the Scottish Lowlands, Europe's first Buddhist monastery turns 40 Retrieved 24 June 2007.
18. Jacques Brosse (1991) *Alexandra David-Neel* (Albin Michel)
19. Jørn Borup. "Article by Jørn Borup on religion.dk ("In Danish")".
20. Kate Rew (2010-01-15). "Scotland's Buddhist retreat". *The Guardian.* http://www.guardian.co.uk/travel/2010/jan/16/buddhism-retreat-meditation-scotland-monastery.
21. Laura Elisabeth Schnabel. "Laura Elisabeth Schnabel "Dalai-Lama: Lad være med at konvertere til buddhismen (Don't convert to Buddhism)". Kristeligt Dagblad (danish newspaper) 30-05-2009.
22. *Le traité de la grande vertu de sagesse de Nâgârjuna (Mahâprajñâpâramitâúâstra)* vol. 1 (1944)
23. Lenoir, Frédéric. Le bouddhisme en France.Paris: Fayard, 1999
24. Loy, David R., "Review of Nietzsche and Buddhism: A Study in Nihilism and Ironic Affinities by R.G. Morrison", *Asian Philosophy* Vol. 8 No. 2 (July 1998), pp. 129–131.
25. Mullen, E.L., "Orientalist commercializations: Tibetan Buddhism in American popular film", *Journal of Religion and Film*, Vol. 2 No. 2 (October 1998).
26. *Northern Ireland Census 2001: Standard Tables*, National Statistics, 2003, page 43.

27. Nydahl, Ole (1992) Riding The Tiger, Twenty Years on the Road - The Risks and Joys of Bringing Tibetan Buddhism to the West, Blue Dolphin Publishing.
28. Obadia, Lionel. "Tibetan Buddhism in France: A Missionary Religion?" Journal of Global Buddhism.
29. Phra Nicholas Thanissaro (1999) *Lezing: Religies in Ieper - Buddhism* Lakenhalle, Ieper 18-10-1999.
30. *Scotland's Census 2001: the Registrar-General's Report to the Scottish Parliament*, General Register Office for Scotland, 2003, page 31
31. *Scotland's Census 2001: the Registrar-General's Report to the Scottish Parliament*, General Register Office for Scotland, 2003, page 31.
32. Shakya, T., "Review of *Prisoners of Shangri-la* by Donald Lopez", *Journal of Buddhist Ethics*, Vol. 6 (1999), pp. 196–199.
33. Shakya, Tsering "Review of *Prisoners of Shangri-la* by Donald Lopez". online
34. The Pew Forum on Religion & Public Life - U.S. Religious Landscape Survey
35. Tworkov, Helen, *Zen in America: Profiles of Five Teachers*, San Francisco: North Point Press, (1989).
36. "University of Aarhus: Religion i Danmark 2009 - Buddhistiske trossamfund og menigheder". Teo.au.dk. 2009-03-16. http://www.teo.au.dk/csr/rel-aarbog09/trossamf/buddhist. Retrieved 2009-08-03.
37. Why is Buddhism the fastest growing religion in Australia? by Darren Nelson.

Bibliography

Avalon, Arthur (1918). *Sakti and Sakta*. Ganesh and Co. http://www.sacred-texts.com/tantra/sas/index.htm.

Avalon, Arthur (1972). *Tantra of the great liberation – Mahanirvana Tantra*. New York: Dover Publications.

Bhattacharyya, N. N. (1999). *History of the Tantric Religion*. New Delhi: Manohar.

Bischoff, Roger (1995) (PDF). *Buddhism in Myanmar-A Short History*. Buddhist Publication Society. ISBN 955-24-0127-5. http://www.buddhanet.net/pdf_file/bud-myanmar.pdf. Retrieved 2006-08-26.

Buckley, Sarah (2007-09-26). "Who are Burma's monks?". BBC News 26 September 2007.

Bühnemann, Gudrun (1988). *The Worship of MahgaGapati According to the Nityotsava*. Institut für Indologie.

Coleman, Graham, ed. (1993). *A Handbook of Tibetan Culture*. Boston: Shambhala Publications, Inc..

Conze, Edward (1993). *A Short History of Buddhism* (2nd ed.). Oneworld.

Curren, Erik D. (2008)*Buddha's Not Smiling, Uncovering the Corruption at the Heart of Tibetan Buddhism Today* Alaya Press.

Dhargyey, Geshe Ngawang; ed. Alexander Berzin, based on oral trans. by Sharpa Tulku (3rd edn, 1978). *Tibetan Tradition of Mental Development*. Dharmsala: Library of Tibetan Works and Archives.

Dr. Guang Xing (2005). *The Concept of the Buddha*, RoutledgeCurzon, London

Dreyfus, Georges (1997). *Recognizing Reality: Dharmakirti's Philosophy and Its Tibetan Interpretations.* New York: State University of New York Press.

E.L. Mullen, "Orientalist commercializations: Tibetan Buddhism in American popular film"

Fields, Rick, *How the Swans came to the Lake - A Narrative History of Buddhism in America.* (Third edition, 1992).

Harper, Katherine Anne and Robert L. Brown (ed.) (2002). *The Roots of Tantra.* State University of New York Press

Harris, Ian (2005). *Cambodian Buddhism*, University of Hawai'i Press.

Harris, Ian (August 2001), "Sangha Groupings in Cambodia", *Buddhist Studies Review* (UK Association for Buddhist Studies) 18 (I): 65–72

Harry L. Wells (2000). *Korean Temple Burnings and Vandalism: The Response of the Society for Buddhist-Christian Studies. Buddhist-Christian Studies.*

Hill, John E. (2009). *Through the Jade Gate to Rome: A Study of the Silk Routes during the Later Han Dynasty, 1st to 2nd Centuries CE.* John E. Hill. BookSurge, Charleston, South Carolina.

Hlaing, Maung Myint (August 1981). *The Great Disciples of Buddha.* Zeyar Hlaing Literature House. pp. 66–68.

Hopkins, Jeffrey (1996). *Meditation on Emptiness.* Boston: Wisdom.

Jackson, Peter (1995). *Thai Buddhist accounts of male*

homosexuality and AIDS in the 1980s. The Australian Journal of Anthropology, Vol.6 No.3, pp.140–153. December 1995. Text online.

John Paraskevopoulos (2009). *Call of the Infinite: The Way of Shin Buddhism*, Sophia Perennis Publications, California.

John Paraskevopoulos (2009). *Call of the Infinite: The Way of Shin Buddhism,* California

Kabilsingh, Chatsumarn (1991). *Thai Women in Buddhism.* Parallax Press.

Keown, Damien; Stephen Hodge, Paola Tinti (2003). *A Dictionary of Buddhism.* Oxford UP.

Lati Rinpoche; trans. & ed.: Elizabeth Napper (1980). *Mind in Tibetan Buddhism: Oral Commentary on Geshay Jam-bel-sam-pel's "Presentation of Awareness and Knowledge Composite of All the Important Points Opener of the Eye of New Intelligence*. Valois, NY: Snow Lion.

Lopez, Donald S. (2005). Critical Terms for the Study of Buddhism. Chicago: The University of Chicago Press.

Loy, David R. (1998). "Review of Nietzsche and Buddhism: A Study in Nihilism and Ironic Affinities by R.G. Morrison", *Asian Philosophy.*

Mullen, E.L. (1998). "Orientalist commercializations: Tibetan Buddhism in American popular film", *Journal of Religion and Film.*

Mullin, Glenn H. (1998). *Living in the Face of Death: The Tibetan Tradition.* 2008 reprint: Snow Lion Publications, Ithica, New York.

Mullin, Glenn H. *The Fourteen Dalai Lamas: A Sacred Legacy of Reincarnations* (2001) Clear Light Publishers.

Nguyen, Cuong Tu & A.W. Barber (1998). "Vietnamese Buddhism in North America: Tradition and Acculturation". in Charles S. Prebish and Kenneth K. Tanaka (eds) .The Faces of Buddhism in America. Berkeley: University of California Press.

Nguyen, Cuong Tu (1997). Zen in Medieval Vietnam: A Study of the ThiÁn UyÃn T-p Anh. Honolulu: University of Hawaii Press.

Norbu, Chögyal Namkhai (1999). *The Crystal and The Way of Light: Sutra, Tantra and Dzogchen*. Snow Lion Publications.

Nyanaponika Thera (1965). *The Heart of Buddhist Meditation*. Boston: Weiser.

Nydahl, Ole (1992). Riding The Tiger, Twenty Years on the Road - The Risks and Joys of Bringing Tibetan Buddhism to the West, Blue Dolphin Publishing.

Obadia, Lionel. "Tibetan Buddhism in France: A Missionary Religion?" Journal of Global Buddhism.

Olson, Carl (2005). The Different Paths of Buddhism: A Narrative-Historical Introduction. New Jersey: Rutgers University Press.

Pabongka Rinpoche; Ed. Trijang Rinpoche, transl. Michael Richards (3rd edn. 2006). *Liberation in the Palm of Your Hand, A Concise Discourse on the Path to Enlightenment*. Somerville, MA: Wisdom.

Page, Tony (1998), *Buddhism and Animals* (Nirvana Publications, London).

Peter Harvey (2000). *An Introduction to Buddhist Ethics*. Cambridge University Press.

Phelps, Norm. (2004). *The Great Compassion: Buddhism and Animal Rights*. Lantern Books.

Powers, John (2004). *History as Propaganda: Tibetan Exiles versus the People's Republic of China*, Oxford University Press.

Queen, Chris; King, Sallie (1996). *Engaged Buddhism: Buddhist Liberation Movements in Asia*. New York: Albany State University Press. p. 36.

Rahn, Kim (2008). "President Embarrassed Over Angry Buddhists". *The Korea Times*. Retrieved October 7, 2008.

Rawson, Philip (1990). *The Art of Southeast Asia*, Thames & Hudson.

Saddhatissa, Hammalawa (1987). *Buddhist Ethics: The Path to Nirvana*. Wisdom Pubns; New Ed edition.

Saraswati, Swami Satyananda (2000). *Sure Ways to Self Realization*. Yoga Publications Trust.

Savada, Andrea Matles (1994). *Laos: A Country Study*. Washington, D.C.: GPO for the Library of Congress. http://countrystudies.us/laos/.

Shakya, T. (1999). "Review of *Prisoners of Shangri-la* by Donald Lopez", *Journal of Buddhist Ethics*.

Smith, E. Gene (2001). *Among Tibetan Texts: History and Literature of the Himalayan Plateau*. Boston: Wisdom Publications.

Sopa, Geshe Lhundup; Jeffrey Hopkins (1977). *Practice and Theory of Tibetan Buddhism*. New Delhi: B.I. Publications.

Spiro, Melford (1982). *Buddhism and society: a great tradition and its Burmese vicissitudes*. University of California Press.

Stcherbatsky, F. Th. 1962 (1930). *Buddhist Logic*. Volume 1. New York: Dover.

Tambiah, Stanley (1970). *Buddhism and the Spirit Cults in North-East Thailand.* Cambridge University Press.

Terwiel, B.J. (1976). "A Model for the Study of Thai Buddhism". *Journal of Asian Studies* 35: 391–403.

Tworkov, Helen (1989). *Zen in America: Profiles of Five Teachers*, San Francisco: North Point Press.

Urban, Hugh (2003). *Tantra: Sex, Secrecy, Politics, and Power in the Study of Religions.* University of California Press.

Wangyal Rinpoche, Tenzin; Dahlby, Mark (1998). *The Tibetan Yogas of Dream and Sleep.*.N.Y.: Snow Lion Publications.

Welch, Holmes (1968). *The Buddhist revival in China.* Cambridge, Mass.: Harvard University Press.

White, David Gordon (ed.) (2000). *Tantra in Practice.* Princeton University Press.

Wyatt, David (2003). *Thailand: A Short History*, New Haven: Yale University Press.

Yeshe, Lama Thubten (1987). *Introduction to Tantra:The Transformation of Desire* (2001, revised ed.). Boston: Wisdom Publications.

Index

●●●